Youth Exclusion and Empowerment in the Contemporary Global Order

Youth Exclusion and Empowerment in the Contemporary Global Order: Existentialities in Migrations, Identity and the Digital Space

EDITED BY

ỌLÁYÍNKÁ ÀKÀNLE

University of Ibadan, Nigeria

University of Johannesburg, South Africa

United Kingdom – North America – Japan – India – Malaysia – China

Emerald Publishing Limited
Howard House, Wagon Lane, Bingley BD16 1WA, UK

First edition 2022

Reprints and permissions service
Contact: permissions@emeraldinsight.com

British Library Cataloguing in Publication Data
A catalogue record for this book is available from the British Library

ISBN: 978-1-80382-778-0 (Print)
ISBN: 978-1-80382-777-3 (Online)
ISBN: 978-1-80382-779-7 (Epub)

ISOQAR certified
Management System,
awarded to Emerald
for adherence to
Environmental
standard
ISO 14001:2004.

ISOQAR
REGISTERED
Certificate Number 1985
ISO 14001

INVESTOR IN PEOPLE

To all organizations, groups, institutions and individuals committed to achievement of youth inclusion, empowerment and sustainable development across the world.

Contents

Abbreviations and acronyms

AU	African Union
CHED	Commission on Higher Education
CSO	Civil society organization
DHET	Department of Higher Education and Training
FAO	Food and Agriculture Organisation
FMF	Fees Must Fall (#FMF)
FTLRP	Fast-track Land Reform Programme
ICT	Information and communications technologies
ILO	International Labour Organization
MOOCs	Massive open online courses
MYD	Ministry of Youth Development
NDP	National Development Plan
NEET	Not in education, employment or training
NYP	National Youth Policy
NYC	National Youth Council
OECD	Organization for Economic Co-operation and Development
RMF	Rhodes Must Fall (#RMF)
SARS	Special Anti-Robbery Squad (Nigeria)
SDGs	Sustainable Development Goals
SRC	Student representative council
STEM	Science, technology, engineering and mathematics
SU	Stellenbosch University
TMT	Temporal motivational theory
UCT	University of Cape Town
UFH	University of Fort Hare
UKZN	University of Kwazulu Natal
UN	United Nations
UNDP	United Nations Development Programme
UNECA	United Nations Economic Commission for Africa
UNFPA	United Nations Population Funds
WFP	World Food Programme
WHO	World Health Organization
Wits	University of Witwatersrand
YDI	Youth Development Index

About the Contributors

Damilola Adegoke is a Research Associate and a Peter da Costa Post-Doctoral Fellow (Future Peace and the State in Africa research cluster) with the African Leadership Centre (ALC), King's College London. His PhD thesis explored the roles and place of big data in security leadership decision-making in crisis situations. He has a BA in Philosophy and an MSc in Sociology of Development from the University of Ibadan, Nigeria. He also holds an MSc in Security, Leadership and Society from King's College London. He is the Head and Chief Data Analyst of the Data Lab (ALC). He is a steering committee member and board member of the Digital Sociology Group of the International Sociology Association. He was a Visiting Research Fellow at the Department of Political Science and Public Policy, University of Buea, Republic of Cameroon. His research interests include artificial intelligence and big data security decision-making, social network analysis and computational sociology.

Qláyínká Àkànle is a Lecturer in the Department of Sociology, Faculty of the Social Sciences, University of Ibadan, Nigeria. He is also a Research Associate in the Department of Sociology, Faculty of Humanities, University of Johannesburg, South Africa. He was a Postdoctoral Fellow at the South African Research Chair Initiative in Social Policy, College of Graduate Studies, University of South Africa, South Africa. He has won other scholarly awards such as being a World Social Science Fellow of the International Social Science Council, Paris, France; Laureate of the Council for the Development of Social Science Research in Africa, Dakar, Senegal; and received the Postgraduate School Prize for scholarly publication from the University of Ibadan, Nigeria. He is a recipient of the Certificate of Achievement from Folke Bernadotte Academy, Swedish Agency for Peace, Security and Development, Sweden. He is a thorough-bred and an internationally affirmed academic, scholar and expert on international development, migration and diaspora studies, social policy, sociological practice and sustainable development. He is a member of funded research groups including Bill and Melinda Gates Foundation Funded Research in DRC, Ghana, Kenya and Nigeria, as well as Arts and Humanities Research Council Funded Research on data and displacement in Nigeria and Sudan. He is a widely published scholar, the author of *Kinship Networks and International Migration in Nigeria* (Cambridge Scholar Publishers, UK, 2015), and has co-edited, among other books, *The Development of Africa: Issues, Diagnosis and Prognosis* (Springer Publishing, Germany, 2018) and *Corruption and Development in Nigeria* (Routledge, UK, 2022).

Kafayat Aminu is a Medical Sociologist who hails from the ancient city of Ibadan. She commenced her higher education at the University of Ilorin where she obtained her Diploma in Social Administration. She later proceeded to the University of Ibadan where she obtained her BSc, MSc and PhD degrees in Sociology. She has special interests in health inequalities, infectious diseases, research methods and ethics, disability studies, virtual communication and others. For her doctoral thesis, she explored the experience of hospital care and social construction of disability in a spinal-cord-injury population. She is a multidisciplinary researcher who has co-authored book chapters and several scientific papers in reputable journals. Her mentors include neurosurgeons and medical sociologists and anthropologists who have influenced her research interests to a great extent. She hopes to reconnoitre other remarkable subjects as she journeys through her career.

Jimoh Amzat is a Full Professor in the Department of Sociology, Usmanu Danfodiyo University, Sokoto, Nigeria, and a Senior Research Associate in the Department of Sociology, University of Johannesburg, South Africa. He was a recipient of Erasmus Mundus scholarships (both as a graduate student and a visiting scholar) and an Alexander von Humboldt postdoctoral fellowship (Germany). He has previously served as a Guest Lecturer to the University of Bielefeld, Germany and EHESP School of Public Health, Rennes, France. He is a scholar of extraordinary insight, with a versatile academic charm and zeal, framed around the tetrad of medical sociology, bioethics, global health and social problems. He has published numerous books and papers in peer-reviewed journals.

Shreya Bhardwaj is a Sociology Doctoral Researcher in the Faculty of Social Sciences at Charles University in the Czech Republic. After working with Tibetan musicians in Dharamshala, India, for her Master's degree in Psychology from the University of Delhi, she has been working with Muslim migrant youth in the Czech Republic under the supervision of Dr Zdenek Uherek (ISS FSV Director, UK), taking a feminist and decolonial approach. She is also involved in a two-year multidisciplinary EU-funded START project aiming to understand how patient advocacy can influence patients' access to justice.

Christophe Dongmo is the Programme Quality and Development Director at Sonna Etienne Foundation, and a non-resident Senior Research Fellow at Leiden University African Studies Centre. He previously served as Senior Regional Executive Officer (Central Africa) of the International Committee of the Red Cross and Country Representative (Cameroon) of Denis and Lenora Foretia Foundation. He holds advanced degrees in international human rights law, American diplomatic history and political science from the University of the Witwatersrand (South Africa), Vanderbilt University (USA) and Johns Hopkins University (USA).

Demilade Ifeoluwa Kayode has degrees in Sociology from Bowen University, Nigeria, and the University of Ibadan, Nigeria. Her research interests include but are not limited to urbanization and migration, social policy, sustainable development, environmental sustainability, qualitative and quantitative methods and entrepreneurship. She has passion for teaching and academic writing.

Amani El Naggare is a PhD candidate at the Graduate School of Sociology at Münster University in Germany. Her PhD thesis examines emotions and political trajectories of youth protesters during the political transition in Egypt from 2011 to the present. Further research interests are youth migrations and activism in exile after the Arab Spring. She has conducted intensive field research in Morocco and Egypt, focusing on youth political participation prior to, and in the aftermath of, the uprisings of 2011. She has participated in several academic conferences during the last decade.

Tatenda Goodman Nhapi holds a Bachelor's degree in Social Work (University of Zimbabwe) and is a graduate of the Erasmus Mundus MA Advanced Development in Social Work joint programme among the University of Lincoln (England), Aalborg University (Denmark), Technical University of Lisbon (Portugal), University of Paris Ouest Nantere La Defense (France) and Warsaw University (Poland). He started his career in Zimbabwe (2008–2013) working in relief and development and social research, focusing on child welfare and gender issues. While employed in Zimbabwe's Department of Social Services, his work focused on policies and protocols implementation pertaining to care and protection of children, older persons, persons with disabilities, disadvantaged persons and households in distress. He is a Research Associate with the University of Johannesburg, and the South African Department of Social Work and Community Development. His research agenda revolves around social policy and implementation of developmental programmes in their attempt to address issues such as poverty, inequality, HIV/AIDS and poverty traps of vulnerable groups such as women, children, older people and youths. He has high academic standing with a growing reputation in research, evidenced by an emerging portfolio of internationally recognised publications.

Terngu Sylvanus Nomishan holds Bachelor and Master's degrees in Archaeology and is presently preparing to commence his PhD programme. He also completed a certificate course in Tourism Management at UNESCO World Heritage Sites, Université Paris 1, Panthéon-Sorbonne. He lectures in the Department of Archaeology and Museum Studies, Federal University Lokoja, Nigeria. His research areas include Cultural Anthropology, Ethnoarchaeology, Cultural Heritage and Museum Studies and Cultural Resource Management CRM. He has published quality articles in both local and international renowned journals. He is an Inaugural Council Member of the Pan African Scientific Research Council.

Ewajesu Opeyemi Okewumi is a Doctoral Researcher at the Department of Sociology, Faculty of the Social Sciences, University of Ibadan, Nigeria. She is a fellow of the Lagos Studies Association. She has attended conferences both locally and internationally and has published articles and book chapters on childhood studies, development studies and sociological theories.

Damola Toyosi Olaniyi holds a Master of Science degree in Sociology and Bachelor of Science degree in Criminology And Security Studies from the University of Lagos and the National Open University of Nigeria, respectively. His areas of interest include sociology of development, crime and delinquency and social issues. Currently, he works as an independent social researcher and has to his credits academic research publications on suicide terrorism, substance abuse and criminality, social supports and widowhood in Nigeria, global issues and African perspectives in sociological theories among others. He has taken part in research studies sponsored by both local and international donors on HIV prevention interventions for female sex worker in Nigeria, Quite Corruption in Lagos State Educational System, among others. Currently, he is an MPhil/PhD student of the Department of Sociology, University of Ibadan.

Ayokunle Olumuyiwa Omobowale (PhD) is a professor of Sociology at the University of Ibadan. He has won the University of Ibadan Postgraduate School Award for scholarly publication, 2007; the Institut Français de Recherche en Afrique Research Fellowship, 2009; the American Council of Learned Societies – African Humanities Programme Post-Doctoral Fellowship, 2010; and the African Studies Association (USA) Presidential Award for 2014. He was also a Visiting Scholar at the Centre for African Studies, Rutgers University, New Jersey, USA, in November 2014. His works have appeared in peer-reviewed journals and edited volumes locally and internationally. He served on the board of editors of *International Encyclopedia of Revolution and Protest* (2009), and he is the author of *The Tokunbo Phenomenon and the Second-Hand Economy in Nigeria* (2013). He is the editor of *Ibadan Journal of Sociology*, and he is also an international partner and participant in the International Network on Women on the Move COST Action (CA19112) 2020-2022.

Mofeyisara Oluwatoyin Omobowale holds a PhD in Anthropology. Her doctoral research was on space, sexuality and power at Bodija Market, Ibadan, Nigeria. She is a recipient of the American Council of Learned Societies – African Humanities Programme (ACLS-AHP) Doctoral Fellowship 2012, the Cadbury Fellowship (Department of Anthropology and African Studies, Birmingham University) 2014 and ACLS-AHP Post-Doctoral Fellowship 2016. Her interests lie in medical anthropology, public health anthropology, cultural studies, sexuality issues and maternal, child and adolescent studies. She is a Research Fellow and Lecturer at the Institute of Child Health, College of Medicine, University of Ibadan, Nigeria. She is a co-investigator on the Global Grand Challenges (Round 23) project on Immunization Strategies for Working Mothers 2019–2021.

Introduction

Ọláyínká Àkànle

There is no other time in human history that this book is relevant than now and into the future. This book is very important in aiding reliable and useful understanding of youth exclusion across the world. Relying strategically on real issues and experiences across many countries and issues, this book adds to existing body of knowledge on the realities of youths as they struggle to survive in contexts of the current systemic societal quagmire prevalent across the world. From poor to rich countries, common experiences of the youths suggest difficult livelihoods driven by widespread exclusion and dis/empowerment. This book therefore intentionally and carefully examines the ramifications and trajectories of youth exclusion across many social systems to x-ray the scenarios common across contexts through objective case studies and global outlooks. This book is practical, pragmatic, scientific and objective yet subjective to sufficiently capture important angles and nuances of the exclusionary and empowerment situations of the youths in spaces and times.

This book is not emptily theoretical and academic. It is both scholarly and pragmatic in manners that are useful for policy and practice. Issues of youth exclusion and empowerment are complex, dynamic, multidimensional, deep-rooted, complicated and formidable. With these in mind, authors in the book adopt a tool kit approach and problem-solving strategies by not only throwing up and engaging the problems but by also providing legitimate and workable solutions. All authors relied on a mix of secondary data, primary data and autoethnography. The methodological triangulation strengthens this book and makes it very strong as a major relevant addition to knowledge. This book is inter/trans/multidisciplinary in orientation and approach. Contributors are from diverse background and countries, and every author contributed something new and innovative in preparing this book. Readers of this book will certainly find this very interesting and relevant to their works and practices. This book is empirical, theoretical, philosophical, historical, scholarly and policy oriented. While this book is specific and contextual, it is also global so as to be relevant to everyone interested in the current realities in which youths exist across the world.

All authors in this book are scholars and stakeholders in youth studies and practices. They are all motivated by passion and desire to make change, thus

Youth Exclusion and Empowerment in the Contemporary Global Order:
Existentialities in Migrations, Identity and the Digital Space, 1–2
Copyright © 2022 by Ọláyínká Àkànle
Published under exclusive licence by Emerald Publishing Limited
doi:10.1108/978-1-80382-777-320221001

their contributions to this book. All authors were very committed throughout the process of writing this book, and they decidedly contributed because they all realized the youths need this scholarly and practice epistemic intervention – this book – for their exclusion to be addressed and better understood globally. Serious work, painstaking commitments and preparations went into writing this book. This book is a very important intervention in a very big problem of youth exclusion. This book has emancipating and liberating objectives to deliver the youths from global exclusion and entrapment. Issues covered include global contextualization and operationalization of youths, youth exclusion and empowerment, historicization, cultural backgrounding and engagement, migration, digital exclusion, riots and violence, identity, health, integration, social media and human rights, among others.

This book has wide application and appeal. It will be useful across many settings and over many years. Issues addressed in this book crosscut with many other issues and are addressed in manners that give this book cutting-edge advantages on the subject of interest – youth exclusion and empowerment. Development partners, governments, practitioners and scholars interested in youths' development, exclusion, inclusion and empowerment will find this book very important and useful. The contributors to this book are well appreciated for seeing this book to publication. All the contributors were very intentional in writing this book knowing fully well this book is to drive change in the right direction for sustainable youth and global development and inclusion. The whole world needs this book even as the world struggles with myriads of development challenges including youth exclusion and sustainable development. It is certain that everyone that reads this book will find it very interesting and useful. We strongly recommend this book for you, and we wish you a fantastic time of reading and experience.

Chapter One

Youths in Global Context: The Anatomy of Exclusion and Processes

Ọláyínká Àkànle, Ewajesu Opeyemi Okewumi and Demilade Ifeoluwa Kayode

Introduction

"Youth are the leaders and hope of tomorrow" is a common old phrase in the mouth of almost every citizen of any country. It is often used as an assurance by the old and a reassurance for the youth to believe that one day, they will get the opportunity to develop the nation and make it better. However, no one really knows when tomorrow is and neither has it come. This phrase of hope now sounds like a broken record. Nations are of the opinion that youths carry the prowess, intellect, exposure and agility to ensure that a nation's wealth does not crumble, yet global situations and facts have shown that the youths are not well represented and not on a par with the adults in various facets of life.

The conceptualization and measurement of youth is complex and vague, but by mere looking at their composure and line of thought, it becomes easier to identify who the youths are. It becomes complex when one needs to analyse the components, issues and anatomical description of youths, especially when a holistic approach is needed. Taking a holistic approach to understand youth or youthhood requires researchers, writers and readers to inquire about the concept from a global perspective that is not Eurocentric about the social anatomy of youth. In studies, different societies and countries define youth differently, based on their unique social characteristics and attributes. More often than not, measuring or defining youthhood using numbers has proved to be the most generalized way of defining youths. However, within this, definitions still vary (Heywood, 2001; World Health Organization, 2014).

The conceptualization of youth has gone far beyond numbers. Rather, it is socially constructed, which in turn is determined by different factors such as the

Youth Exclusion and Empowerment in the Contemporary Global Order:
Existentialities in Migrations, Identity and the Digital Space, 3–15
Copyright © 2022 by Ọláyínká Àkànle, Ewajesu Opeyemi Okewumi
and Demilade Ifeoluwa Kayode
Published under exclusive licence by Emerald Publishing Limited
doi:10.1108/978-1-80382-777-320221002

agents of socialization, institutions and the society at large. The age of youth-hood has now developed to represent a group of people who are affected posi-tively or negatively by the same situation and who have developed a subculture which then guides their behaviour and activities with other members of their group as well as with society at large (Oparina et al., 2020). The youths exist within a complex social system with elements such as norms, traditions, history, demands from society and an individual's future prospects all adding up to form the lives of youths. Consciously or unconsciously, they are wired to accept new roles and ways of life, which are some of the attributes that differentiate adults from youths or adolescents from youths.

It is important to note that within society, a symbiotic relationship exists between the society as an independent entity and its people. The structure of the society (polity, economic state) directly or indirectly influences its citizens while individual activity also plays an indispensable role in structural formation of the society. With respect to exclusion of youths within society, it is prerogative to understand that the structural composition of a country helps to include the youth or exclude them from institutions depending on how these structures have been institutionalized. Guilia (2013) defined exclusion as a state of been deprived. This deprivation could come in different forms, such as material or non-material deprivation, and social, political and economic deprivation of a group of people who have been regarded as subordinate or subjected to those in power, who are marginalized.

For instance, African countries are well known for high levels of corrupt prac-tices, neglect of citizens' fundamental human right, unfair remuneration and election issues. Youth vying for political positions within Africa countries is a situation that might never see the light of day because the structure of society has given much power to adults and the political elite. Moreover, issues such as job opportunities and education for all cannot be excluded from what youths are experiencing in Africa as a continent (UNDP, 2007). Social exclusion of youths or any marginalized group does not happen independently of external catalysts or factors. One of the major catalysts of social exclusion of youths from institu-tions has to do with the high level of inequality, including unequal access to job opportunities or wealth creation and the political composition of most countries, which has contributed immensely to exclusion of youths from the system and even marginalized within the system.

More often than not, youths are only recognized when it comes to negative happenings within the society. For instance, drug abuse, prostitution, gangsters, violence and protest are issues often related as the doings of the youths, neglecting that these issues are a product of what society throws at this particular group of people (youths). Regardless of how society might have constructed the youth to be of great concern to the society at large, it is important to point out that within this same cohort, some youths have been impacting their society positively in eco-nomic and political sectors. However, compared to the totals of those involved in those sectors, the youths are less well represented. This chapter will give an insight into how much the youths have been excluded, the causes of their exclusion and the way forward for a sustainable society by ensuring youth inclusiveness.

The Age of Youths: Issues in Conceptualization and Measurements

To affirm or assert that there is a universal definition of the term "youth" or "youthhood" is trying to constrain or limit the usage of the term. Unlike pure sciences, where a singular term or word means the same in all situations and events, discussions and terminologies in social sciences do not enjoy that privilege. With regard to conceptualizing and measuring youth, there has been no acceptable definition by different scholars or disciplines as to what should be the central definition of youth. For Bourdieu (1993), the concept "youth" has evolved over time and is still evolving, and it is now viewed as a term that came to be as a result of social construction. A virtue of Bourdieu's (1993) orientation is that a socially constructed term varies among societies, countries and continents, and therefore a universal yardstick cannot be applied as who should be regarded as a youth.

The youthhood stage is that phase of life that is shortly after childhood or adolescence and shortly before adulthood. This period or phase might not be given much cognisance simply because of conceptualizations in which they are regarded as adolescent for some countries and adult for others. Nevertheless, organizational bodies, researchers and scholars have come up with various definitions and yardsticks for ascertaining that an individual is in their youthful stage. For the United Nations (UN), youths are determined by an age range: a youth is expected to be 15–24 years old. This had to be ascertained in this manner for data collection, census purposes and statistical purposes. It should, however, be noted that the definition of youth by the UN is without prejudice of other forms of definitions propounded by nation-states (UNDP, 2010). By merely making use of age to define youths, there arises a contradicting notion because the age that is regarded as youth in some definitions is defined as a period of adolescence in others. World Health Organization (2014), for instance, defined the youth as those between the ages of 10 and 24, while in the United States, the Office of Disease Prevention and Health Promotion (2018) sees youth as those aged 18–25. The African Youth Charter explained that only those within the ages 15–35 should be regarded as youths while the National Policy on Youth Development consider only those whose age falls within 18–35. To this end, one can deduce that there is usually a misconception of youth as adolescent and adolescent as youth. Beyond using numeric explanation to define who a youth is, subjectively, some of these definitions that assume an adolescent or child as a youth can as well be right from their own lenses, such that a child that is five or seven is regarded as a youth as far as they are independent and can survive without their mothers (Heywood, 2001, p. 11).

In Western societies, youthhood is the period characterized by independence that proceeds from adolescence but precedes adulthood (Kehily, 2007). Moreover, Frith (2005) explained youthhood as more of a social construction than a biological one. For Firth, the biological transition of a child into a young adult or youth occurs at the adolescent stage, which is characterized by puberty or the hormonal or psychological changes. The definition of youth can be culturally inclined as well. From a social anthropologist's perspective, issues such as family pattern, beliefs, behaviour, norms and the political and social organization of a particular community can determine who the youth are (Kehily, 2007, p. 47). The environment, the culture, religion and economy of a particular society determines how the youths of that society are defined.

For social anthropologists, an individual can only be regarded as a youth if they have passed through all the necessary procedures known as the "rites of passage." For instance, in Nigeria, the Igbos are popularly known for a passage rite known as the Iwa Akwa, which is a ritual that allows the little ones to transit into a much-matured group. An individual is affirmed to be ready for the rite when he shows some level of independence as well as physical attributes. This Iwa Akwa is solely for the male gender and until he passes through the rite, such individual cannot be regarded as a man. In European countries, the rite of passage can be characterized as becoming employed, entering college and becoming self-sufficient and even getting married. Honwana and De Boeck (2005) defined the age of youth as a period that is characterized by expectations and responsibilities and only those that have the resources and capability to shoulder those responsibilities are referred to as youth. To this end, the age of youth is defined by cultural markers in which the group is characterized by distinct social status, specific social roles, rituals and relationships.

In conceptualizing youth, it is important to understand it from quantitative perspective, a socially constructed orientation, a psychological opinion and socio-culturally, so that the definition of youth is holistic. One could go further to describe the age of youthhood as a period of experimentation with roles and identities, and that, although they are not pressurized into the norms of the society, they are steadily preparing for that phase of life of becoming burdened with societal expectation or obligation.

Theorizing Youthhood

In theorizing the youth as a group of people, it is first of all important to understand these groups of individuals as humans before categorizing them into youths or those who make up the youthhood cohort. Since it has been established that all youths are humans but not all humans are youths, when theorizing youth, it simply means understanding the totality of youths from a theoretical perspective. It should also be brought to bear that societies construct what youths are termed to be, and prior to individuals attaining the youthhood state, there has been a transition – a metamorphosis from the childhood state, or the adolescent state, all through to the youthhood state. It should also be noted that each of these stages are characterized by different activities, different levels of self-identification and different facets to the socialization process, and they are opportune to face, experience, learn and unlearn different aspects of life just by merely growing. Moreover, the total make-up of human nature is the synthesis of nature and nurture. Therefore, irrespective of what the youths have become or been structured to be based on external and internal factors, they are formed by the composition of biological and environmental conditioning. Hence, in theorizing youthhood, one is theoretically explaining human beings of a particular group of people (Erikson, 1968).

As it was earlier claimed that human nature is as a result of the synthesis of nature and nurture. This claim however falls under the psychosocial theory. This theory opined that the composition of human life is as a result of the interaction of three elements; the biological system, psychological system and the societal system (Erikson, 1968; Coulshed and Orme, 2006, p. 109). Sensory capacities, circulatory and motor responses, and genetic composition make up the biological system while mental processes, personality traits, emotions, and cognitive reasoning are the component of the psychological system. The last element, which is the societal system, has to do with family, the socialization process, societal expectations, and the social and cultural environment. Moreover, all the systems are in continuous interaction with one another with and among every individual.

One of the psychosocial theorists is Erikson, who identified the different stages of human development with respect to the age group that falls within each stage (Austrian, 2008; Higley, 2019). Stage one to stage four cover the childhood and adolescent groups, which are characterized by being needful, having a sense of dependence and separate identity, experimentation and role playing. Stages five and six cover the youth, which is the central concern of this chapter. In stage five, individuals are in a state of identity formation, independent from societal demands, parents' opinion and peer pressure, while stage six has to do with forming relationships and intimacy. The adequate development of each of the stages is an essential prerequisite for the succeeding stage. This means that if stages one to four are not adequately managed by the various agents of socialization, the youthhood stage can be negatively altered, which will become detrimental to the society. It is therefore important that before reaching the age of youths, children and adolescents should be helped to deal with barriers that can be detrimental at their youthful age (Austrian, 2008; Higley, 2019).

Still theorizing youthhood, it is necessary to understand the nature of their needs during their youthful period. Judging from Abraham Maslow's "Hierarchy of Needs," humans' needs develop in a progressive manner, in which a particular need of the lower level needs to meet before the succeeding need can be met. Abraham Maslow was able to point out the five-step hierarchy of needs of human starting from physiological needs such as clothing, food and shelter. Following the physiological need are safety and security needs, social needs, the need for self-esteem and, lastly, self-actualization. According to Maslow, every individual is expected to pass through the needs from the lowest to the highest needs, and until the preceding needs are satisfied, the succeeding needs cannot be attained. Judging from the assumption of Maslow's theory, all youths are expected to satisfy their needs in a progressive manner, starting from the physiological needs; hence the reason a graduate who has been unable to get their desired job settles for lesser employment, in a bid to satisfy physiological needs rather than being concerned about their social status.

In explaining youthhood as a fraction of a larger society, social system theory gives a vivid theoretical lens on youths as a subsystem of the larger system. The social system theory postulated that "the whole is more than the sum of the parts." The basic assumption of social system theory is that, in every society or system, there exists a smaller fraction of elements known as the subsystem.

From this theory, one gets to understand that youths are part of society and they are indispensable. More importantly, although they form their own cohort group, they are as well found within the various systems or institutions that make up the whole. They form their own subculture and way of life as an entity and in turn infuse their subculture into other systems of society. According to Davies (2004, p. 380), the youths impact the system and they are impacted by it. Just as the youths get to influence or affect the society in which they live, the environment – be it the political or economic system or religion or social media – also influences their composition, mindset and way of life; hence the reason youths differ among societies or countries.

Take as examples the #EndSARS situation in Nigeria, which was a hash tag that was started by Nigerian youth through social media or the Black Lives Matter movement in United States. Each situation occurred as a result of the larger system (polity, unemployment, discrimination) being incapable of protecting the lives of their citizens, especially youths, from the hands of the armed forces and the whites, respectively, hence a subculture among the youths was created. This subculture (peaceful protest, use of social media for awareness) was a response from the youths to actions from the larger society (police brutality, colour discrimination), which, for some, was termed a positive reaction while negative for others. From social system theory, it is important that both the subsystem (youthhood) and the system at large (society) should be understood in order to be able to understand how the youths act, what influences their actions and how their actions influence society at large.

Further explaining youthhood as a subsystem of the larger system, advocacy theory explains how this group of people have been marginalized, discriminated against, incapacitated by the larger society and how their rights have been trampled upon. This is as a result of the unequal distribution of resources and power within a society, in which a group of people who are not the youth have been able to acquire both power and resources overtime. From the standpoint of advocacy theory, the youths are involved in ensuring these resources and power are equally distributed among all groups (Peteru, 2008, p. 26). These struggles are evidently seen in the clamour of youths wanting to be involved in politics not just as a voter or political campaigner but holding relevant positions within the system. Apart from wanting to be involved in politics, there has been agitation about the failure of society to safeguard their rights and lives as well. Other theoretical orientations that can be used to explain youthhood are the functionalist theory, the looking glass self by Cooley (1902), who opined that individuals are a reflection of how the society in which they live views them – hence if a society expects positive behaviour from youths, according to Cooley, the individuals (youths) will exhibit positive behaviour and vice versa.

The State of Youths: Currents and Perspectives

The UN estimates that 41% of the world's population is under the age of 24 (UNDP, 2010). However, regardless of this proportion which some have termed the "youth bulge," youths have not been well represented in decision-making in either public or private sectors (Acosta, Szlamka, and Mostajo-Radji, 2020). To address this issue, the UN developed the Adolescents 2030 initiative in 2018, stressed the need to empower youth to attain their greatest potential (United Nations Youth Strategy, 2018). The strategy adopted to achieve these goals included engaging youth voices to achieve a peaceful, just and sustainable world, increasing young people's access to education and health services, improving access to decent and productive employment through empowerment as well as promoting and protecting their human and civil rights.

From a global perspective, the state of youth and their experiences can be described using one term or analogy, which is the "state of dilemma": asking questions that have answers yet they are asked rhetorically, and it is a new stage of life where crucial decisions are made. These decisions can either make or mar the youths involved. Keniston (1970) described the youths as those who "seem not to be able to settle down" and are unable to give answers to the issues of life, such as what relationship to venture into, their desired vocation or profession, whether they are willing to unlearn and relearn new social lifestyles and if they are really independent in action. Using the description of Keniston (1970), youths arc characterized by "pervasive ambivalence toward self and society," a "feeling of absolute freedom, of living in a world of pure possibilities" and "the enormous value placed upon change, transformation and movement," and though they are the age group paid less attention, they contribute significantly to the demographic make-up of the society.

As this state is a crucial phase of life, it is important to note that external factors such as the political, economic, infrastructural and religious environment, as well as family, social media and peer groups, all contribute significantly to youthful development and provide a favourable environment for self-actualization. However, rather than helping to facilitate youth development, some of these institutions are contributing to the negative state of youths in society. It is noteworthy that the youths, irrespective of their social construction, are energetic, futuristic, optimistic, enterprising and the hope of tomorrow. When external factors do not seem to favour their goals, the end result is for them to become pessimistic, dangerous and deviant and their behaviours end up causing their environment to deteriorate. Observing the state of youths through five basic lenses – politics, economy, religion, family and social media – this chapter gives an overview of both the positive and the negative state of the youths in their various societies.

Politically, statistics have shown that youths are usually marginalized when it comes to political involvement such as occupying a political position and getting involved in political decisions. Globally, fewer than 2% of youths are members of a parliament, although youths make up about 10% of members of parliament in countries such as Ecuador, Norway, Sweden and Finland (Inter-Parliamentary Union, 2016). The United Nations Development Programme (UNDP, 2012) also asserted that, when it comes to occupying formal political positions, youths (below 35 years of age) are rarely found within politics; moreover, at the national level, the age of eligibility is 25 years and more. This points to the fact that the youths are not as represented as they should be within political institutions and every other activity.

Youth studies encompass a wide range of viewpoints. It is trans-disciplinary and structured around a social core. Geographical, historical, anthropological, educational, cultural and media studies, as well as strands of adolescent psychology and economics, are all represented (Woodman and Bennett, 2015). However, there are some parallels that can serve as shared points of reference for young people. The development of effective youth policy largely depends on the blend of political priorities, professional programmes and perspectives of young peoples (Williamson, 2019). Young people, who are more connected than ever before, want to and are already contributing to their communities' resilience by providing innovative solutions with the use of technology, initiating organizations both for profit and not for profit, to push forward social progress and inspire political change across board (United Nations Youth Strategy, 2018).

There is a likelihood that the older generation would interpret their environment differently than today's youthful generation, who have witnessed the intensification of an Internet-ruled world, the global financial crisis of 2008 and the current debates over transcontinental migration, during their formative years (Philipps, 2018). Young women and men are more connected than ever before, and they are increasingly affecting the direction of their communities and countries (World Bank, 2014). The reactions of new generations to such global connection are not always favourable to globalization. Young people are rising to the occasion by pioneering the use of ICT and setting trends in an industry that is undergoing rapid growth (Alao and Brink, 2020). This has contributed greatly to several achievements towards accomplishing the Sustainable Development Goals (UNDP, 2010). Simultaneously, this generation suffers numerous challenges, including marginalization, alienation and a denial of access to opportunities and a voice in decision-making.

The Drivers and Processes of Youth Exclusion

The exclusion of young people from key socio-economic sectors has significant social and economic implications, and it may even lead to social and political instability (OECD, 2021). At best, Everatt (2015) contends, global exclusion is disregarded, or worse, reified by essentially ignoring the importance of the Global South's youth and converting them to things of remote interest, terror or predatory peering. This undervaluing of youths and their potentials puts development at risk. The 2030 Agenda pushes that everyone should benefit from wealth and enjoy minimum standards of well-being. This is encapsulated in the 17 Sustainable Development Goals, which aim for equal access to health, education, work, food, well-being and security, among other things. Acknowledging that these goals will be difficult to accomplish without making institutions work for the poorest and most vulnerable people, the Agenda includes broad goals designed to promote the statutes of the law, ensuring justice and equality and encouraging inclusiveness and participation of everyone, old and young, in decision-making.

Unfortunately, today's youth experience tremendous economic and social marginalization. Many factors contribute to youth exclusion, including illiteracy and unemployment. Furthermore, exclusion is a process that marginalizes particular persons rather than a condition. Boudarbat and Ajbilou (2007) identify the key reasons as well as situations in Morocco that exacerbate youth economic exclusion, such as low macroeconomic performance, widespread urbanization, persistence of poverty, labour markets that are underperforming and the dynamics of the family. These reasons are not, however, peculiar to Morocco, although they might differ in degree across the board. The structural character of unemployment is exacerbated by the protracted periods of unemployment that young people experience (Lahusen and Giugni, 2016; National Bureau of Statistic, 2020). There's also a mismatch between educational skills and labour market needs, slow job growth and a tenacious preference among youth for paying public sector work.

Most discussions of youth exclusion have tended towards economic exclusion with the focus on poverty and unemployment as glaring consequences. Exclusion due to labour market failure impacts not just unemployed youths who are educated but also their families (Boudarbat and Ajbilou, 2007). This is especially true for parents who are also struggling to make ends meet and who have made significant sacrifices to ensure their children get educated and subsequently become gainfully employed. The exclusion of educated youths, in particular, causes dissatisfaction resulting in different forms of social tensions displayed in riots and protests. On the other hand, because of low economic capacity, young people now delay marriages since they cannot afford the rising cost of living.

However, the exclusion of youths has broadened beyond just the economic implications resulting in massive unemployment to include social, political and cultural dimensions (World Bank, 2014). Because social exclusion is related to marginalization along numerous axes, policies that address only one component of marginalization, such as greater access to education, may be insufficient to address exclusion more broadly (World Bank, 2014). The quest to improve youth inclusion led to the #NotTooYoungToRun bill, which came into effect in 2018 ahead of the 2019 elections in Nigeria. This bill was sponsored to improve youth participation in governance and increase their political influence. However, despite the provisions of this new law and the recommendation to adopt it in other sister countries in Africa, youthful representation still remains below par. Instead, youths remain pawns in the political game, acting as the power hands of those in power, wielded to knock down opponents. The approach to youth development is now poised to move away from fragmented initiatives and towards a comprehensive set of policies and investments that maximize financial resources (World Bank, 2014). To ensure equity, national youth policies and any related reforms that span sectors but have a shared focus on young inclusion are the best way to go.

Consequences of Youth Exclusion

Over the years, there has been much attention paid to the subject of poverty in Africa by the international community, governmental and non-governmental organizations, as well as several seasoned scholars from different countries. In Nigeria, it has been observed that the country is plagued by poverty, which may be related to misuse of existing abundant resources, both in terms of human capital and natural resources (Abada and Omeh, 2019). The bulging population of youths in Africa and globally creates the expectation of a large working population, but this is not often the case as this available human resource is mismanaged. Various government regimes have implemented various programmes aimed at eradicating poverty among youngsters. While only a few of them saw major improvements, others were unable to achieve the aim as little attention was paid to the root cause of poverty in the programme designs.

Youth exclusion has also been linked with violence, insecurity and instability in many countries, especially in nations with a surge in youth population (Hilker and Fraser, 2009). Unoccupied youths are easy recruits for violent activities. Continued exclusion of youths has also been noted to lead to youth discouragement and inactivity, which is considered to be worse than unemployment (World Bank, 2014). Exclusion in the political arena also has implications for democracy, especially in African nations. Needless to say, the youths are at more of a disadvantage if democracy crumbles in Africa due to the massive generational gap between those making the policies and the majority of the citizens (Signe, 2019). Countries such as Equatorial Guinea, Cameroon, Uganda, Sudan, Chad, Eritrea, Congo, Algeria, Djibouti, Rwanda and DRC have had presidents serving consecutively for more than 15 years (Adegoke, 2017). Africa has the oldest presidents in the world even though it has highest percentage of youths globally (60%).

Conclusion

The phrase "youth are the future of tomorrow" still stands, but without proper inclusiveness of this group of people, the future can be categorically ascertained to be unsure. Right from the conceptualization of youth, they have been experiencing exclusion as the definition of youth cannot stand without comparison with either adolescents or adults. More often than not, they are characterized as people who are yet to know what they aspire to for themselves, hence they are considered incapable of thinking and ruling their countries in any sphere of life. Nevertheless, it is imperative to affirm that the youths are the most agile, strongly willed group of people, hence the agitation for inclusiveness. Moreover, the world is evolving to be more technologically inclined: automation and artificial intelligence keep increasing and the youths make up the majority of the population who have been able to develop skills that accommodate twenty-first-century technology. To this end, lawmakers, institutions and governments need to be proactive in engaging youths if development and sustainability of the country is to be assured.

The continuous exclusion of youths from social, political, economic and cultural processes is as a result of the absence of strong youth policies that ensure inclusion. In places where such policies are in existence, little is done to ensure inclusion. The success of present youth policies and initiatives is another area where more research and evaluation is required. Often times, in an attempt to solve the problem of unemployment and the different forms of economic exclusion, programmes and policies are formulated that appear to address the issues while ignoring the preferences and needs of young people. A fundamental precondition for addressing youth economic exclusion in countries will be a radical reassessment of each country's development strategy, pushing it towards a more youth-oriented growth model. In countries such as Tunisia and Egypt, that have experienced uprising as a result of youth frustrations and exclusion, little has been done to realign policies to ensure more youth inclusion. In-depth political transformation and a substantial reorganization of the present political-economic dynamics, which are notably youth-hostile, will be required for a serious reorientation of past economic policies (Akanle & Omotayo, 2020). Such policies and reorientation cannot be possible when youths remain excluded from decision-making processes. In addition, a bottom-up approach to implementing policies should be implemented. With this approach, the youth will be involved in the formulation process of the policy and their needs can be reflected within the policy's actions and objectives.

It is noteworthy that youth do not live in isolation; external factors such as the agents of socialization and institutions all play a contributing role to the make-up of youths within a country. Hence, a cohort of youth in Africa can act differently from their contemporaries in the United States. The synthesis of nature and nurture also varies among countries. For this reason, it might be difficult to assume that what works for one country can be implemented in another nation. Basically, policies surrounding youths should be indigenized and utmost attention needs to be given to the nature and nurture environment as it can either make or mar the youth (Erikson, 1968).

References

Abada, I. M. and Omeh, P. H. 2019. Social intervention schemes and poverty alleviation among Nigerian youths, *International Journal of Scientific and Research Publications (IJSRP)*, 9(9), 9394. https://doi.org/10.29322/ijsrp.9.09.2019.p9394

Acosta, M., Szlamka, Z. and Mostajo-Radji, M. 2020. Transnational youth networks: an evolving form of public diplomacy to accelerate the Sustainable Development Goals. SocArXiv 8247s, Center for Open Science. Handle: RePEc:osf:socarx:8247s doi: 10.31219/osf.io/8247s.

Adegoke, Y. 2017. The world's youngest continent will keep being run by its oldest leaders. *Mind Gap. QuartzAfrica*. December 28, 2017. Available at: https://qz.com/africa/1162490/the-youngest-continent-keeps-on-being-run-by-the-oldest-leaders/

Akanle, O. and Omotayo, A. 2020. Youth, unemployment and incubation hubs in Southwest Nigeria. *African Journal of Science, Technology, Innovation and Development. 12*(2), 165–172.

Alao, A. and Brink, R. 2020. Impact of ICTs for sustainable development of youth employability. In *Promoting Inclusive Development in Fourth Industrial Revolution*. http://dx.doi.org/10.4018/978-1-7998-4882-0.ch006

Austrian, S. G. 2008. *Developmental Theories Through the Life Cycle*, 2nd ed., Chichester, NY, Columbia University Press.

Boudarbat, B. and Ajbilou, A. 2007. *Youth Exclusion in Morocco: Context, Consequences, and Policies*, The Middle East Youth Initiative Working Paper 5. Dubai School of Government.

Bourdieu, P. 1993. Youth' is just a word. In *Sociology in Question*, Ed. P. Bourdieu, pp. 94–102, Thousand Oaks, CA, Sage.

Cooley, H. C. 1902. *Human Nature and the Social Order*, pp. 179–185, New York, NY, Scribner's.

Coulshed, V. and Orme. J. 2006. *Social Work Practice*, 4th ed., China, Palgrave Macmillan.

Davies, M. 2004. *The Blackwell Encyclopaedia of Social Work*, Oxford, Blackwell Publishing.

Erikson, E. H. 1968. *Identity: Youth and Crisis*, No. 7, New York, NY, WW Norton and Company.

Everatt, D. 2015. The politics of non-belonging in the developing world. In *Handbook of Children and Youth Studies*, Eds J. Wyn and H. Cahill, pp. 63–78, Singapore, Springer. ISBN 978-981-4451-14-7.

Frith, S. 2005. Youth/music/television. In *Sound and Vision*, pp. 68–83, London, Routledge.

Guilia, P. 2013. Youth social exclusion and lessons from youth work. Report produced by the Education, Audiovisual and Culture Executive Agency (EACEA). Available at: file:///C:/Users/KAYODE%20DEMILADE/Documents/YOUTHHOOD/eurydice-study-social-exclusion-2013.pdf

Heywood, C. 2001. *A History of Childhood*, Cambridge, Polity Press.

Higley, E. 2019. Defining young adulthood. DNP Qualifying Manuscripts 17. Available at: https://repository.usfca.edu/dnp_qualifying/17

Hilker, L. M. and Fraser, E. 2009. Youth exclusion, violence, conflict and fragile states. In *Report Prepared for DFUD's Equity and Rights Team*. https://doi.org/10.1007/BF01164663

Honwana, A. and De Boeck, F. Eds 2005. *Makers and Breakers: Children and Youth in Postcolonial Africa*. Oxford, James Currey; Trenton, NJ, Africa World Press; Dakar, Codesria.

Inter-Parliamentary Union. 2016. *Youth Participation in National Parliaments*, Chemin du Pommier 5 CH - 1218 Le Grand-Saconnex, Geneva. Available at: www.ipu.org

Kehily, M. J. 2007. *Understanding Youth: Perspectives, Identities and Practices*, Milton Keynes, Open University Press.

Keniston, K. 1970. Youth: a "new' stage of life," *American Scholar*, *39*(1970), 632–636.

Lahusen, C. and Giugni, M. Eds. 2016. Experiencing long-term unemployment in Europe: youth on the edge. In *Experiencing Long-Term Unemployment in Europe: Youth on the Edge*, London Borough of Camden, Palgrave Macmillan https://doi.org/10.1057/978-1-137-50487-6

National Bureau of Statistic. 2020. Labor force statistics: unemployment and underemployment report, *Labor Force Statistics Unemployment and Underemployment Report*, *1*(December), 1–88. Available at: https://www.proshareng.com/news/NigeriaEconomy/Unemployment-Rate-Rises-to-18.8Percent-i/37757

Office of Disease Prevention and Health Promotion. 2018. Adolescent health. Healthy People 2020. Available at: https://www.healthypeople.gov/2020/topicsobjectives/topic/Adolescent-Health

OECD (Organization for Economic Co-operation and Development). 2021. The updated youth OECD action plan. Report of meeting of OECD Council Members. May 11–June 1 2021.

Oparina, N., Kazakova, I. S., Abramov, Y. V., Shapovalov, N. I. and Ilyin, V. A. 2020. Youth subculture and modern society, *Journal of Critical Reviews*, 7(13), 363–365.

Peteru, P. S. 2008. Youth development: a Pacific content, *Journal of Commonwealth, Youth and Development*, 6(1), 23–35.

Philipps, J. 2018. A global generation? *Youth studies in a postcolonial world, Societies*, 8, 14. doi:10.3390/soc8010014

Signe, L. 2019. Africa youth leadership: building local leaders to solve global challenges. *Africa in Focus. Brookings.edu March 27*, 2019. Available at: https://www.brookings. edu/blog/africa-in-focus/2019/03/27/africa-youth-leadership-building-local-leaders-to-solve-global-challenges/

UNDP (United Nations Population Division). 2007. Summary of the virtual round table on social exclusion. United Nations Development Programme [pdf] Available at: http://hdr.undp.org/en/nhdr/networks/replies/161.pdf [Accessed 11 March 2013]

UNDP (United Nations Population Division). 2010. *UN-DESA World Population Prospects: 2010 Revision 3*. Available at: https://www.un.org/en/development/desa/population/index.asp

UNDP. (United Nations Population Division). 2012. *Enhancing Youth Political Participation Throughout the Electoral Cycle: A Good Practice Guide*, New York, NY, UNDP.

United Nations Youth Strategy. 2018. *Youth 2030: The UN Youth Strategy Office of the Secretary-General's Envoy on Youth*. Available at: https://www.un.org/youthenvoy/youth-un/

Williamson, H. 2019. *Youth and Policy*, 1st ed., London, Taylor & Francis. Available at: https://www.perlego.com/book/1503476/youth-and-policy-pdf

Woodman, D. and Bennett, A. 2015. Cultures, transitions, and generations: the case for a new youth studies, *Youth Cultures, Transitions, and Generations*, 1–15. https://doi.org/10.1057/9781137377234_1

World Bank. 2014. Breaking the barriers to youth inclusion, *New Directions for Youth Development*, *141*, 9–14. Available at: http://www.ncbi.nlm.nih.gov/pubmed/24753274

World Health Organization. 2014. Health for the world's adolescents: a second chance in the second decade. Available at: http://apps.who.int/adolescent/seconddecade/section2/page1/recognizing-adolescence.html

Chapter Two

Youth and Desperate Migration: A Historical and Cultural Perspective

Terngu Sylvanus Nomishan

Introduction

The phenomenon of migration dates back to the origins of humankind (Adepoju, 1995, 2008).

> Migration is a constant behaviour in human history, and has been effective in all human races throughout the world. No human group can claim not to have migrated from one region to another and also to its present abode. (Nomishan, 2020, p. 31)

Historical records from many centuries past show that people from all parts of the world have moved to other locations for various purposes – whether for settlement, agriculture, technology or trade, among other reasons. For instance, there are well-established trade routes among western Africa and the Arabian Peninsula and India, and the trans-Saharan connects either end of the Sahara. These were developed through caravan trade (Afani, 2013). Today, migration takes place in different forms for different reasons. And as the population continues to grow, migration has also progressively become more dynamic in its nature and scope on a daily basis. Both adults and youths may migrate consistently from one location to another. However, for the purpose of this chapter, concentration is on desperate youth migration and its historical and cultural dimensions.

The concept of "youth" is best understood as a period of transition from the dependence of childhood to adulthood's independence and awareness of our interdependence as members of a community (UNESCO, 2016). Youth is a more fluid category than a fixed age group. The United Nations General Assembly defined youth as those persons falling between the ages of 15 and 24 years (United Nations, 2001). This definition is based on the premise that the age of 15 years represents the earliest acceptable school-leaving age, while 24 years is

Youth Exclusion and Empowerment in the Contemporary Global Order:
Existentialities in Migrations, Identity and the Digital Space, 17–31
Copyright © 2022 by Terngu Sylvanus Nomishan
Published under exclusive licence by Emerald Publishing Limited
doi:10.1108/978-1-80382-777-320221003

the age at which most people will have completed tertiary education (O'Higgins, 2002). There are more young people in the world presently than there have ever been. Statistics show that there are about 1.8 billion young people in the world (UNFPA, 2014). This indicates that they are the largest category of people in the history of the world. Based on the 2017 revised report of the United Nations, Trends in International Migrant Stock, there were 258 million international migrants, out of which 11% were under the age of 24. Also, the United Nations reported in 2011 that youths have a higher propensity to migrate than their adult counterparts. Youths get connected to each other as they live in a world of unlimited potential, constituting a tremendous and essential asset worth investing in, to open the door to an unparalleled multiplier effect through them (IOM, 2020).

However, given lack of youth training, empowerment or inclusion in strategic decision-making, policy planning and design and leadership, among so many other factors, there is generally a constant situation of desperation among the youths. This has also led to desperate migration of youths from different locations to others perceived to possess better or brighter potentials to explore. The launch of the United Nations Youth Strategy (United Nations, 2018b) was made necessary by the problems youths come across during migration. This is in addition to the general non-inclusion of youths in development policy frameworks and decision-making, among many other factors.

Priority 1 of the United Nations Youth Strategy, which is "Engagement, Participation and Advocacy," is to serve as reference for collective efforts to enhance migration governance, develop policy frameworks and foster greater cooperation, partnerships and networks for future action. The 2018 World Youth Report emphasizes that the goals, targets and instruments incorporated in the 2030 Agenda for Sustainable Development offer increased opportunities to advance youth development objectives in the context of socially, economically and environmentally sustainable development efforts (IOM, 2020).

There is a conviction that

> when young people are empowered and well equipped with required skills, they can use their energies, creative thinking and expertise to turn uncertain landscapes into dozens of opportunities in the world. If engaged in a community development plan, through meaningful participation in policy and decision making, they are more likely to support their communities towards much positive growth. They can play a key role in policy discussions; defend their rights by making convincing demands for better opportunities, through round-table negotiations. An example of this is the world youth movement against climate change. (IOM, 2020, pp. 3–4)

Further, the main objective of the United Nations Youth Strategy is

> to facilitate increased impact and expanded global, regional and country-level action to address the needs, build the agency and advance the rights of young people in all their diversity around

the world. It is also to ensure their engagement and participation in the implementation, review and follow-up of the 2030 Agenda for Sustainable Development, as well as other relevant global agendas and frameworks (United Nations, 2017, cited in IOM, 2020, p. 5)

Without this, youths are likely going to be moving (desperately and in great numbers) from one location to another in search of greener pastures which, most of the time, results in frustration, manipulation, intimidation, segregation, discrimination and maltreatment.

Historical and Cultural Perspectives on Youth (Desperate) Migration

Intra and inter-continental migration is a culture that dates back to the origins of humankind (Adepoju, 1995, 2008). Archaeologists, anthropologists, historians and other scientists of the prehistoric era have established that, in the hunter-gatherer days, human beings (whether young or old) moved from place to place in search of food (Beekman and Christensen, 2003; Christenson, 1980; Clark and Yi, 1983; Harari, 2014; Nomishan, 2020).

Pre-modern migration of human populations began with the movement of *Homo erectus* out of Africa across Eurasia some 1.75 million years ago. By 150,000 years ago, *Homo sapiens* appeared to have occupied all of Africa. However, from recent studies, it appears that some members of *Homo sapiens* moved out of Africa into Asia about 125,000 years ago (Bae, Douka, and Petraglia, 2017). Another recent study places as early as 270,000 years ago (Posth et al., 2017; Zimmer, 2017).

The coming of agriculture brought another impressive dimension to migration in human history. This time, humans began to move from place to place in search of arable land and water for themselves and for their domesticated plants and animals.

Further, the advent of science and technology in the history of humans made migration even more complex and dynamic. At this point, humankind began to aggressively move to areas where they could find abundant resources to use. For example, almost all the early humans moved from one place to the other in search of fertile land to farm. Also, people who knew the techniques of making clay pots had to move to locations where quality clay could be found, just as people who had the knowledge of iron smelting moved to locations with availability of iron ore, and so on.

Moreover, the complexity in human migration soared in the era of intra and inter-continental trade (in goods and slaves). It was already mentioned that records from many centuries past show well-established trade routes among western Africa, the Arabian Peninsula and India, and between either ends of the Sahara through the trans-Saharan caravan trade (Afani, 2013). North African Arabs initiated and sustained the trans-Saharan trade for gold and slaves from sub-Saharan regions for a long time.

Further, as kingdoms and empires with powerful and influential kings and emperors began to spring up, another complex dimension came to human mobility. At this time, powerful empires and kingdoms started fighting and overthrowing less powerful or influential ones. They conquered and controlled lesser kingdoms and thereby imposed harsh conditions of living on members of the conquered kingdoms. This usually led to desperate movement of members of these less powerful kingdoms to new and virgin locations in order to avoid being sent into extinction or captured and turned into slaves. The Bantu expansion and the (putative) north-south migration of Hamites, and the migration of Germanic tribes into the Roman Empire, are some of the examples of migrations for the purposes of conquest and dominance that took place in human history.

Therefore, migrations took place in the past for different reasons at different times. And this culture continued into what is known as religious intended movements (for purposes of conversion and, more recently, pilgrimages in a limited context). All these movements have always involved young people, and many of the migrations were carried out under pressure and desperation. In historical terms, major incidences of migration have included the influx of immigrants to the United States from the mid-1800s to the twentieth century and flows of people (old and young) at the end of World War II, when tens of millions of people, particularly in Europe, were sundered from their native countries by years of violent conflict. The movement of more than 17 million Africans (young and old) within their continent in the twenty-first century is variously considered as the major incidents that mark the beginning of youth migration across the globe (Meisel, 2017).

Today, opportunities are often found in urban locations, and many young people in the world – particularly those in Africa, who have been described as belonging to an immensely mobile continent (Bruijn, Rijk and Dick, 2001; Curtin, 1997; IOM, 2005) – migrate to work or attend school in other parts of the world, preferably America, Asia and Europe. They thereby leave behind their parents and natal homes (Heckert, 2015). As already established above, the migrant population, both in terms of volume and the effect they have on the giving and receiving countries, keeps growing at a concerning rate.

A 2014 report by the United Nations Inter-Agency Network Global Migration Group on migration and youth indicates that, in 2013, young migrants aged 15–24 represented 12% of the total migrant population of 28.2 million people. A summary of the international migrants indicates that 10.2% of migrants from developed countries, 14.9% from developing countries and 20.9 from the least-developed countries were young people. In developed countries, young women made up 8.9% of young migrants and 43% of young migrants in developing countries. Within this period, a total of 27 million young people left their countries of birth to seek employment abroad as international migrants.

This means that migration is a cultural phenomenon which starts from places with fewer opportunities and ranges to those with more or moderate opportunities. For example, rural youth often migrate to urban settlements because of certain disadvantages (considered in the next paragraph) which characterize rural dwelling. Desperate youth migration from some African countries to other continents (usually refers to as developed countries) also has some root in these disadvantages.

Some Relevant Cases of Desperate Youth Migration

These cases are sourced from research conducted by the American Bar Association (ABA) Center on Children and the Law regarding the experiences of illiterate migrants (ABA, 2018), as well as Plutzar and Ritter's (2012) research for the Council of Europe, Language and Policy Division. The cases centre on the needs of illiterate migrants in Australia and experiences of desperate migrants in the United States. They are therefore relevant to the present research because they reveal the negative effects of desperate migration on migrants (particular the youths).

The case of Mira from Serbia

According to Plutzar and Ritter (2012, p. 2), Mira, a migrant from Serbia to Australia,

> could not attend school in Serbia when she was a child because her mother died when she was only 7 years old. As she was the eldest daughter, she had to deal with the household duties and care for her siblings from then on. This enabled all her brothers and sisters to go to school, while for Mira this was not possible.

After some time, Mira migrated to Austria, having a husband and two young children.

> Her husband got work on a construction site, and was in and out of work for years, until he had an accident on a construction site that left him deaf. Mira herself worked for 11 years in the kitchen of a Viennese restaurant.

Life was not easy for Mira because she had no formal education that could give her a white-collar job. She continued to struggle with life until she was able to get scholarship for her children to acquire good education and get good jobs in later times (Plutzar and Ritter, 2012).

The case of Yousof from Afghanistan

Yousof desperately migrated to Austria as an asylum seeker at the age of 35 years, with his wife and two kids. After some time, his application for asylum was granted by the Austrian authorities, and Yousof was then allowed to work in Austria. He began to search for a job desperately in order to make a living for himself and his family. In the words of Plutzar and Ritter (2012, p. 3), like over 50% of male adults and over 87% of female adults in Afghanistan (UNESCO Institute for Statistics, 2006), Yousof did not go to school. In Afghanistan he worked as a mechanic for many years, learning from a master of the trade, like many other illiterate male immigrants. While in Afghanistan he was a crafts-man sustaining his family, but in Austria it is hard for him to get a job because of his low level of literacy.

This problem affected Yousof's efforts to find a job and afford a better life for himself and family. He then decided to enrol himself in adult education where he was able to learn a little German. Yousof continued to face discrimination at the level of looking for a job because literacy skills were not good enough, even if the job required little or no high level of education or language competence.

The case of Maka-Laye from Ivory Coast

Maka-Laye was 21 years old when he migrated to Austria in 2008 as an asylum seeker. According to Plutzar and Ritter (2012, p. 4), Maka-Laye:

> is plurilingual and speaks Tula (mother tongue), Arabic, Yoruba, some Fula, very good oral French and intermediate oral German. He is partially literate having had three years of schooling in the Ivory Coast. He wanted to sit for the school-leaving certificate examinations, which would enable him to start an apprenticeship. However, he was not yet qualified for a secondary school course because he lacked reading and writing skills.

A further obstacle in Maka-Laye's way was that in Austria, there are few lan-guage and literacy courses for asylum seekers. Even though he was young and very eager to learn, Maka-Laye's opportunities were very limited. At the age of 21, he still had to attend a youth course to acquire literacy training before seeking skills that would help him fend for himself. This kind of treatment is not applica-ble to Maka-Laye alone but to almost all migrants in his category.

The case of Victor and Christopher from El Salvador

The ABA Centre on Children and the Law published that

> Victor and his four-year-old son Christopher fled El Salvador to the United States of America in 2015, and crossed the border with his child without inspection. Victor decided to flee because his wife (Christopher's mother) had been killed in an attack on a bus while coming home from work and he felt unsafe trying to raise his son there.

In the United States, Victor started suffering from depression and post-trau-matic stress disorder. Initially, he was able to work as a day labourer and found day care for Christopher. Because of his depression, however, Victor eventually became unable to work; therefore, it became a huge struggle to care for his young child. After a while, Victor's son Christopher began to suffer frequent illness and huger; he also had asthma that appeared to be untreated. And even though a caregiver at Christopher's day care noticed all these problems,

> she hesitated to contact Child Protective Services (CPS). This was because of Victor and Christopher's lack of immigration status and because she was not sure CPS would have many services to assist non-English speakers. (ABA, 2018, p. 9)

The case of Lizette, Tomas and Ana from Guatemala

Lizette's husband was killed by a gang in Guatemala and she decided to migrate to the United States with Tomas, her four-year-old son.

> She and Tomas were stopped at the border, then released and issued Notices to Appear in Immigration Court. An Immigration Judge subsequently issued *in absentia* removal orders for each of them when they did not appear for proceedings. Tomas turned 11 years old in 2018, and has a six-year-old sister, Ana, who was born in the USA, and whose father left the family soon after Ana's birth. (ABA Center on Children and the Law, 2018, p. 5)

The US Immigration and Customs Enforcement (ICE) arrested and detained Lizette during a raid and pickup of any employee who could not provide evidence of lawful immigration status. When the ICE asked if anyone needed to make plans for children in their care before being detained, Lizette didn't tell the ICE about her children because she was scared Tomas could be detained as well. However, when Lizette failed to pick up her children from school, the school authorities called Lizette's emergency contact, a family friend named Marta. Though Marta agreed to take care of Lizette children, she soon became highly overwhelmed with the burden of caring for Lizette children in addition to hers. This forced Marta to start searching for Lizette in immigration detention but she could not get any tangible information about her. Thus, Marta decided to call the Child Protection Services and ask the agency to place Tomas and his sister in foster care while their mother remained in immigration detention.

The above cases represent a tiny proportion of the cases of desperate youth migration and the conditions they commonly find themselves in around the world.

Factors that Trigger Youth Desperate Migration

"Generally speaking, migration, in its broadest meaning – spatial mobility – can be regarded as part of the human condition" (Bilger and Kraler, 2005). Normally, human beings are dynamic creatures and have high tendencies to move from place to place at different times (as seen in human historiography and archaeological records). However, the desire to move out of a particular location in favour of another does not just arise. Migration among humans is largely influenced by "political, economic, cultural, ecological and the social context in which it occurs" (Bade, 2000, p. 11, cited in Bilger and Kraler, 2005, p. 5).

As noted earlier, the desire to migrate from a given location to another is usually or mostly triggered by unfavourable factors experienced at the initial point. In the case of the youth, particularly in recent times, factors that trigger migration among them, especially at the international level, include environmental changes, lack of quality or productive education, low-wage employment, unemployment, underdevelopment, poverty, drugs, crime and overpopulation. Pull factors for youth desperate migration include prospects for getting a better education, marriage, increasing earning power and improved living conditions through access to better infrastructure and public amenities, among others. The above is particularly true in the case of youth in many (if not all) African countries, who desperately migrate to developed countries of the world such as the United Kingdom, United States, Canada, China, Japan, France, Germany, Italy and Spain, among others, in search of greener pastures.

Further, environmental factors such as climate change, desertification and lack of arable soil have been instrumental in triggering desperate migration of millions of young people from one place to another, both in the past and present. For example, the expansion of the Sahara Desert in the northern part of Africa has, over time, forced great numbers of people to move out of the desertified region to other locations within and outside Africa with the hope of finding better prospects for agriculture and animal grazing, among other life fortunes.

The syndrome of the spread of Fulani herders and its effect on the West African subregion is also blamed on the expansion of the Sahara Desert. And this is also a strong factor triggering desperate migration of the youths from the North African region to other parts of the continent and to other countries of the world in search of better opportunities. No wonder the desert and the Mediterranean Sea have over time had their bellies swollen with human corpses.

In the same vein, factors such as unemployment and lack of access to education have been uprooting large numbers of youths from African countries to their American, Asian and European counterparts. For example, the desperate migration of the youths to Global North countries is precipitated by the recruitment of foreign labour by these countries, where the twin factors of an ageing population and a declining birth rate are at play (Akinyemi and Ikuteyijo, 2009).

Youth desperate migration affects mostly African countries because leadership policies in African countries have, over time, neglected proper youth training (in terms of relevant skill acquisition) and their engagement, empowerment and enhancement for national progress and development, as well as inclusion in policymaking, thereby leaving youths in an unlimited and uncontrolled anxiety and desperation that leads them to take risky actions intended to avert the perturbation.

Further, overpopulation is recently becoming a huge factor in youth desperate migration. Youths have continued to migrate from overpopulated areas to locations with less population. This is because overpopulated areas suffer inevitable diminishing resources that should support their teaming inhabitants. In some cases, this triggers crises or disputes in a community, resulting in the death of several people, especially youths. Thus, the youths, being the worst affected by these adverse effects of overpopulation, turn to aggressively or desperately move out to areas with more, sufficient or surplus resources. Even in the developed countries, overpopulation has an adverse effect on the youths in certain locations. And because the youths are mostly in the category of people searching for employment opportunities, they largely turn to migrate in great numbers from locations or states with large population and few opportunities, to those with sufficient opportunities.

War or conflict also triggers youth desperate migration. A practical example is the incidence presently taking place in Afghanistan, where Afghan citizens, residents, tourists and students, among others, are desperately migrating to other parts of the world for fear of being killed by the Taliban authority. It has been reported that approximately 125,000 people, including about 6,000 US citizens and their families, were evacuated from Afghanistan on 31 August 2021 (Macias, 2021). This is in addition to several million Afghan citizens presently living in other countries of the world. Also, the conflict between Middle Belt farmers and Fulani herders in Nigeria has forced millions of young people in Benue, Plateau, Taraba, Nasarawa and Southern Kaduna, among others, to move to urban areas for safety and better opportunities.

Consequences of Youth Desperate Migration

Archaeological and historical records indicate that migrants were usually faced with several challenges depending on the conditions surrounding such migrations. For instance, people who were affected by epidemics and pandemics in history experienced high vulnerability (Huremović, 2019; Jarus, 2020; Rosenwald, 2020), some of whom desperately migrated to other places. In their bid to migrate, they got attacked by natural or human forces resulting in more casualties (Robert Wood Johnson Foundation, 2013). Some of these epidemics and pandemics disproportionately affected previously healthy young adults (Craig, 2017; Huremović, 2019; Reid, 2015), thereby, triggering more aggression in youth migration.

The above narrative is not far from what has been happening to young migrants in recent times. Desperate youth migrants facing a lot of challenges, ranging from natural to human induced. Cortina, Taran and Raphael (2014, p. 3) posits that "migrant youth face risks compounded by their age, gender, migration status, and cultural identity." They are generally resilient, ambitious and adaptable and, therefore, most sought after by employers. However, while migrant youth commonly face social exclusion, disruption of family and absence of social protection, young women and girl migrants are more at risk of abuse, discrimination and gender-based violence, including sexual violence.

In many cases, the arrival of rural migrants to urban areas increases the unemployment rate and expands the pool of young urban job seekers, which, in effect, reduces the pressure on employers to offer competitive wages and favourable working conditions to this category of workers. This also promotes willingness to by-pass set labour standards in a bid to bastardize the system to the detriment of the migrants.

Moreover,

> youth migrants belonging to specific ethnic or cultural groups, as well as youth with disabilities, face particular difficulties. Available data shows that youth, particularly migrant youth, are more likely to experience unemployment, lack of access to decent work, exploitative working conditions, inadequate access to skills and vocational training, and social marginalization and exclusion (Cortina et al., 2014, p. 3),

inter alia.

Furthermore, "environmental drivers also contribute to make the situation worse – when factors such as prolonged droughts, rising sea levels and coastal erosion further reduce employment opportunities" in migrant-receiving societies (Martin and Herzberg, 2014, p. 3).

It has been observed that urban areas are becoming extremely overcrowded and overburdened, putting pressure on insufficient infrastructures, schools, health facilities, sanitation and water systems. This escalating urbanization deficit has created a new context of poverty in which urban centres are overtaxed and unprepared to absorb increasing youth unemployment. In absolute numbers, youth unemployment becomes more prevalent in urban areas than rural areas (Min-Harris, 2019).

Female youth are

> often especially at risk and/or face additional gender-related challenges. Young women migrants increasingly work in [a] diverse number of sectors, such as manufacturing, construction, or nursing and homecare globally – where they may face general gender-related problems, workplace constraints, including lower wages or lack of childcare. More so, a large share of unskilled or undocumented women migrants finds work as domestic servants. Such women, who often work and live in their employers' homes, can be invisible to authorities and become subject to low pay, restricted freedom, and sexual exploitation. (S4YE, 2017)

among other social vices.

Further, migrant youth "face more acute constraints than host or local youth in accessing entrepreneurship opportunities" (S4YE, 2017, p. 13). As indicated in the S4YE baseline report of 2015, "young people are generally among the most entrepreneurial worldwide in terms of nascent start-up activity, seeing it as a path out of poverty and joblessness." While labour market barriers may push migrants towards self-employment, they are often faced with constraints in accessing available opportunities.

> A key constraint among international migrants is the difficulty relative to hosts, or locals, in obtaining credit. Relative to adults, young people generally are disadvantaged in accessing business start-up loans as they lack experience, borrowing and repayment histories, and collateral assets to assure lenders. (S4YE, 2017, pp. 13–14)

Conclusion

Ensuing from the above, youth migration is seen to be a cultural phenomenon (Massey et al., 1993; Punch, 2007), which directly or indirectly aids interactions between the youths, places and materials and also shows how people (young and old) get interlinked or entangled in their relationship with places and materials during movement. This process promotes both tangible and intangible heritage that should be held in high esteem.

According to the text of the UNESCO 2003 Convention for the Safeguarding of the Intangible Cultural Heritage,

> intangible cultural heritage means the practices, representations, expressions, knowledge, skills – as well as the instruments, objects, artefacts and cultural spaces associated therewith – that communities, groups and, in some cases, individuals recognize as part of their cultural heritage. (UNESCO, 2003, cited in Labadi, 2013, p. 129)

One of the important points raised by this definition

> relates to the constantly re-created dimension of intangible cultural heritage in response to the communities' environment, their interaction with nature and their history. This recognizes the porous, creolized and moving nature of intangible heritage that is transformed by the migration of cultural bearers, their contacts with other cultures and external influences. (Labadi, 2013, p. 131)

Further, the Faro Convention Action Plan 2018–2019, published by the Council of Europe, "ultimately aims at creating a space for multiple narratives, perspectives and a better quality of life through heritage" (Faro, 2018, p. 7). To this end, all peoples and nations of the world must begin to envisage or conceive migration, especially among young people, as being part of the means by which intangible cultural heritage is transformed.

Moving on from the point above, local authorities and other stakeholders – whose obligations include ensuring the training, empowerment, enhancement and employment of the youths, and guaranteeing their inclusion in policymaking, which in turn leads to quality and sustainable life for young people – must begin to prioritize these responsibilities. This is because it is more profitable to discourage migration of the local population (especially the youths) to more economically prosperous regions – an action which indeed presents a major threat to native communities, seeing that the action usually leads to the abandonment, disappearance and slow degradation of the tangible and intangible cultural heritage of the local communities (Labadi, 2013).

This should be done to promote favourable conditions of living, on one hand, for the young people who chose to stay at home and pursue progress and, on the other hand, to eliminate the challenges that pose barriers to migration (both at the giving and receiving ends), so as to guarantee safety, confidence and good life to young people who chose to move in pursuit of the same ends. This is because, since migration is a culture, associated with almost all peoples of the world (Nomishan, 2020), it is practically impossible to eliminate it, and so it should be granted a favourable environment to keep it going. This conscious effort, if given priority, would reduce or end frustration and desperation among young people, thereby eliminating not youth migration per se, but *desperate or hasty migration* among the youths.

References

ABA Center on Children and the Law. 2018. Immigrants in the child welfare system: immigrant children and families in the U.S. Available at: https://www.americanbar.org/groups/child_law/project-areas/immigration.html

Adepoju, A. 1995. Migration in Africa. In *The Migration Experience in Africa*, Eds J. Baker and T. A. Aina, Sweden, Nordic Africa Institute.

Adepoju, A. 2008. Migration in Sub-Saharan Africa. In *Current African Issues No. 37*, Sweden, Nordic Africa Institute. Available at https://www.files.ethz.ch/isn/91432/37_Migration-in-Sub-Saharan-Africa.pdf

Afani, A. 2013. ECOWAS and migration. In *The Encyclopaedia of Global Human Migration*, Ed. I. Ness, Hoboken, Wiley-Blackwell.

Akinyemi, A. and Ikuteyijo, L. 2009. Emigration of health professionals in Nigeria: Review and evidence on determinants, patterns and trends. Paper presented at the Inaugural Scientific Conference of the Network of Migration Researchers in Africa (NOMRA), Lagos State, Nigeria.

Bade, K. J. 2000. *Europa in Bewegung. Migration vom späten 18. Jahrhundert bis zur Gegenwart*, München, C.H. Beck.

Bae, C. J., Douka, K. and Petraglia, M. D. 2017. On the origin of modern humans: Asian perspectives, *Science, 358*(6368), eaai9067. https://doi.org/10.1126/science.aai9067

Beekman, C. S. and Christensen, A. F. 2003. Controlling for doubt and uncertainty through multiple lines of evidence: a new look at the Mesoamerican Nahua migrations, *Journal of Archaeological Method and Theory, 10*(2), 111–164.

Bilger, V. and Kraler, A. 2005. Introduction: African migrations; historical perspectives and contemporary dynamics, *Stichproben. Wiener Zeitschrift für kritische Afrikastudien*, 8(5), 1–17.

Bruijn, M. D., Rijk, V. D., Dick, F. 2001. Mobile Africa: changing patterns of movement in Africa and beyond. In M. D. Bruijn, R. V. Dijk (Eds.), *African Dynamics*, Vol. *1*, pp. 1–8, Leiden, Brill.

Christenson, A. 1980. Change in the human niche in response to population growth. In *Modeling Change in Prehistoric Subsistence Economies*, Eds T. Earle and A. Christenson, pp. 31–72, New York, Academic Press.

Clark, G. A. and Yi, S. 1983. Niche-width variation in Cantabrian Archaeofaunas: a diachronic study. In *Animals and Archaeology L" Hunters and their Prey*, Eds J. Clutton-Brock and C. Grigson, pp. 183–208, Oxford, BAR International Series S-163.

Cortina, J., Taran, P. and Raphael, A. Eds 2014. *Migration and Youth: Challenges and Opportunities.* Geneva, Global Migration Group.

Craig, R. 2017. *The Mystery of a 1918 Veteran and the Flu Pandemic*. The Conservation. Available at: https://theconservation.com/the-mystery-of-a-1918-veteran-and-the-flu-pandemic-86292?xid=PSsmithsonian

Curtin, P. 1997. Africa and global patterns of migration. In *Global History and Migration*, Ed. W. Gungwu, pp. 63–94. Boulder, Westview Press.

Faro. 2018. The Council of Europe Framework Convention on the value of cultural heritage for society. Available at: http://www.coe.int/en/web/culture-and-heritage/faro-action-plan

Harari, Y. N. 2014. *Sapiens: A Brief History of Humankind*, Toronto, McClelland & Stewart, a division of Random House of Canada Limited, a Penguin Random House Company. Available at: www.randomhouse.ca

Heckert, J. 2015. New perspective on youth migration: Motives and family investment patterns, *Demographic Research*, *33*, 765–800. https://doi.org/10.4054/DemRes.2015.33.27

Huremović, D. 2019. Brief History of Pandemics (Pandemics throughout History). In *Psychiatry of Pandemics*, Ed. D. Huremović, pp. 7–35. Springer Cham. https://doi.org/10.1007/978-3-030-15346-5_2.

IOM (International Organization for Migration). 2005. *World Migration 2005. Costs and Benefits of Migration*, Geneva, IOM.

IOM (International Organization for Migration). 2020. *Youth and Migration: Engaging Youth as Key Partners in Migration Governance, Unlocking the Potential of Youth to Respond to the New Challenges and Opportunities of Migration, International Dialogue on Migration*, No. 29, Geneva, IOM.

Jarus, O. 2020. *20 of the Worst Epidemics and Pandemics in History*. LiveScience. Available at: https://www.google.com/amp/s/www.livescience.com/amp/worst-epidemics-and-pandemics-in-history.html

Labadi, S. 2013. *UNESCO, Cultural Heritage, and Outstanding Universal Value: Value-based Analyses of the World Heritage and Intangible Cultural Heritage Conventions.* Lanham, AltaMira Press.

Macias, A. 2021. 85 Americans have left Afghanistan since U.S. completed its withdrawal. Available at: https://www.cnbc.com/amp/2021/09/20/85-americans-have-left-afghanistan-since-us-withdrawal.html

Martin, S. and Herzberg, D. G. 2014. Climate change, international migration and youth. In *Migration and Youth: Challenges and Opportunities*, Eds J. Cortina, P. Taran and A. Raphael, Geneva, Global Migration Group.

Massey, D. S., Arango, J., Hugo, G., Kouaouci, A., Pellegrino, A. and Taylor, J. E. 1993. Theories of international migration: a review and appraisal, *Population and Development Review*, *19*(3), 431–466. https://doi.org/10.2307/2938462

Meisel, A. 2017. *The Past, Present, and Future of Human Migration*, The School of Arts and Sciences, University of Pennsylvania. Available at: https://omnia.sas.upenn.edu/story/past-present-and-future-human-migration

Min-Harris, C. 2019. Youth migration and poverty In Sub-Saharan Africa: empowering the rural youth, *Topical Review Digest: Human Rights in Sub-Saharan Africa*. Available at: https://www.du.edu/korbel/hrhw/researchdigest/africa/.

Nomishan, T. S. 2020. Perspectives on the origin, genealogical narration, early migrations, and settlement morphology of the Tiv of Central Nigeria, *International Journal of Academic Pedagogical Research (IJAPR)*, 4(8), 26–32. Available at: http://ijeais.org/wp-content/uploads/2020/8/IJAPR200808.pdf

O'Higgins, N. 2002. Youth employment in Asia and the Pacific: analytical framework and policy recommendations. Report prepared for ILO/Japan tripartite regional meeting on youth employment in Asia and the Pacific, Bangkok. Available at: http://www.ilo.org/public/english/region/asro/bangkok/conf/youth/constu/synthes.pdf

Plutzar, V. and Ritter, M. 2012. *Language Learning in the Context of Migration and Integration – Challenges and Options for Adult Learners*. A Publication of the Council of Europe: Language Policy Division. Available at: http://rm.coe.int/09000016802fc1d6

Posth, C., Wißing, C., Kitagawa, K., Pagani, L., Holstein, L. V., Racimo, F., Wehrberger, K., Conard, N. J., Kind, C. J., Bocherens, H. and Krause, J. 2017. Deeply divergent archaic mitochondrial genome provides lower time boundary for African gene flow into Neanderthals, *Nature Communications, 8*, 16046. https://doi.org/10.1038/ncomms16046

Punch, S. 2007. Migration projects: children on the move for work and education. Paper presented at Independent Child Migrants: Policy Debates and Dilemmas organized by the Development Research Centre on Migration, Globalisation and Poverty, University of Sussex and UNICEF Innocenti Research Centre, Westminster, London, September 12.

Reid, A. 2015. The effects of the 1918–1919 influenza pandemic on infant and child health in Derbyshire, *Medical History*, 49(1), 29–54. https://doi.org/10.1017/s0025727300008279

Robert Wood Johnson Foundation. 2013. *The Five Deadliest Outbreaks and Pandemics in History*. Robert Wood Johnson Foundation. Available at: https://www.rwjf.org/en/blog/2013/12/the-five-deadliesto.html

Rosenwald, M. S. 2020. History's deadliest pandemics, from ancient Rome to modern American, *Washington Post*. Available at: https://www.washingtonpost.com/graphics/2020/local/retropolis/coronavirus-deadliest-pandemics/

S4YE. 2017. *Toward Employment Solutions for Youth on the Move*, Solution for Youth Employment. Available at: https://www.s4ye.org/s4ye-publications

UN Inter-Agency Network. 2014. *Global Migration Group: Migration and Youth*, Geneva, Global Migration Group. Available at: http://www.globalmigrationgroup.org/sites/default/files/0.CoverandAcknowledgements%281%29.pdf

UNESCO. 2003. *Convention for the Safeguarding of the Intangible Cultural Heritage*, UNESCO. Available at: http://unesdoc.unesco.org/images/0018/001870/187086e.pdf

UNESCO. 2016. *Definition of Youth*, UNDESADSPD. Available at: http://undesadspd.org/Youth.aspx. [Accessed 4 March 2021].

UNESCO Institute for Statistics. 2006. Global education digest 2006: Comparing education statistics across the world. Available at: http://uis.unesco.org/sites/default/files/documents/global-education-digest-2006-comparing-education-statistics-across-the-world-en0.pdf

UNFPA. 2014. *Between the Ages 10 and 24 Years, According to UNFPA, State of the World Population: The Power of 1.8 Billion*, UNFPA. Available at: www.unfpa.org/sites/default/files/pub-pdf/EN-SWOP14-Report_FINALweb.pdf

United Nations. 2001. *Implementation of the World Programme of Action for Youth to the Year 2000 and Beyond: Report of the Secretary-General*, Youth Policy. Available at: http://www.youthpolicy.org/basics/2001WPAYImplementationReport.pdf

United Nations. 2018b. *United Nations Youth Strategy*. Available at: www.un.org/youthenvoy/wp-content/uploads/2018/09/18-00080UN-Youth-StrategyWeb.pdf

Zimmer, C. 2017. In Neanderthal DNA, signs of a mysterious human migration, *New York Times*, 11 October 2021.

Chapter Three

Youth Digital Exclusion, Big Data Divide and the Future of Work

Damilola Adegoke

Introduction

The implications of digital human relations have moved from speculations and idle scholarly discussions at the margins into mainstream policy agenda across the globe. There are tomes of literature about youth exclusion and its implications so that it has almost become a cliché in discursive engagements on youth issues. Similarly, there is virtually no known platform for discussing digital exclusion without some form of mention of "youth exclusion." However, fascinating mainstreaming of these challenges is, there is very little focus on practicable ways out that are contextual. Rather, we have had one-size-fits all sweeping suggestions for possible alternatives. The unintended consequences of the big data divide (structural inequalities) and digital exclusion on youth and their future work experiences have received perfunctory attention from policy actors and scholars. In a few cases, individual countries (mainly developing states) are the subject of interest. The assumption that this exclusion is limited to developing countries is misleading as countries in the Global North, including the OECD states (Canada, United States, United Kingdom, France, Sweden, Spain, Netherlands, and so on), are not exempted from the harsh realities of youth digital exclusion and the big data divide.

The effects of these on the future of employment are now gaining attention in popular policy circles and academic conversations. This chapter explores the challenges of digital exclusion and the big data divide on the future of youth employment and employability using multiple cases across different countries around the world and to also propose solutions to help mitigate the impending crises that these challenges portend. This chapter contains a comparative analysis of the problems, opportunities and solutions in the selected countries. This chapter shows that youth big data digital exclusion is not only about access to big and smart technologies and tools but includes other challenges such as the

Youth Exclusion and Empowerment in the Contemporary Global Order:
Existentialities in Migrations, Identity and the Digital Space, 33–47
Copyright © 2022 by Damilola Adegoke
Published under exclusive licence by Emerald Publishing Limited
doi:10.1108/978-1-80382-777-320221004

structure, culture (language) and algorithms of these technologies. This chapter also reveals, from examples from the developed countries, that youth exclusion and inclusion in relation to big data digital technologies is not limited to the less developed countries; the challenges are also matters of concerns to excluded youths in the developed countries.

Youth Digital Exclusion and the Big Data Divide

Youth Digital Exclusion: A Global Problem

Other than being the antonym of digital inclusion, digital exclusion is the unevenness and power differentials accentuated by social inequalities which disenfranchise a large segment of society – mainly the vulnerable and disempowered – from accessing digital tools necessary for effective participation in society. The vulnerable in this regard include the elderly, the youths, children, the disabled and people with learning disabilities. Youth digital exclusion is the primary focus of this chapter. Robert Sanders defined digital exclusion as being where a section of the population has continuing unequal access and capacity to use information and communications technologies (ICTs) that are essential to fully participate in society (Sanders, 2020).

According to the 2021 world population statistics, 25.3% of the world's population are under the age of 15 years and 65.1% are aged 15–64 (United Nations Population Fund, 2021). Controlling for outliers such as the Middle East and sub-Saharan Africa, the rest of the world can be described as ageing: but 40% of the entire population of Africa (the most youthful continent in the world) is aged 0–15 years (Statista, 2021). Nonetheless, the exclusion of the youths who are typically described as the digital natives – based on the supposition that a large proportion of those in the category grew up in the digital age – are excluded from the infrastructure that now defines their world while potentially determining the direction of their future. Aged adults (especially those above 65) who are considered *digital immigrants* do not fare any better on digital inclusion indices either. Each generation has its own defining work challenges: it was industrial machines for those born in the nineteenth and early twentieth centuries; for the millennials, it is digital infrastructure. Implicit in these definitions are accessibility and age. However, there are corollary and ancillary meanings associated with digital exclusion or digital divides (some literature also uses *digital disparities, digital poverty* or *digital gaps*) that raise challenges other than access, particularly with reference to youths. The 2018 United Nations e-Government Survey identifies other descriptors (see Table 3.1) including affordability, bandwidth, education, location, gender and migration.

The Riga Ministerial Declaration in Latvia (11 June 2006) defines e-inclusion as

> both inclusive [Information and Communication Technologies] (ICT) and the use of ICT to achieve wider inclusion objectives. It focuses on participation of all individuals and communities in all aspects of the information society. e-Inclusion policy, therefore,

Table 3.1.   Descriptions of Digital Divides.

Divide	Description
Access	It starts with access or the lack thereof: although Internet penetration has increased, it continues to be a key barrier as more people globally remain offline rather than online.
Affordability	The gap between rich and poor affects affordability of ICTs and serves as an important difference in adoption within countries as much as between them.
Age	Older people are generally using ICT to a lesser extent than younger populations, despite the notion that they could benefit from online social and health services.
Bandwidth	International bandwidth and the capacity to transmit and receive information over networks varies greatly among countries but also within them, limiting potential useful endeavours.
Content	Relevant content in local language(s) is important to stimulate adoption.
Disability	Those with disabilities face additional hurdles to using ICT if websites are not compliant with web accessibility guidelines.
Education	Like social divides, education and literacy rates are fundamental challenges to bridge digital divides.
Gender	There is a small but persistent difference in online usage between men and women.
Migration	Migrants may not possess the same levels of digital skills as the population in their new country, and if they do, they may be subject to content and language divides.
Location	Rural and remote areas are often at a disadvantage in terms of speed and quality of services compared to their urban counterparts.
Mobile	Mobile devices provide opportunities to bridge the access gap but can also introduce new forms of divides in terms of technology, speed and usage.
Speed	The gap between basic and broadband access is creating a new divide as speed is important to reap the full benefits of a digital society.
Useful usage	What people do with their access is a key difference in whether users take full advantage of ICT, such as e-government services.

Source: United Nations (2018, p. 34).
Note: The above table is intended to be illustrative and not exhaustive.

aims at reducing gaps in ICT usage and promoting the use of ICT to overcome exclusion, and improve economic performance, employment opportunities, quality of life, social participation and cohesion. (European Commission, 2006, p. 1)

The assumption that we now live in a digital world is commonplace, but the reality that a very large majority are not connected to the Internet seems at variance with this supposition. According to a 2020 report by UNICEF and the International Telecommunication Union (ITU), two thirds of the world's school-aged children have no Internet access at home; that is, 2.2 billion – or 2 in 3 – children and young people aged 25 years or less do not have Internet access at home (United Nations Children's Fund and International Telecommunication Union, 2020). The chart in Fig. 3.1 illustrates the digital divides across the different regions of the world, especially during the Covid-19 lockdown in 2020. Globally, more children and youths have no access to the Internet than those who do. When disaggregated by region, the inequalities appear more pronounced.

This connectivity inequality holds although 85% of the world's population lives in areas covered by 4G; added to this dire situation is the factor of cost, given that mobile broadband is 18 times more expensive in low-income countries inhabited by 650 million people than in the developed countries (O'Halloran, 2021). These accessibility and cost factors highlight the digital exclusion faced by youths and the vulnerable in disadvantaged communities. We must not presuppose that this exclusion is limited only to poor countries as data from the so-called developed countries in recent times does not bode well either. In France, Covid-19 lockdown revealed the underbelly of the digital inequalities experienced by ethnic minorities and the poor population compared with those in more affluent

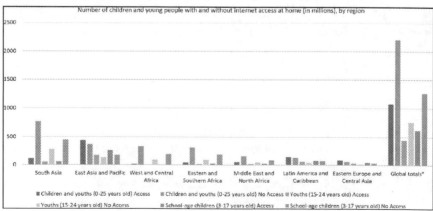

Fig. 3.1.   Youth Internet Access at Home (in Millions), by Region.
Source: UNICEF and ITU (2020).
*Note: The global totals exceed the sum of the regional values because the global totals include countries in regions not listed.

demography. In 2020, the French education ministry reported that 4% of students (about 500,000 young people) dropped out of school due to the digital gap, although this is a conservative estimate, as teachers reported 30% dropped out among low-income students from disadvantaged groups in France (Marlowe, 2020). The digital gap is deepening more than ever. The United Kingdom, Canada and the United States have reported cases of youth digital exclusion, in some cases exacerbated by the Covid-19 pandemic (Carmi and Yates, 2020; Pawluczuk, 2020).

Youth, Gender and Language in Digital Exclusion

Gender digital divide is an aspect of this inequality and is a factor now beginning to gain traction in scholarly and policy discussions. This cuts across all the regions of the world. While affordability, access and location are factors prevalent in poor countries, the gulf between male and female access to digital infrastructure is deepening and widening. Only 8% of countries globally have women using the Internet more than men, "while gender equality in Internet use is found in just over one-quarter of countries" (ITU, 2020). ITU put the gender gap in global Internet use at 12.5% (ITU, 2021). Fig. 3.2 showcases this gap. The economically developed countries of the world are on the same level as the least-developed countries for gender disparity in Internet use. France, Canada, Italy, Finland and Chile have higher rates of male Internet users than female. In fact, the Democratic Republic of Congo has more gender equality in the rates of Internet use than these countries.

The United Nations e-Government Survey report (see Table 3.1) and many other studies on the subject identify education and literacy as factors responsible for the youth digital divide. The low literacy rate among youths in disadvantaged communities across the globe has been considered a bottleneck to digital access for affected people. What is often overlooked is the language of digital communication and how this contributes to the deepening of the digital divide. Literacy is not only limited to the world's dominant languages, but there are also people who write and speak in fluent Zulu, Yoruba, Punjabi and so on, who may not be able to speak other languages. Cyberspace is dominated by 10 languages, including English, which constitutes 30% of the language in cyberspace, followed by Chinese, Spanish, Arabic and Portuguese (Young, 2016). According to Visual Capitalist's data stream, English is the most used language on Twitter (60.4%), followed by Russian (8.8%) and Spanish (4%) (Bhutada, 2021). This power asymmetry further disadvantages youths with no proficiency in these major languages. This is further spotlighted against the background that only 5% of the world are native English speakers with the remaining half of the entire global population catering to this small demographic (Harper and Nikki, 2019). Mark Graham and William Dutton of the Oxford Internet Institute noted that "Rich countries largely get to define themselves and poor countries largely get defined by others" (Graham and Dutton, 2014). Most of the content available online is not produced in the languages of excluded communities. Any youth who does not understand the dominant languages is

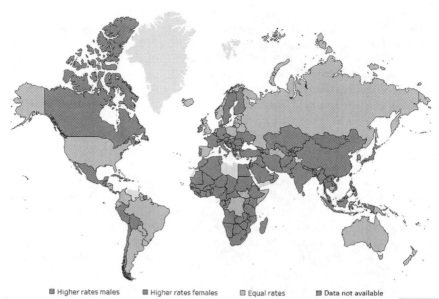

Fig. 3.2.   Global Gender Internet Divide. *Source*: ITU (2020).
Note: ITU estimate. Penetration rates in this chart refer to the number of women/men that use the Internet, as a percentage of the respective total female/male population. The ratio is considered equal when the difference between the male and female Internet penetration rate is less than two percentage points.

automatically alienated from the benefits accruable to the content produced in those languages.

Another point is the structure of the language of digital expression. Twitter has a limit of 140 characters, which is not a problem for Japanese, Korean and Chinese characters; in fact, you can say more with 140 characters in these languages than you can in English (Aliza and Ihara, 2017). You might be able to whittle down your statements without losing meaning in English, but many other languages are adversely affected by this policy as the structure of the languages prevent such adjustments. "Abbreviations, contractions can be easily implemented in English, but not so in some Asiatic and sub-Saharan languages" (Trevino, 2020). Miguel Trancozo Trevino also notes that more than 80% of Wikipedia articles are from Europe and North America. Also worthy of note is the fact that 75% of the web's top-level domains, from .com to .org, come from the same two regions (Trevino, 2020). This contributes to widening the gap. Whose information, whose knowledge, is available online?

The structure of the language of digital technologies also excludes youths. Take, for instance, the issue of lexical ambiguity occasioned by the orthography of some languages of people underrepresented in cyberspace. Most Niger-Congo languages such as Yoruba and Igbo have words with similar characters but different meanings, only made interpretable by tonal diacritics (accent markings).

In Yoruba, *igbá* (calabash), *igbà* (climbing harness), *igba* (the number 200) and *igbá* (garden egg) are typical examples. Without tonal diacritics, the Igbo *akwa* would have lexical ambiguity, given that it could mean *ákwá* (cry), *àkwà* (bed/bridge), *ákwà* (cloth) or *àkwá* (egg) (Ezeani et al., 2018). The English language reportedly has approximately 6,139 homonyms – similar words with different meanings, such as bark, which is a tree's outer layer and the sound a dog makes (Nicholls, 2002); however, since the popular Internet platforms and algorithms are in English, this complexity is increasingly being addressed because digital products can decipher the meaning through contextual interpretation, made possible by natural language understanding and deep learning. Youths whose primary language is not English, however, have been excluded because of these unintended nuances.

The implication becomes glaring when using search engines such as Google with keyboards that have no such accent marks. Also, most content and information available on the Internet does not include this peculiarity, hence excluding millions of youths who are not literate in the more popular languages of the Internet. Other language-based discrimination includes non-recognition of tonal accents by digital voice assistants such as Alexa (Amazon), Google Assistant, Cortana (Microsoft) and Siri (Apple). There are instances where people who speak English with non-native accents have had their query not understood by these digital assistants. Even those who spoke English with Scottish accents have had the same complaints (Carrie, 2018). This has serious implications for those using interactive digital products who are second language speakers with foreign accents. All these could lead to language homogenization where a few dominant languages, even in the digital sphere, lead to the disappearance of minority languages as experienced with Spanish in Mexico (Trevino, 2020).

Disability and Digital Exclusion

Also excluded are the physically challenged, since most digital products are not designed with their uniqueness in mind. Most digital divide discussion does not even include youths in that category as part of the main agenda. According to the UK Office for National Statistics in 2017, "60% of Internet non-users aged between 16 and 24 years were people with disabilities, a proportion that is the same as for those aged 75 years and older" (Serafino, 2019). Although, there has been a little spike between 2019 and 2020 (about 3%) in Internet use by disabled adults, there is still more to be done in ensuring more digital inclusion for youths (Prescott, 2021). The situation is noticeable in the so-called developed countries. Findings from a study by Scholz, Yalcin and Priestley that compared data from 27 European countries "found a distinct disability effect in regard to digital divides and that people with disabilities are over-represented among those who are digitally excluded" (2017; see also Johansson, Gulliksen and Gustavsson, 2021). Other than digital access, other concerns include the quality of digital experience available to those with disabilities. A typical example is the search engines, which are necessary information portals to effectively navigate the vast world and opportunities of the Internet; these engines are ableist in design and conception. Those who have visual or audio impairments might not to be able to use these portals without the aid of additional assisted technologies that are expensive and not available to excluded youth communities.

Big Data Divide: From Digital Divide to Big Data Divide

If digital exclusion is bad, big data exclusion is worse. Since computer algorithms learn from available data (that which they are exposed to), it therefore follows that their outputs and solutions would reflect only those data used in training them to the exclusion of the data poor. A 2016 report published by the Federal Trade Commission, Big Data: A Tool for Inclusion or Exclusion? identified four discrete phases during the transformation process of "little" data to "big" data: they were (1) collection, (2) compilation and consolidation, (3) analysis and (4) use (Panori, 2016). Although the report dwelt on the exclusion occasioned by the analysis phase of big data, all the phases of the transformation process are embedded with potential mechanisms of digital exclusion, albeit largely inadvertently.

A lot of work has been done on big data and exclusion, especially of disadvantaged groups across the world (Chin-Yee and Upshur, 2019; Favaretto, De Clercq and Elger, 2019; Gillis and Spiess, 2019). Discriminations generated passionate debate around disparate impact (unintended policies or consequences of big data discriminations) and disparate treatment (intended). Solon Barocas and Andrew Selbst opined, within the context of the United States, that unbridled or unchecked dependence on data mining "can deny historically disadvantaged and vulnerable groups full participation in society" (Barocas and Selbst, 2016). They also noted that the nature of this discrimination is almost always benign given that it is algorithmic, thereby making it difficult to identify (Barocas and Selbst, 2016). As societies become largely datafied, with data-based realities unfolding rapidly nearly every day, there are huge challenges associated with these emergent experiences for youths and other disadvantaged people in society. The most glaring is the exclusion of youths from poor homes, who are disconnected from digital technologies such as smartphones, computers and other big data technology devices, consequently detaching them from the pool of data collected through sensors embedded in these devices that are usually the basis for advanced data mining and big data analytics.

The implications of reliance on big data for big decision-making – often automated – are beginning to unfurl, with claims of racial profiling and criminalization of black youths in America in what some observers have tagged "school-to-prison predictive policing" (Heaven, 2020). Due to disproportionate arrests of black youths in the past and systemic racism against other ethnic minorities in the United States, the algorithms designed to use variables such as location-based predictive policing, which depend on historical events data, will likely mark more black areas as prone to crime than white areas, thereby leading to increasing police surveillance and arrests. These algorithms extend to critical decisions such as pretrial hearings, sentencing and determination of recidivism (Heaven, 2020). This racial profiling enabled by big data technologies has been observed by affected minority ethnic groups, mainly youths, in Brazil, Colombia and the European Union (Nebehay, 2020).

In Nigeria, using data gathered from Bank Verification Numbers (BVN), a system of biometric identification linked to financial transactions, the government blocked the bank accounts of 20 youths leading the #EndSARS anti-police-brutality protests of October and November 2020 (Reuters, 2020). This is another example of youth exclusion from governance and civil participation by government agents using big data technologies (Human Rights Watch, 2020). On 5 June 2021, the Nigerian government shut down Twitter services in Nigeria because the president's tweet was deleted for violating the terms of service of the company and primarily because it was the social media platform of choice for Nigerian youths to ventilate their grievances against state oppression (Akinwotu, 2021). There are concerns in India about the government's big data identification project to capture biometric data of the citizens and how homeless individuals are excluded; there are concerns that social "undesirables," the lower rung of the social strata, are excluded as they are most likely to be workers with worn-out fingerprints and cataract sufferers, compared to the more affluent class (Arora, 2016). The consequences include exclusion of this demographic from the larger datafied society. The youths within this class are not exempted from the digital gentrification process.

The youths are particularly affected by the new fad of big data as they are subjected to the challenges of acquiring relevant skills to meet the modern work reality, much different from what previous generations had to contend with. The ever-changing, rapidly updating technologies meant that they must learn new programming, software and other digital tools as their skills get obsolete fast (Ra et al., 2019). Their data are mined and used to make decisions with major impact such as their credit scores, their housing and education, where they shop, what they buy and eat and their access to financial support (Open Society Foundations, 2019). Even their democratic rights are been threatened by algorithms that can manipulate opinions through filtered and customized feeds as seen during the Cambridge Analytical scandal and the Russian interference with the US elections. The sensors in the numerous data hungry devices that they interface with everyday determine their destiny with no recourse to their privacy, and the anonymity of their data is no longer guaranteed.

Implications for the Future of Work

With the transformation of Facebook to Meta, the leading social media platform has made a landmark move with reverberations for human–machine interactions in cyberspace, including the introduction of Metaverse as the next phase of digital engagements. Advancements in virtual reality technologies, led by the gaming industry, have generated new modes of human social relations dominated by avatars and augmented reality. Just as in the early days of the Internet, when certain jobs were replaced by computers leading to loss of jobs, the youths are now under considerable pressure from these new technologies, because they demand newer skillsets and qualifications (Chambers, 2019). The older generation might not be as much affected by this sudden change as the youth since the education systems of most countries have not risen to accommodate the challenges of this emergent future. How many youths have programming skills? How many even own or can afford a computer? There are serious concerns among youths that their skills and knowledge will not be in demand in the future workplace (Chambers, 2019). The implication is particularly dire for countries with high "youthening" of their populations, most of which are in the developing countries. This demographic characteristic, once celebrated as an opportunity for economic growth, is now considered a factor fuelling conflict in most of the affected countries where social mobility has been hampered by rapid underdevelopment and economic disempowerment (Beehner, 2007; Brand South Africa, 2018). Most of the countries in sub-Saharan Africa, Asia and Latin America are going to be adversely affected by the migration to digital space that the future workplace will likely entail. The current technological inequality will be further widening as society moves into a digital economy from which the most disadvantaged youths are going to be excluded.

Before the dystopian epoch of the Metaverse, automated management decision-making in recruitment has been blamed for being unfair to people of colour and other minority groups. Most of the systems have opaque algorithms that are not innocuous in terms of human bias, and the implication is felt more by youths aspiring to entry-level positions. Reversed ageism, where experience is conflated with age, is a factor suffered by many youths who are not selected for even first-stage interviews. In some countries such as Nigeria, and in some African and Asian countries, applicants have to be of certain age with years of "work experience" for entry-level positions, thereby potentially excluding youths who could have benefited from potential mentoring and learning opportunities associated with the positions. Since large companies even in these countries rely on automated databases, youth are filtered out through the criteria programmed into the algorithms. Examples of algorithm bias in recruitment abound: one of the better-known cases led to Amazon shutting down its artificial intelligence recruitment tools and models when they were audited and discovered to be biased against women (Dastin, 2018).

A lot of big companies now rely on predictive hiring algorithms to handle their human resources, ranging from resume filtering and hiring to retention, salaries and promotion (Engler, 2021). Platforms such as Jobberman, LinkedIn, Glassdoor and Indeed have databases for job applicants which are driven largely by artificial intelligence (Engler, 2021). In the coming decades, the youths are going to be subjected to decisions made by machines, presenting new challenges. In some cases, recruiters have invasive programmes for scouring social media accounts of applicants to determine their suitability for jobs. The youth are under more intense scrutiny, surveillance and pressure than youths of previous generations. The future of work for them is challenging. Some jobs are even more demanding to the extent that they have soft skills such as "interpersonal relationship" communication to make them more appealing – none of this was demanded nor expected of their peers in previous generations.

There are already concerns of labour market discrimination against minorities, with reports that people with white-sounding names get invited more often than those with black sounding names (Bertrand and Mullainathan, 2004).

Recent studies have shown that computerized recruitment has not proved better either, as there are reports of more implicit bias against people with black names than those with white names, leading to some adding or switching their names to white names ("whitening") to beat the machine bias (Barhat, 2016; Gerdeman, 2017; Pearson, 2016). These discriminations are not limited to African Americans: there are instances of people with Chinese or Singaporean names experiencing this labour discrimination in New Zealand, Australia, France and the United Kingdom (see Barhat, 2016). Youths are likely to be the most affected by these challenges since they are more likely to change jobs and experience regular employment migration than other demographic categories. The future of work for these youths will be more challenging because human social laws (discriminations) have not been dispelled by present technologies: there is no guarantee that the next phase of digital technologies, embodied Internet and virtual reality will not create new forms of extending old biases.

Conclusion

In the coming decades, work is going to be redefined. At the moment, youths are beginning to experience what the potential future of work portends. The skills that they are exposed to are not sufficient nor practically disconnected from current technology-led employments; although this factor directly affects those who live in urban communities across the globe, most of the world's youth population are technologically off-grid. For these youths, who are excluded from the present Internet, one can only imagine their place in a future driven by advanced big data technologies. The first step must adequately include these excluded marginals. The digital space should be opened to more youths to prepare them both for the challenges and opportunities of the future workplace. There must be concerted efforts by governments across the globe to create more opportunities for youths, particularly those in poor rural communities, to participate digitally. The curriculum of schools (especially elementary and secondary schools) should be revamped to reflect the demands of the present workplace while anticipating expectations of the future of work. Youths must be prepared and empowered to enable them to actively engage in the digital economies of the present and the future. Just like reading and numeracy, digital skillsets must feature prominently in the education plan of the school systems. On big data technologies, ethical algorithms should be encouraged by governments across the globe to deter discriminations and biases in computer programmes used by big companies.

There must be compliance and standards enforced to regulate the use, storage and transmission of data mined by big technology companies. Already, most European countries have implemented the General Data Protection Regulation 2016/679 (GDPR) on data protection and privacy to protect data of citizens in the region (GDPR, 2020). Other regional bodies can demand and implement similar measures to curtail the abuse of data of their citizens by big technology firms. Following the Cambridge Analytica scandal, it became imperative for governments to understand the implications of unregulated big data technologies. The immense capabilities of these private interests to influence elections, manipulate opinions and propagate fake news call for a more reflective approach that will not stifle freedom of expression while also not making citizens vulnerable to sinister influences, especially from external foreign powers. Since the bulk of big data are from social media, and since youths are the largest constituents of these platforms (Ghani et al., 2019), it is only logical to assume that youths are more likely to be affected than other age categories (Auzier and Anderson, 2021). Youths should be exposed more to digital media literacy; it is essential for them to understand the implication of what they read or post on their future job prospects and health. Employers now scour and mine social media accounts of job applicants for insights into their prospective employees. They must also be taught how to assess messages as they come as online so as not to be easily influenced by negative persuasions or misinformation.

While it is difficult to fully understand the experiences of youths in the future, opportunities can be provided to mitigate the impacts of big data and digital technologies exclusion on youths with strategies and policies made up-scalable for their future work life. This chapter reveals that algorithmic and big data have further accentuated and alienated youths from excluded communities in more nuanced ways, contrary to what was previously assumed. Also fundamental is the spread of these exclusions across different global economic strata. Youths are excluded not only in the "underdeveloped" countries but also in the acclaimed advanced economies. This chapter shows that providing these big technologies to disadvantaged youths is not enough to bridge the gaps because of several factors, including language, gender, disabilities, the orthography of Internet technologies, lack of relevant skills, reversed ageism in workplaces and the limitations imposed on excluded youth by algorithm biases in artificial intelligence solutions. This chapter tied these experiences to the impacts on the future of work and the workplace for these youths. This chapter, in all, has provided a useful template for a global wholistic approach to studying the subject of youth big data digital exclusion across different social and economic strata of the world.

References

Akinwotu, E. 2021, June 4. Nigeria suspends Twitter access after president's tweet was deleted, *The Guardian*. Available at: https://www.theguardian.com/world/2021/jun/04/nigeria-suspends-twitter-after-presidents-tweet-was-deleted

Aliza, R. and Ihara, I. 2017, September 26. Giving you more characters to express yourself. Twitter. Available at: https://blog.twitter.com/en_us/topics/product/2017/Giving-you-more-characters-to-express-yourself

Arora, P. 2016. Bottom of the data pyramid: Big data and the global south, *International Journal of Communication*, *10*, 19.

Auzier, B. and Anderson, M. 2021, April 7. *Social Media Use in 2021*. Washington, DC, Pew Research Centre. Available at: https://www.pewresearch.org/Internet/2021/04/07/social-media-use-in-2021/

Barhat, V. 2016, September 16. Should you change your name to get a job? BBC. Available at: https://www.bbc.com/worklife/article/20160915-should-you-change-your-name-to-get-a-job

Barocas, S. and Selbst, A. D. 2016. Big data's disparate impact, *California Law Review*, *104*, 671.

Beehner, L. 2007, April 13. The effects of 'youth bulge' on civil conflicts. Council on Foreign Relations. Available at: https://www.cfr.org/backgrounder/effects-youth-bulge-civil-conflicts

Bertrand, M. and Mullainathan, S. 2004. Are Emily and Greg More employable than Lakisha and Jamal? A field experiment on labor market discrimination, *American Economic Review*, *94*(4), 991–1013.

Bhutada, G. 2021, March 26. Visualizing the most used languages on the internet. Visual Capitalist. Available at: https://www.visualcapitalist.com/the-most-used-languages-on-the-internet/

Brand South Africa. 2018, November 18. Young population a goldmine for sub-Saharan countries: UN. Brand South Africa. Available at: https://www.brandsouthafrica.com/south-africa-fast-facts/news-facts/population-a-goldmine-for-sub-saharan-countries

Carmi, E. and Yates, S. J. 2020. What do digital inclusion and data literacy mean today? *Internet Policy Review*, *9*(2). https://doi.org/10.14763/2020.2.1474

Carrie, E. 2018, August 21. Alexa and Google Home are no threat to regional accents – here's why. The Conversation. Available at: https://theconversation.com/alexa-and-google-home-are-no-threat-to-regional-accents-heres-why-101866

Chambers, N. 2019, September 3. Young people don't feel ready for the future of work. The Forum Network. Available at: https://www.oecd-forum.org/posts/53006-young-people-don-t-feel-ready-for-the-future-of-work

Chin-Yee, B. and Upshur, R. 2019. Three problems with big data and artificial intelligence in medicine, *Perspectives in Biology and Medicine*, *62*(2), 237–256.

Dastin, J. 2018, October 11. Amazon scraps secret AI recruiting tool that showed bias against women. Reuters. Available at: https://www.reuters.com/article/us-amazon-com-jobs-automation-insight-idUSKCN1MK08G

Engler, A. 2021, March 12. Auditing employment algorithms for discrimination. Brookings. Available at: https://www.brookings.edu/research/auditing-employment-algorithms-for-discrimination/

European Commission. 2006, June 12. Internet for all: EU ministers commit to an inclusive and barrier-free information society. European Commission. Available at: https://ec.europa.eu/commission/presscorner/detail/en/IP_06_769

Ezeani, I., Hepple, M., Onyenwe, I. and Chioma, E. 2018, June). Igbo diacritic restoration using embedding models. In *Proceedings of the 2018 Conference of the North American Chapter of the Association for Computational Linguistics: Student Research Workshop* (pp. 54–60). Available at: https://aclanthology.org/N18-4008.pdf

Favaretto, M., De Clercq, E. and Elger, B. S. 2019. Big data and discrimination: perils, promises and solutions. A systematic review, *Journal of Big Data*, *6*(1), 1–27.

GDPR. 2020. Complete guide to GDPR compliance, GDPR.EU. Available at: https://gdpr.eu/

Gerdeman, D. 2017, May 17. Minorities who 'whiten' job resumes get more interviews, *Havard Business School*. Available at: https://hbswk.hbs.edu/item/minorities-who-whiten-job-resumes-get-more-interviews

Ghani, N. A., Hamid, S., Hashem, I. A. T. and Ahmed, E. 2019. Social media big data analytics: a survey, *Computers in Human Behavior*, *101*, 417–428.

Gillis, T. B. and Spiess, J. L. 2019. Big data and discrimination, *The University of Chicago Law Review*, *86*(2), 459–488.

Graham, M. and Dutton, W. H. 2014. *Society and the Internet: How Networks of Information and Communication are Changing Our Lives*, Oxford, Oxford University Press.

Harper, S. and Nikki G. 2019, December 19. Lost in translation: building a multilingual space at RightsCon. RightsCon. Available at: https://www.rightscon.org/lost-in-translation-building-a-multilingual-space-at-rightscon/

Heaven, W. D. 2020, July 17. Predictive policing algorithms are racist. They need to be dismantled, *MIT Technology Review*. Available at: https://www.technologyreview.com/2020/07/17/1005396/predictive-policing-algorithms-racist-dismantled-machine-learning-bias-criminal-justice/

Human Rights Watch. 2020, November 13. Nigeria: punitive financial moves against protesters. Human Rights Watch. Available at: https://www.hrw.org/news/2020/11/13/nigeria-punitive-financial-moves-against-protesters#

International Telecommunication Union. 2020. The digital gender gap is growing fast in developing countries. ITU. Available at: https://itu.foleon.com/itu/measuring-digital-development/gender-gap/

International Telecommunication Union. 2021, July). Bridging the gender divide. ITU. Available at: https://www.itu.int/en/mediacentre/backgrounders/Pages/bridging-the-gender-divide.aspx

Johansson, S., Gulliksen, J. and Gustavsson, C. 2021. Disability digital divide: the use of the Internet, smartphones, computers, and tablets among people with disabilities in Sweden, *Universal Access in the Information Society*, *20*(1), 105–120.

Marlowe, L. 2020, July 20. Coronavirus: France's 'lost' school year highlights issues with its education system, *The Irish Times*. Available at: https://www.irishtimes.com/news/world/europe/coronavirus-france-s-lost-school-year-highlights-issues-with-its-education-system-1.4308247

Nebehay, S. 2020, November 26. U.N. decries police use of racial profiling derived from big data. Reuters. Available at: https://www.reuters.com/article/uk-un-rights-race-idUKKBN28620F

Nicholls, D. 2002, November) Watt is a homonym? *Med Magazine*. Available at: http://macmillandictionaries.com/MED-Magazine/November2002/02-language-interference-homonym.htm#how%20many%20homonyms%20are%20there%20in%20the%20English%20language

O'Halloran, D. 2021, September 21. Take the 1 billion lives challenge to close the digital divide. WeForum. Available at: https://www.weforum.org/agenda/2021/09/take-the-1-billion-lives-challenge-to-close-the-digital-divide-edison-alliance-inclusion-internet-connectivity/

Open Society Foundations. 2019, May). Life in a quantified society. Open Society Foundations. Available at: https://www.opensocietyfoundations.org/explainers/life-quantified-society

Panori, A. 2016, January 6. Big data: a tool for inclusion or exclusion? Understanding the issues (FTC report). Federal Trade Commission. Available at: https://www.ftc.gov/system/files/documents/reports/big-data-tool-inclusion-or-exclusion-understanding-issues/160106big-data-rpt.pdf

Pawluczuk, A. 2020. Digital youth inclusion and the big data divide: examining the Scottish perspective, *Internet Policy Review*, *9*(2). https://doi.org/10.14763/2020.2.1480

Pearson, J. 2016, August 26. It's our fault that AI thinks white names are more 'pleasant' than black names: A new study reveals some unsettling trends in our mechanical friends. Vice. Available at: https://www.vice.com/en/article/z43qka/its-our-fault-that-ai-thinks-white-names-are-more-pleasant-than-black-names

Prescott, C. 2021, April 6. Internet users, UK: 2020. Office for National Statistics. Available at: https://www.ons.gov.uk/businessindustryandtrade/itandinternetindustry/bulletins/internetusers/2020/pdf

Ra, S., Shrestha, U., Khatiwada, S., Yoon, S. W. and Kwon, K. 2019. The rise of technology and impact on skills, *International Journal of Training Research*, *17*(supl), 26–40.

Reuters. 2020, November 7. Nigeria's central bank freezes accounts of police brutality protesters. Reuters. Available at: https://www.reuters.com/article/nigeria-protests-banking-idUSL4N2HT06D

Sanders, R. 2020, Aril 9. Digital inclusion, exclusion and participation. Iriss. Available at: https://www.iriss.org.uk/resources/esss-outlines/digital-inclusion-exclusion-and-participation

Scholz, F., Yalcin, B. and Priestley, M. 2017. Internet access for disabled people: understanding socio-relational factors in Europe, *Cyberpsychology: Journal of Psychosocial Research on Cyberspace*, *11*(1), Article 4. https://doi.org/10.5817/CP2017-1-4

Serafino, P. 2019. Exploring the UK's digital divide. Office for National Statistics. Available at: https://www.ons.gov.uk/peoplepopulationandcommunity/householdcharacteristics/homeinternetandsocialmediausage/articles/exploringtheuksdigitaldivide/2019-03-04/pdf

Statista. 2021. Proportion of selected age groups of world population in 2021, by region. Available at: https://www.statista.com/statistics/265759/world-population-by-age-and-region/

Trevino, M. T. 2020, April 15. The many languages missing from the Internet. BBC. Available at: https://www.bbc.com/future/article/20200414-the-many-lanuages-still-missing-from-the-internet

United Nations. 2018. *United Nations e-Government Survey 2018: Gearing e-Government to Support Transformation Towards Sustainable and Resilient Societies*, New York, NY, United Nations. Available at: https://www.unescap.org/sites/default/files/E-Government %20Survey%202018_FINAL.pdf

United Nations Children's Fund and International Telecommunication Union. 2020. *How Many Children and Young People Have Internet Access at Home? Estimating Digital Connectivity During the COVID-19 Pandemic*, New York, NY, UNICEF. Available at: https://data.unicef.org/wp-content/uploads/2020/11/How-many-children-and-young-people-have-internet-access-at-home-2020_v2.pdf

United Nations Population Fund. 2021. World population dashboard. Available at: https://www.unfpa.org/data/world-population-dashboard

Young, H. 2016. The digital language divide: How does the language you speak shape your experience of the Internet? *The Guardian*. Available at: http://labs.theguardian.com/digital-language-divide/#information-inequality-7879

Chapter Four

Re-imagining Violence Against Africa's Youth Within the Framework of the 2008 Hunger Riots

Christophe Dongmo

Introduction

Precipitated by a global inflation of commodity prices, a global food crisis unfolded at an alarming speed in African countries in 2008, leading to widespread hunger riots. According to the May 2017 United Nations Food and Agricultural Organization (FAO) Food Price Index, in the year preceding the hunger riots, the price of wheat has risen by 130%, soya by 87% and rice by 74% (FAO, 2017). Schneider (2008) shows that, throughout the continent, youth demonstrators combined demands for lower food prices with calls for greater democracy, good governance and transformative political reforms. These events affected the majority of Africa's poor, causing protests and presenting policymakers with the challenge of simultaneously addressing hunger, poverty, economic planning and political stability.

The basic assumption is that Africa marginalizes its youth from participation in labour markets and mainstream political leadership institutions. Although the past decades have seen advances in terms of policy commitments to youth development, the 2008 hunger riots show that African countries have not matched such gains with actions. Far too many young people are still jobless and struggle to access public resources and quality social services. They are barely involved in policy formulation and programme design as their participation in politics and decision-making is limited (UNECA, 2017). The growing role of youth in changing societies is particularly relevant to Africa. In less than three generations, its youth population will represent more than 40% of the world's young people. However, young Africans who should give momentum to the continent's transformation are largely hungry, undereducated, alienated, discriminated against and marginalized from socio-political markets. African countries will adequately

Youth Exclusion and Empowerment in the Contemporary Global Order:
Existentialities in Migrations, Identity and the Digital Space, 49–64
Copyright © 2022 by Christophe Dongmo
Published under exclusive licence by Emerald Publishing Limited
doi:10.1108/978-1-80382-777-320221005

measure success in development cycles if they weigh policies against actions to foster transformative and inclusive youth-oriented development.

This chapter primarily used a documentary research methodology. The study involved a desk-based literature review and consultations with a small number of key informants. It reviewed key policy and academic literature on hunger riots, youth, exclusion and violence in order to examine the nature of the evidence on the linkages among these artefacts, the consensus, contradictions and gaps. In so doing, this chapter critically tested and analysed comparative data on youths' involvements during the 2008 hunger riots. The paper compiled statistical data from reference materials such as those produced by government agencies and human rights organizations. At national level, this chapter references primary source documents, providing new statistical data to help ensure that policymakers take into account youth's role within the political market. Secondary sources included books, academic articles and conference papers. The study also consulted a group of stakeholders specialized in youth empowerment, peacebuilding, and political participation issues. Overall, the paper took a holistic approach to state violence – recognizing that, in practice, different forms of violence (political, religious, ideological, extremism, intergenerational) overlapped and that some of the same structural and proximate factors may drive youth engagement in different forms of political expressions and self-determination against the state.

This chapter critically reviews the significance of Africa's youth roles in the global order in the context of the 2008 hunger riots. Young people, defined by the UN Resolution 2250 (2015) as those aged 18 through 29 years, constitute a substantial share of the population of most sub-Saharan African countries and of the continent as a whole. This creates a need for public policies and related programmes to engage youth effectively in all development projects. Referring to the 2008 hunger riots, this chapter argues that failure to have policies in place that support young people's contribution to development processes could have negative political and socio-economic consequences. In this light, food security and malnutrition – being complex development problems – require a "conceptual framework" to distinguish different types and levels of interrelated causal factors. To strengthen my argument, the first part of this chapter provides a review of literature about youth-led political violence and hunger in Africa. Second, central to this chapter are the geographies of the 2008 hunger riots in selected African countries. Lastly, this chapter provides a strategic and policy framework for analysing circular linkages between youth policies and social unrest in Africa.

In the end, the originality of this chapter to social sciences scholarship lies in the recognition of the significance of youth's political participation as a tool for social inclusion, leadership and self-empowerment in Africa's fragile states. Indeed, there is a growing evidence from different countries that the social and economic statuses required for welfare are increasingly attainable for young people. Although the relative importance of factors that stall the African youth's socio-economic conditions may vary from one context to the next, this chapter raises recent trends underlying youth exclusions and lack of opportunities, which trigger the likelihood of youth engagement in violence. As such, this chapter brings in new scholarly evidence of linkages between youths, as social capital, and risks of state violence. This shows that African countries are likely to be at higher risk of social conflicts and exclusions. Therefore, state organs, alongside international stakeholders, should engage with youth to take preventive actions (UNDP, 2006; USAID, 2005).

Literature Review on Youth-Led Political Violence and Hunger in Africa

In the context of youth violence, social sciences scholarship summarizes the current research on risk, protection and resilience. Some scholars shed new light on the role of youth political violence in African politics. In States of Violence, Edna Bay and Donald Donham (2006) use wide-ranging power struggles in Sierra Leone, nationalism in postcolonial Zimbabwe and the Bakassi boys of Nigeria to offer probing examinations of such defining events as the Rwandan genocide and the bloody Egypt's Alexandria rebellion during the first six months of 1986.

Social sciences scholarship discusses the so-called Africa's lost generation – the generation of politicized youth who dedicated their lives to the liberation of their country, and who have "lost" everything in the process. Monique Marks' (2008) *Young Warriors* is about both this social group and a critique of the very concept of a "lost generation." It is the story of activists who have become leaders, political executives and national ministers in a democratic society. While focusing on the lives of young men and women in Diepkloof, a South African black "township," the book is also a narrative of the lives of many black South Africans who "grew up" within the liberation movement led by the African National Congress.

Black Consciousness ideology and school-based organizations were instrumental in shaping the character and form of youth-led revolts in African politics. The Soweto uprising, for instance, was a true turning point in South Africa's political history, as it marked the beginning of the demise of apartheid. Noor Nieftagodien's (2014) *The Soweto Uprising* looks at the crucial role of the black youth and examines both the underlying causes and the immediate factors that led to this watershed event towards a democratic South Africa. What began as a peaceful and coordinated demonstration rapidly turned into violent protests posing political demands on the apartheid state. By drawing on a rich body of oral histories, Nieftagodien explains the uprising and its aftermath from the perspective of its core participants, the youth.

Youth involvement in politics moved violent protests to the public sphere and helped establish the patterns of popular action and state responses. Referring to South Africa, Julian Brown's (2016) *The Road to Soweto* is an extremely important contribution to the historiography of youth-led protests in African politics. It links black and white student protests – too often studied in isolation from one another – to workers' movements by looking at the changing forms of protest during the 1960s and 1970s, and the apartheid government's changing responses.

Encapsulating the long build-up of unrest in South Africa's youth black underclass, and situating the uprising in this context as a powerful corrective to previous attempts to consider it in relative isolation, Brown throws new light on the background to the Soweto revolts. In so doing, the author provides insight into white and black student politics, worker protest and broader dissent. Brown argues that, far from there being "quiescence" following the 1976 Sharpeville massacre and the suppression of African opposition movements, during which they went underground, this period was marked by experiments in resistance and attempts to develop new forms of politics that prepared the ground for youth uprisings. Students at South Africa's segregated universities began to reorganize themselves as a political force. New ideas about race reinvigorated political thought and debates around confrontation shaped the development of new forms of protest.

Referring to authoritarian regimes and racial democracies, social sciences scholarship marks a definitive shift in sociological studies of youth and the field of moral education by demonstrating the power of empirical research into moral formations. Sharlene Swartz (2009), in *The Moral Ecology of South Africa's Township Youth*, provides an engaging account of the moral lives of young black South Africans once the struggle against apartheid ended and took away their object of political resistance. In the best ethnographic tradition, Swartz's deeply moving study of the moral thinking and behaviour of young black people in a South African township shows how partial parenting, partial schooling and pervasive poverty contribute to how a group of young people construct right and wrong and what rules govern their behaviour. As such, moral ecology is an innovative development in social scientific research, not only because it places the morality of youth at the heart of social scientific analysis but also because it demonstrates the importance of subjecting the moral fibre of all societies to the social scientific axiom.

Unemployment shapes political identities and motivates youth violence. High youth unemployment is a major issue across Africa. It is a matter of concern for both economic development, a threat to social stability and a challenge to state stability. Youth unemployment is a key indicator for social progress. Drawing on rich empirical data about young people on the margins of the informal economy in Sierra Leone's capital, Freetown, in the wake of its civil war (1991–2002), Luisa Enria's (2018) *The Politics of Work in a Post-Conflict State* moves beyond reductive portrayals of unemployed youth as "ticking bombs" to show how labour market experiences influence them to mobilize politically. Enria argues that violence is not inherent to unemployment, but that social factors and the specific nature of the post-war political economy mediate the impact of joblessness on political activism. Referring to Freetown's youth, she views labour market exclusion as having implications for social status, identities and social relations, ultimately keeping them in exploitative patterns of dependence. This, in turn, shapes their political subjectivities and claims on the state and structures the opportunities from and constraints on their collective action.

Centuries of inequity have made young people the brunt of unspeakable exploitation and violence. Youth are still marginal in the postcolonial present, embodying most acutely the ghosts of catastrophes past. The young people of the Cameroon Grassfields, for instance, have been subject to a long history of violence and political marginalization. For centuries the main victims of the slave trade were the young people as they became prime targets for forced labour campaigns under a series of colonial rulers. Today's youth remain at the bottom of the fiercely hierarchical and polarized Grassfields societies. Such abiding trauma finds little voice in the state's modern and monolithic narratives. In *The Intestines of the State* (2008), Nicolas Argenti undermines linear historical narratives and describes – through witnessing, remembering and performing "re-enactments" of violence – the transformation of the Oku tribe youth into a political force. The book's most compelling argument is that these unspoken histories of violence and slavery have prompted a non-discursive embodied practice – masquerading –which, Argenti argues, is itself the lived practice of remembering. In this compelling scholarly output, Argenti shows how a myriad of masks "unmask" the complex and ambiguous discourses of elites' domination, violence and subjection.

Youth political participation and identity politics are salient feature of Africa's political market. A deeply nuanced ethnography of historical consciousness, Lesley Sharp's (2002) *The Sacrificed Generation* challenges many cross-cultural investigations on youth. Lesley refutes dominant assumptions that African children are the helpless victims of postcolonial crises, incapable of organized, sustained collective thought or action. Grounded in vivid depictions of local life, Sharp relates these to larger questions about the postcolonial exercise of political and economic power, when international organizations unattached to any particular state ostensibly control sovereign states. Referring to these radically changing circumstances, the author questions the construction of young people's capacity to understand their past, present and future. Given the linkages between autobiography and national history, Sharp asserts that the classroom, the home and the streets forge political consciousness.

Hunger is an increasingly violent agent of progress within the discourse of political economy that emerged in the eighteenth century and subsequently shaped modern social and political life. Examining the works of Charles Dickens, Harriet Martineau, George Eliot, Elizabeth Gaskell, Henry Mayhew and Charlotte Bronte, Lesa Scholl (2016) argues, in *Hunger Movements in Early Victorian Literature*, for the centrality of hunger in social development and understanding. She shows how the rhetoric of hunger moves beyond critiques of physical starvation to a paradigm in which the dominant narratives of civilization are predicated on the continual progress of literal and metaphorical taste. Through the lens of early Victorian writers and the pre-eminent political, social and economic thinkers of the age, *Hunger Movements* reminds us of what hunger was during the West's modernization, and what it still may be, thus telling the story of these bleak times. By exploring the ways in which the language of starvation interacts with narratives of emotional and intellectual want to create a dynamic, evolving notion of hunger, Lesa Scholl's revelations on want, riots and migration give interesting new perspectives that trigger fresh exploration of Victorian classics.

Social sciences scholarships acknowledges the linkages among hunger, political stability and social unrest. Marco Lagi, Karla Betrand and Yaneer Bar-Yam (2011) identify a correlation between international food prices, as measured by the FAO Food Index, and media reports of food riots. Similarly, Marc Bellemare (2012) also found that increases in the FAO Food Index led to increased media reports of food riots. Both of these papers present compelling findings of statistical correlations between food prices and riots, but they both use international commodity prices as the measure of food prices. In the same vein, based on specific case studies (Egypt, Mozambique and Niger), which represent different responses to the food crisis, Julia Berezneva and David Lee (2013) stress the key role of pro-poor long-term policies and investments, highlight the importance of pro-poor policies and investments and improved governance in addressing the problems facing the poor and in helping secure political stability. Berezneva's and Lee's empirical analysis demonstrates that higher levels of poverty (as proxied by the Human Poverty Index), urbanization, restricted access to and availability of food, more oppressive regimes and stronger civil societies are associated with a higher likelihood of riots occurring.

Rising food prices are a contributing cause not just of food riots but also of social unrest more broadly defined, including labour strikes, street demonstrations, communal conflict and other riots. Todd Smith (2013) provides some insight into potential causality between hunger and political instability. From a theoretical perspective, he introduces some theoretical and methodological innovations and tests the impact of national consumer food price indices on social unrest because these better represent the prices that people actually pay for food. Michael Lofchie's and Stephen Commins' (1984) *Food Deficits and Agricultural Policies in Sub-Saharan Africa* tackles the problem of continuing famine, examining drought, the theory of underdevelopment and agricultural policies, thus recommending short- and long-term changes.

Hunger defines popular protest and popular politics. It is due to the lack of balanced development in many countries and the disregard for agriculture's role in economic development cycles. Bacon once observed in *The Essays of Francis Bacon* (2014, p. 44) that "rebellions of the belly are the worst." In resonant, delicately crafted verse, James Ragan's (1996) *The Hunger Wall* explores the parallels between riot-torn cities and reflects on the nature of divisions (ethnic, cultural and political). In a metaphorically rich language, Ragan studies what it means to set a "border," whether it be political, racial or economic. *The Hunger Wall* examines a continually changing world – a world of shifting cultural identities in which the widening gap between the rich and the poor is dangerously explosive.

Relevant policies must go beyond economic reforms and seek a solution to the entrenched political problems that are dividing the continent. By delving into the past and providing details of the underlying factors that contributed to the creation of the problem of famine, hunger and starvation, Karefah Marah (2006) discusses and puts the issue in its proper historical context in *Famine, Hunger and Starvation in Africa*. In the same vein, David Bigman's (2011) *Poverty, Hunger, and Democracy in Africa* evaluates alternative policy options for African countries to overcome the food crisis and the changing structure of world trade to sustain their impressive growth beyond the 2000s.

In the end, social science authors have made substantial insights into critical reasoning in the context of youth-led violence, political participation, identity politics, racial biases, class struggles and hunger. However, few of them have bothered to get inside political sociology to uncover how to orient their scholarship towards the 2008 hunger riots that brought upheaval to African countries. This paper attempts to fill that gap.

Geographies of the 2008 Hunger Riots in Selected African Countries

Hunger riots broken out in several African countries in 2008. Inflation was more pronounced in the developing world where 50%–60% of income goes to food, compared with just 10%–20% in the developed world. In Africa, rising food prices have an undeniably disproportionate impact on poor populations who often devote more than half of their income to food (Haddad, Ruel and Garrett, 1999; Kendall, Olson and Frongillo, 1996; Maxwell et al., 2000). Increased food demand from developing countries, the use of crops for biofuels, global stocks at 25-year lows and market speculation boosted prices of staples such as wheat, maize and rice to record highs (Pomeroy, 2008). Economic hardships resulting from rising food prices led to violence and social unrest. Mindi Schneider's (2008) *We Are Hungry*, a detailed survey of the geography of the 2008 hunger riots in selected African countries, forms the basis of this analysis. This chapter will now survey the following countries: Burkina Faso, Cameroon, Côte d'Ivoire, Egypt, Ethiopia, Guinea, Madagascar, Mauritania, Morocco, Niger and Senegal.

Burkina Faso's food price riots erupted in February and March 2008, especially in the cities of Ougadougou, Bobo Dioulasso, Ouhigouya and Banfora. Rioters protested against taxes and inflation. Police arrested and detained more than 300 demonstrators. As a result, public authorities suspended import duties on staple food imports for three months. Two weeks before the outbreak of food riots, the government took two specific measures against inflation: the release of emergency stocks onto the market and tax rebate on basic goods (IRIN, 2008a). Despite these initiatives, unions called a general strike in early April, demanding further price cuts for food and a 25% increase in public sector salaries and pensions (Bonkoungou, 2008).

Cameroon's hunger riots took place in several key cities. Human rights campaigners accused the government of covering up the true death toll. The communication minister, Jean-Pierre Biyiti Bi Essam, acknowledged 17 deaths. However, Madeleine Affite, the Littoral Region coordinator for Action of Christians for the Abolition of Torture (ACAT), contended that the true death toll was higher. Security forces arrested and detained, without charge or trial, youth opposing the Cameroon government. Charges coalesced around the criminal offences of public disorder and destruction of private and government property, complicity in looting, destruction of property, arson, obstructing streets, degrading public or classified property and forming illegal gatherings (Amnesty International, 2009). Public authorities subjected more than 1,500 people, mostly youths, who had been arrested during the February 2008 riots to speedy trials. At least 300 protesters were detained at the Yaoundé Kondengui central prison. In Douala, more than 460 were found guilty of various criminal offences. The Cameroon Bar rose up against such illegal practices (Musa, 2008).

Cameroon's youth demonstrators decried human rights abuses and plans by the ruling Cameroon Peoples' Democratic Party (CPDM) to amend the 1996 constitution to make it possible for President Paul Biya, who had been in office since 1982, to run for the presidency yet again when his term expired in 2011. The National Assembly approved the amendment on 10 April. Although opposition parties' members of parliament staged a walkout to protest the move, there was little immediate public outcry.

The Cameroonian government enacted several measures to dissipate some of the hunger-related issues and bring down the prices of mass consumption commodities. On 20 May 2008, President Paul Biya decreed a conditional amnesty for hunger-riot prisoners. However, several dozen did not benefit from the amnesty and remained in custody, either because they had appealed against their conviction and sentence or because they had been unable to pay fines imposed by the judicial system. For example, of the 466 released from the Douala New Bell prison on 10 June, 245 remained in custody because they had appealed while a further 147 continued to be detained for failing to defray court-related fines. Only 74 were immediately released. In response to the demands of demonstrators, the government agreed to cut the price of a litre of gasoline from XAF 600 to XAF 594 (about US$1.36) (Reuters, 2008). Additionally, Paul Biya announced an increase of civil servants salaries by 15% and the suspension of customs duties on cement and basic foodstuffs, including fish, rice and cooking oil (FAO GIEWS, 2008).

Protestors against high food prices took the streets of Côte d'Ivoire on March 31, demanding that the government take action to curb food prices (IRIN, 2008a). The riots left one person dead and 20 wounded (BBC, 2008a). Following two days of rioting, President Laurent Gbagbo cancelled customs duties and cut taxes on basic household commodities.

Described as "the Mahalla intifada," Egypt's violent hunger protests began on 6 April in the Nile Delta textile town, Mahalla el-Kobra, two days ahead of nationwide local council elections (Cairo News, 2008). From March through April, rice prices had more than doubled. Many people depended on state-subsidized bread, sold for 20% of its market price. Fights in the long bread lines left at least six people dead, and the government called in the army to bake bread for the public (Borger, 2008; Moore, 2008). On 6 April, security officers thwarted a strike planned by workers at the Misr Spinning and Weaving plant to protest increased prices of food, mostly bread, and to demand a rise in the minimum wage. On 5 April, almost 100 political activists were arrested, and the plan was abandoned (Beinin, 2008). Egypt's civil society organizations endorsed a hunger strike. These included the Egyptian Movement for Change Kifaya, the Islamist Labour Party, the Nasserist Karama Party and the Bar Association.

Still in Egypt, Prime Minister Nazif announced a set of measures during a visit to Mahalla el-Kobra on 8 April. He promised bonuses for textile workers; increased investment in the Misr plant; and more subsidized bread, rice, oil, sugar and flour (Gamal, 2008). In March, in an effort to put an end to bread queues that had people waiting in long lines for subsidized bread, President Mubarak ordered the army to increase bread production and distribution. Likewise, the government used foreign reserves to purchase wheat on the international market

(BBC, 2008b). By May, Egypt opened its ration card system until 30 June and doubled the amount of rice that cardholders could receive (FAO, 2008). The following month, the country extended the rice export through April 2009.

In Ethiopia, the prices of basic foods in Addis Ababa jumped 30%–70%. The government banned cereal exports and subsidized wheat for low-income city households.

As for Guinea, in January and February 2007, anti-government demonstrations led to a crackdown that claimed nearly 200 lives and provoked a deep crisis. The grievances were both political and economic, combining dissatisfaction with the government and popular dismay over worsening living conditions. Sporadic street protests flared throughout that year. In mid-February 2008, rioting over high food prices broke out again in Ratoma, just outside the capital city, Conakry.

Madagascar witnessed food riots in April 2008 (Mineguruji, 2008). The following month, in an effort to preserve domestic food supplies, the government banned rice exports (IRIN, 2008b).

Mauritania faced violent demonstrations against the high cost of staple foods by November 2007 (Reuters, 2007). Annual inflation on some locally grown foodstuffs had reportedly reached 28%. The price of wheat products had gone up even more, from US$200 a tonne to US$356 a tonne (Gambia News Community, 2007). Nouakchott and nine other cities exploded in mass protests. Young people looted food stores and attacked law enforcement officers. In May, the government implemented a "Special Plan of Intervention" for the subsequent six months, including credits and distribution of inputs for farmers. In May, it reduced import taxes on cereals (FAO, 2008).

Successive waves of sit-ins to protest high food prices hit Morocco from March to September 2007. Protestors violently clashed with police after a 30% increase in the price of bread. These events in Sefrou left 50 injured. In April, riots also broke out in Rabat, in front of the parliament (Harsch, 2008). From September 2007 to February 2008, the judiciary sentenced 34 rioters to jail.

To contain the hunger riots, the government of Niger set up a cabinet-level ministry to coordinate action on commodity prices. Public authorities acted quickly to remove tariffs on rice, which everyone eats. That quick action kept people from taking to the streets.

In November 2007 and March 2008, Senegal's 18 unions marched to protest the spiralling cost of basic food. Further unrest in March led to clashes with police and at least 24 arrests. Angered by sharply rising prices of basic foodstuffs, transport, electricity and other essentials, Senegal's youth poured onto the streets to express their frustrations and demand that their governments act quickly to halt the spiralling inflation.

Strategic and Policy Frameworks for Analysing Circular Linkages Between Youth Policies and Social Unrest in Africa

The potential of young people is Africa's driving force for structural transformation and growth. In less than three generations, Africa's population is projected to represent over 40% of the world's young people. By 2050, the teeming numbers of young Africans are forecast to form over a quarter of the world's labour force. Moreover, there is a growing consensus that Africa's youthfulness will continue to grow for the next 50 years, while the other continents are ageing (UNECA, 2017, p. i).

Young people constitute a substantial share of the population of most sub-Saharan African countries. This creates a need for transformative policies and related programmes to engage youth effectively in all development schemes. Failure to have such policies could have grim political and socio-economic consequences (UNECA, 2007). Using an overview chart of the framework of the World Programme of Action for Youth, the governments of Ethiopia (2004), Ghana (2007 draft), Kenya (2007), Nigeria (2001 draft) and Uganda (2004) enacted youth policies to promote effective development and inclusion of young people. Nigeria adopted a National Youth Development Agenda. Here, major policy reforms included a review of the National Youth Policy created in 2001, a reform of the National Youth Service Corp, the inauguration of a Youth Parliament, the strengthening of the National Youth Council, creating a Youth Development Index and the release of a Youth Development Report. Major priority issues therein included training, status of girls and young women, employment, economic development, information and communications technology, conflicts, globalization, drug abuse, HIV/AIDS, juvenile delinquency and intergenerational issues. In its 2006/2007 budget, Kenya set aside one billion Kenya shillings (about US$15,000) to fast track the youth initiative and provided the necessary legal framework to govern its monitoring and operations. In January 2007, the country set up an 11-member advisory board of the Youth Enterprise Development Fund, aiming to facilitate youth employment by providing loans to existing micro-finance institutions, registered non-governmental organizations, and savings/credit co-operative organizations for lending to youth corporations.

Engaging the youth of Africa and meeting the expectations for a more inclusive future requires a better understanding of their needs, interests, challenges and potential as well as their diversity. This is the basis and inspiration for Africa's youth and prospects for inclusive development. In line with global commitments on youth, the United Nations Economic Commission for Africa (UNECA) provides a detailed assessment of the major issues and challenges faced by young people in Africa. By way of innovative examples, the institution illustrates how governments and other key actors could ensure that policy and service delivery achieve meaningful results for Africa's youth, particularly those who are disadvantaged and marginalized. Indeed, Africa's children can scale the ladder of hope based on decisions policymakers take. As UNECA's Africa's youth and prospects for inclusive development regional situation analysis report (2017, p. i) suggests, "young people must be meaningfully involved in the implementation and tracking of the Sustainable Development Goals and the African Union Agenda 2063."

Young African people are marginalized from participation in mainstream institutions. During the 2008 hunger protests, they catalysed the political order to some extent. As is evident in the hunger riots and protest movements in African countries, young people are increasingly finding outlets for political expression outside of partisan politics and civil society. The picture of youth catalysing ruptures and engaging in "unruly politics" is consistent with one of the threads of youth literature and policy discourses about generational differences and tensions (Khanna, 2012). The idea is that young people tend to resist and attempt to (in a different way) engage with or change the political and social structures that they come to meet (Honwana, 2012).

The involvement of Africa's youth in mass protests is not a consistent part of their repertoire. It is used in response to particular situations. The picture of young people's agency in creating new spaces and forms of political and civic engagement is not promising. According to UNECA (2017, p. 57), "these new informal modes may further alienate young people from formal structures and processes where much of the decision-making about national development occurs." An analysis of youth protest activity across six rounds of the Afrobarometer survey, from 2000 to 2014, using data from the six countries that had the highest levels of youth participation in protests, shows no clear trend (UNECA, 2017, pp. 55–56).

Creating jobs that are more productive is even more pressing for Africa. Employment and entrepreneurship refer to the enhancement of natural capacity to develop gender sensitive strategies for decent work for young people. Employment and entrepreneurship ensure greater opportunities for youth to secure decent work and income over the life cycle, contributing to a virtuous cycle of poverty reduction, sustainable development and social inclusion. The rapid growth in Africa's population and consequently its workforce increases pressure on the continent's labour market. According to the African Development Bank, Organization for Economic Cooperation and Development and United Nations Development Programme (UNDP) (2012), the continent's workforce is expected to increase by 910 million people between 2010 and 2050, of which 80 million will be in North Africa. About 19 million young people joined the labour market in all other parts of Africa (excluding North Africa) in 2015, and approximately 4 million will do so in North Africa. It is projected that the number of young people joining the labour market will increase to 370 million in all other parts of Africa (excluding North Africa) by 2030, while the figure for North Africa will increase to 65 million in the same year. This yields a yearly average of 24.6 million and 4.3 million new entrants, respectively.

Opportunities for Africa to benefit from the youth demographic dividend are quickly slipping away (International Labour Organization (ILO), 2015). Young Africans aspire to productive, formal employment opportunities that provide them with a decent wage, relative security and good conditions of work. Yet far too few of them are able to match their aspirations to reality. Estimates of youth labour force participation rates for 2013 globally were 47.4%, and for Africa, 46.8%. Young males in Africa had a higher participation rate, at 51.9%, relative to young females, 41.9%.

Eastern Africa had the highest youth labour force participation rate, averaging 61%, while Northern Africa had the lowest rate at about 33%. The high labour force participation rates for the subregion are mainly attributed to the United Republic of Tanzania (80.5%), Zimbabwe (79.5%), Madagascar (78.8%), Eritrea (77.2%), Ethiopia (76.6%), Zambia (66.9%) and Burundi (64.6%). Countries that had relatively low rates were Gabon (25.7%), South Africa (26.3%), Algeria (28.9%), Tunisia (31.5%), Namibia (31.8%) and Egypt (34%). Overall, there is a gender gap in labour force participation rates in all subregions in favour of males, with the disparity being the largest in northern Africa (UNECA, 2017, p. 60). With regard to the ILO key indicators of the labour market pilot countries, Mozambique had the highest youth labour force participation rate at 65.5%, compared to 44% for Sierra Leone and 39.5% for Kenya (ILO, 2014). This means that a higher proportion of the youth in Mozambique is actively engaged in the labour market than in Sierra Leone and Kenya.

Concluding Thoughts: Unlocking Africa's Youth Transformative Leadership Potentials

Africa's youth population is growing rapidly and is expected to double to more than 830 million by 2050. This increase in working-age population presents an opportunity to boost productivity and facilitate inclusive growth across the continent. Many governments are addressing these challenges by revising existing youth policies and creating new strategies that aim to increase the support available to young people to participate fully in their societies (UNECA, 2007, p. 4). However, much of this demographic dividend remains untapped. Although 10–12 million youths enter the workforce every year, the continent creates only around 3 million formal jobs annually. As a result, one third of African youth aged 15–35 years are unemployed. Another one-third are vulnerably employed or underemployed, mostly in the informal sector. While much of the literature on youth employment calls for the creation of jobs and opportunities to absorb them in the labour market, little is known about the youths themselves, their demographics and their expectations. Policymakers should gather more information on the impact of youth demographics on their social welfare, social protection, education and health as well as their skills and ability to meet labour market demands in a globalized world.

There exists complex and circular relationships between hunger and social unrest in Africa. The linkages between rising food prices and hunger riots are central in both academic studies of political stability and political and economic policy calculations. Provided public policies prioritize their needs, younger people are potential assets who would contribute to sustainable development. Key current challenges include gender disparity, the low correlation between economic growth and job opportunities and the fact that a significant number of jobs created are of low quality. There is a need to fill existing knowledge gaps in the analyses of employment, labour markets and economic and social policies related to youth welfare and aspirations. The 2008 hunger riots caused protests in African countries and presented policymakers with the challenge of simultaneously addressing food security, poverty, rural exodus, democratic reforms and political instability. Youth protesters violently reacted against sharply rising prices of basic foodstuffs, transport, electricity and other essentials. They poured into the streets to express their frustrations and demand that governments act quickly to contain the spiralling cost of living.

African youths' hunger is an extreme form of deprivation with huge political, security, social and economic costs. Against this backdrop and in light of the great potential, dynamism, resourcefulness, resiliency and aspiration of its younger population, Africa continues to face daunting challenges of maximizing benefits from this social capital. It fails to adequately invest in youth empowerment and development. The majority of African youth continue to face political marginalization, unemployment, underemployment, lack of skills and relevant education, limited access to capital and unmet need for health-related information and services including those related to diagnosis, treatment and care of tropical and communicable diseases (AUC, 2011). Along with other groups (women, disabled people), Africa's youth bear the brunt of internal and external crises, be it those related to financial, food and hunger crisis, climate change or human insecurity (AUC, 2011).

African countries should harness the demographic dividend through investments in the youth. They must foster interregional collaboration for youth development in Africa and encourage the alignment of national youth policies with the regional commitments encapsulated in the African Youth Charter (AYC) (UNECA, 2007, p. 4). There is a collective need to strengthen Africa's national platforms of youth organizations in order to have strong partners in all stages of implementation of national youth policies (UNECA, 2017). In other words, stakeholders responsible for youth development require further support and assistance to mainstream youth development initiatives in national planning and to integrate youth issues across government structures and departments (UNECA, 2017). To give substance to this commitment to the development of African youth, the AUC has since developed progressive policy frameworks. The AYC prescribes responsibilities to member states for the development of youth. The July 2006 AYC is a political and legal document to support policies, programmes and actions for youth development in Africa. The AYC, which serves as the strategic framework for youth empowerment and development at the continental, regional and national levels, addresses key issues affecting youth, including employment, sustainable livelihoods, education, skills development, health, youth participation, national youth policy, peace and security, law enforcement, youth in the diaspora and youth with disabilities (AUC, 2006).

Engaging the youth of Africa and meeting the expectations for a more inclusive future requires a better understanding of their needs, interests, challenges and potential as well as their diversity. That assertion is the basis and inspiration for Africa's youth and prospects for inclusive development (UNECA, 2017). Based on the foregoing, UNECA has identified key initial areas for potential follow-up recommendations. The institution prescribed the sharing of experiences across youth ministries to learn from and build upon each other's implementation of policies; the provision of further support and assistance to state organs in charge of youth development to mainstream youth development initiatives in national planning and to integrate youth issues across government structures and departments; the undertaking of collective action to strengthen national platforms of youth organizations to have strong partners in all stages of implementation of the national youth policies; the promotion and harmonization of international, regional and national commitments to youth; and to leverage these to promote youth development activities (UNECA, 2007).

In the final analysis, Africa's policymakers should advance opportunities for the youth as a priority within the framework of the sustainable development goals and the post-2015 development agenda. They should increase access to decent work and livelihood opportunities, promote access to essential financial and non-financial resources to increase entrepreneurship opportunities and develop public–private partnerships to stimulate job creation and youth employment. Likewise, African governments should ensure all young people have access to inclusive, adequate and high-quality formal, non-formal and vocational education and training, which enables them to lead a healthy and productive life, equips them with skills that are relevant to market needs and fosters global citizenship, leadership and political participation.

Overall, this chapter is an original contribution to our understanding of youth and exclusion in the global order. Based on the 2008 hunger riots, it has shown that youth, especially the unemployed, have a higher propensity than other groups to engage in violence against the state. Referring to African countries, the paper has demonstrated that "hunger," "greed" or "opportunity" perspectives stress the material and other benefits, such as protection, that engagement in violence might offer, particularly for those – like poor, disgruntled unemployed youth – for whom the opportunity cost of engaging in violence is much higher. Here, "grievance" perspectives stress the relative deprivation of social, economic and political exclusions suffered by youth as a motivation for their political engagement through violence. Finally, this chapter has brought out the fact that gerontocracy, structural exclusion and lack of opportunities faced by youth effectively prolong their transition to adulthood through economic self-sufficiency and can lead to frustration, disillusionment and, in some cases, their engagement in violence (Social Development Direct, 2009).

References

African Development Bank, Organization for Economic Cooperation and Development, United Nations Development Programme. 2012. *African Economic Outlook 2012: Promoting Youth Employment in Africa.*

AUC. 2006. *African Youth Charter, 6th Ordinary Session.*

AUC. 2011. *African Youth Decade 2009–2018 Plan of Action Accelerating Youth Empowerment for Sustainable Development.*

Amnesty International. 2009. *Cameroon Impunity Underpins Persistent Abuse, AI Index: AFR 17/001/2009,* London, Amnesty International Publications.

Argenti, N. 2008. *The Intestines of the State: Youth, Violence, and Belated Histories in the Cameroon Grassfields,* Chicago, University of Chicago Press.

Bacon, F. 2014. *The Essays of Francis Bacon,* Morrisville, NC, Lulu Press Inc.

Beinin, J. 2008. Egypt: bread riots and mill strikes, *Le Monde Diplomatique,* May.

Bonkoungou, M. 2008. Burkina general strike starts over cost of living, Reuters, 8 April.

Bay, E. G. and Donham, D. 2006. *States of Violence: Politics, Youth, and in Contemporary Africa,* Charlottesville, University of Virginia Press.

BBC. 2008a. Riots prompt ivory coast tax cuts, BBC, April 2.

BBC. 2008b. Egypt army to tackle bread crisis, BBC, March 17.

Berezneva, J. and Lee, D. R. 2013. Explaining the African food riots of 2007–2008: An empirical analysis, *Food Policy*, *39*, 28–39.

Borger, J. 2008. Feed the world? We are fighting a losing battle, UN admits, *The Guardian*, 26 February.

Brown, J. 2016. *The Road to Soweto: Resistance and the Uprising of 16 June 1976*, Melton, James Currey.

Bellemare, M. 2012. *Rising Food Prices, Food Price Volatility, and Social Unrest*, SSRN Scholarly Paper, Rochester, Social Science Research Network.

Bigman, D. 2011. *Poverty, Hunger, and Democracy in Africa: Potential and Limitations of Democracy in Cementing Multiethnic Societies*, London, Palgrave Macmillan.

Cairo News. 2008. Egyptians protest against rising cost of living, Cairo News, August 4.

Enria, L. 2018. *The Politics of Work in a Post-Conflict State: Youth, Labour & Violence in Sierra Leone Western Africa Series*, Melton, James Currey.

FAO. 2008. Economic and social department, "policy measures taken by governments to reduce the impact of soaring prices," Crop prospects and food situation, No. 3, July.

FAO. 2017. *FAO Food Price Index*, FAO.

FAO GIEWS. 2008. Crop prospects and food situation, No. 2, April.

Gamal, W. 2008. Two die after clashes in Egypt industrial town, Reuters, 8 April.

Gambia News Community. 2007. Mauritania: high food prices spark protests, 14 November.

Haddad, L., Ruel, M. T. and Garrett, J. L. 1999. Are urban poverty and undernutrition growing? Some newly assembled evidence, *World Development*, *27*(11), 1891–1904.

Harsch, E. 2008. Price protests expose state faults rioting and repression reflect problems of African governance, *Africa Renewal*, July.

Honwana, A. 2012. *The Time of Youth: Work, Social Change, and Politics in Africa*, Sterling, VA, Kumarian Press.

IRIN. 2008a. Food riots shut down main towns, All Africa Global Media, 22 February.

IRIN. 2008b. Madagascar: rice exports banned to keep home market supplied, Humanitarian News and Analysis: UN Office for the Coordination of Humanitarian Rights, 14 May.

ILO. 2014. *Key Indicators of the Labour Market*, 8th ed., Geneva, ILO.

ILO. 2015. *The Global Employment Trends for Youth 2015: Scaling Up Investments in Decent Jobs for Youth*, Geneva, ILO.

Karefah Marah, J. 2006. *Famine, Hunger and Starvation in Africa: Challenge to African and World Leaders*, Bloomington, Author House.

Kendall, A., Olson, C. M. and Frongillo, E. A. Jr. 1996. Relationship of hunger and food insecurity to food availability and consumption, *Journal of the American Dietetic Association*, *96*(10), 1019–1024.

Khanna, A. 2012. Seeing citizen action through an 'unruly' lens, *Development*, *55*(2), 162–172.

Lagi, M., Betrand, K. Z. and Bar-Yam, Y. 2011. The food crises and political stability in North Africa and the Middle East, *arXiv*, 1108.2455.

Lofchie, M. F. and Commins, S. K. 1984. *Food Deficits and Agricultural Policies in Sub-Saharan Africa*, The Hunger Project Papers.

Marks, M. 2008. *Young Warriors*, Johannesburg, Wits University Press.

Maxwell, D. G., Levin, C. E., Armar-Klemesu, M., Ruel, M. T., Morris, S. S. and Ahiadeke, C. 2000. *Urban Livelihoods and Food and Nutrition Security in Greater Accra, Ghana, Research Report*, Washington, DC, International Food Policy Research Institute.

Mineguruji. 2008. Soaring cereal prices leading to food riots, MERINEWS, 13 April.

Moore, F. C. 2008. Earth Policy Institute using "clashes over food prices trouble political leaders," Reuters, 2 April.

Musa, T. 2008. Cameroon activists say riots kill more than 100, Reuters, 5 March.

Nieftagodien, N. 2014. *The Soweto Uprising Ohio Short Histories of Africa*, Columbus, Ohio University Press.

Pomeroy, R. 2008. Food riots to worsen without global action: U.N., Reuters, 11 April.

Ragan, J. 1996. *The Hunger Wall: Poems*, New York, NY, Grove Press.

Reuters. 2007. Price protests grip southeast Mauritania, one dead, Reuters, 9 November

Reuters. 2008. Anti-government rioting spreads in Cameroon, *International Herald Tribune*, 27 February.

Schneider, M. 2008. "We are hungry!" A summary report of food riots, government responses, and states of democracy in 2008, *Research Gate*, pp. 8–27.

Scholl, L. 2016. *Hunger Movements in Early Victorian Literature: Want, Riots, Migration*, London, Routledge, Taylor & Francis.

Sharp, L. A. 2002. *The Sacrificed Generation: Youth, History, and the Colonized Mind in Madagascar*, Los Angeles, University of California Press.

Smith, T. G. 2013. Food price spikes and social unrest in Africa, Climate Change and African Political Stability (CCAPS), Research Brief No. 11, April.

Social Development Direct (Edited by Lyndsay McLean Hilker and Erika Fraser). 2009. *Youth Exclusion, Violence, Conflict and Fragile States. Report prepared for DFI's Equity and Rights Team*, London, Social Development Direct.

Swartz, S. 2009. *The Moral Ecology of South Africa's Township Youth*, London, Palgrave Macmillan.

UN. 2015. *Security Council Resolution 2250 on Youth, Peace and Security*, New York, NY, UN.

UNDP. 2006. *Youth and Violent Conflict: Society and Development in Crisis*, New York, NY, UNDP.

USAID. 2005. *Youth and Conflict: A Toolkit for Intervention*, Washington, DC, USAID.

UNECA. 2007. *Building Capacity to Assess National Youth Policies Workshop Report*, Addis Ababa, Ethiopia, UNECA.

UNECA. 2017. *Africa's Youth and Prospects for Inclusive Development Regional Situation Analysis Report*, Addis Ababa, Ethiopia, UNECA.

Chapter Five

Rural Youth Migration and Development in Zimbabwe

Tatenda Goodman Nhapi

Background and Introduction

This chapter explores intractable socio-economic challenges triggering youth exclusion and resultant migration of rural youths. Undeniably, as Arslan et al. (2021) suggest, in Global South countries, increasing numbers of rural youth and their perceived disenchantment with society and economy have raised policy concerns globally. As will be shown later, dominant narratives in Africa and Zimbabwe generally point to exclusionary socio-economic development policies which favour a gerontocratic model of development. Despite a policy architecture amplifying youth inclusion, the implementation modalities of policies sideline youths from political and local government development as they continue to be labelled as immature. It is increasingly acknowledged that productive youth employment is among the major development challenges of our time. The small size of the manufacturing and formal service sectors and the informal sector economies in Africa magnify this challenge; the likelihood is that a significant proportion of youths will continue to live in rural areas for decades to come.

As outlined by Sumberg and Yeboah (2020), an emerging orthodoxy supports the proposition that a rural economy built around agriculture but encompassing much more can be a sweet spot of employment opportunities for millions of youths in the foreseeable future. The African Development Bank Group (2017) reinforces Sumberg and Yeboah's (2020) assertions, observing that, given the anticipated doubling of Africa's youth to more than 830 million by 2050, increased productivity and more inclusive economic growth across the continent could be the result of harnessing the youth dividend (African Development Bank Group, 2017). On the same note, the Food and Agricultural Organization (FAO, 2018) notes that, of Africa's estimated 1.2 billion people, 60% are aged below

Youth Exclusion and Empowerment in the Contemporary Global Order: Existentialities in Migrations, Identity and the Digital Space, 65–83
Copyright © 2022 by Tatenda Goodman Nhapi
Published under exclusive licence by Emerald Publishing Limited
doi:10.1108/978-1-80382-777-320221006

25 years and the majority are in rural areas with few jobs, and growing uncertainty exists over the continent's preparedness to tap this resource. It is important to note that, before the onset of Covid-19, income disparities across Africa were on the rise (United Nations Economic Commission for Africa (UNECA), 2021). UNECA further posits that while extreme poverty had almost vanished in North Africa, more than 50% of the population in Central Africa lived below the extreme poverty line. UNECA observes that about 9 out of 10 extremely poor people in the world currently live in Africa and warns that Covid-19 will push an additional 5–29 million below the extreme poverty line.

Furthermore, Arslan et al. (2021) outline that the conclusion of a positive youth trajectory would be development of a mature adult possessing a positive sense of self, with developed agency, a set of core competencies and effective economic and societal engagement skills. For Arslan et al. (2021), a negative trajectory would be one where the person does not develop self-esteem and agency, leading to risky or destructive behaviour such as teen pregnancy, crime and violence, poor health habits and disengagement from society. All these destructive behaviours can lead to household poverty and lower economic growth (Arslan et al., 2021).

Certainly, Dzinotyiwei (2021) observes that it is disconcerting that Zimbabwe has not sufficiently factored in the economic benefits of empowering youths. Most economically productive years for youths are being wasted at a time when their development should be accelerated to meet the growing demands of advancement in modern society (Dzinotyiwei, 2021). Besides costly education and equipment, Zimbabwe lacks the necessities to train medical doctors, resources to equip our engineers, materials for our artists and a functioning economy for our budding accountants and economists to maintain (Dzinotyiwei, 2021).

Certainly, demographic transition, unemployment and underemployment have become rife and a fundamental development challenge in Africa. According to SNV (2020), data from the 2019 Labour Force and Child Labour Survey (LFCLS) indicates higher unemployment in rural than in urban areas (24.6% and 17.2%, respectively). For women in rural areas, the unemployment rate is 24.1%, and for men, it is 24.9%. In urban areas, there is a significant difference, where female unemployment is at 21%, which is 7% higher than male unemployment at 14.2% (SNV, 2020). During International Migrants' Day in 2017, the African Development Bank (2017) called on African countries to reconstruct rural areas from zones of economic misery to zones of economic prosperity for expansion of youths' economic opportunities to stem migration.

Considerable debate has been generated in southern Africa with regard to people's movement across political boundaries, with a compelling need for harmonization of southern African countries' regional migration policies (Crush & Tevera, 2010). However, Crush and Tevera contend that development-level disparities are still evident in the economies of the region. The challenges facing rural areas, in which three quarters of the world's poor reside, are a pressing concern for national governments and international organizations (ILO, n.d). Undoubtedly, as suggested by Sumberg and Yeboah (2020), African agriculture should be transformed for provision of decent or simply secure and remunerative employment for youths. This is achievable, according to Sumberg and Yeboah (2020), by equipping women and youth entrepreneurs with skills, resources and mentoring to drive Africa's growth. In most accounts, the transformation that is envisaged is described in terms of intensification and commercialization and involves increasing use of technology (Sumberg & Yeboah, 2020).

Henceforth, this chapter's objective is to explore programmatic interventions by state and non-state actors that galvanize rural youth horizons in terms of economic freedom, and build resilience to shocks and stressors. This chapter is grounded in an extensive review of literature focusing on youth development and migration dynamics within socio-economic domains currently obtaining in Zimbabwe. It synthesizes literature and provides insights for policy direction. Specifically, it reviews evidence on some of the migration policies, entrepreneurship and other social protection programmes. This chapter aims to create a starting point for a research agenda and to pose strong research questions with regard to rural youths' migration.

Methodology

This chapter is grounded in a historiography of commissioned studies and critiques on youth development. The search engine Google was used to locate websites operated by the Government of Zimbabwe, ministerial bodies and non-governmental organizations involved in youth development interventions. Targeted searches were conducted for documents produced between 2018 and 2021 through identifying publications in reference lists and expert recommendations. This discourse analysis included academic journals, books, newspapers, blogs, reports, research studies and magazines. Exploring official reports of youth development interventions helped to inform the study with such data as the beneficiaries of rural youth development interventions, the numbers reached, the finances involved, gaps that need attention and the impact on rural youth migration, among other issues.

Social Economic Overview

My discussion begins by critiquing current trends and dynamics in Zimbabwe's socio-economic trajectory. While 2021 began with prospects of a better harvest due to improved rainfall, and therefore a reduction in severe food insecurity, the country continues to face multiple hazards that include the lingering structural and flood-induced food and nutrition insecurity, the ensuing health crises, the ongoing impacts of Covid-19 and the chronic economic crisis. According to Reuters (2021), official data showed that Zimbabwe expects to harvest up to 2.8 million tonnes of maize in 2021, three times the 2020 output thanks to higher than usual rainfall. Zimbabwe endured devastating droughts from 2018 to 2020, which cut the maize harvest to 900,000 tonnes in 2020, half its annual requirements (Reuters, 2021). Despite a steady decrease in year-on-year inflation for the month of March 2021 (240.55%, down from 321.6% in February 2021), Zimbabwe is still in hyperinflation, severely impacting affordability of basic services for most of the population (UNICEF Zimbabwe, 2021).

On the basis of the 2020 Zimbabwe Vulnerability Assessment Committee (ZimVAC), the World Food Programme Zimbabwe (2021a) noted that 42% of urban households inability to meet cereal requirements in 2021 compared to 30% in 2019 has been due to Covid lockdowns which depleted livelihoods and diminished employment prospects. ZimVAC is a technical advisory committee comprised of government representatives, development partners, United Nations (UN) agencies such as the World Food Programme (WFP), non-governmental organizations (NGOs), technical agencies and academics.

Lockdown impositions to contain the spread of Covid-19 dealt a severe blow to poor urban communities, many of whom were daily wage earners living hand to mouth. While unable to find work in cities, the ban on travel has meant that seasonal employment in rural areas is no longer an option. With work opportunities disappearing, the ZimVAC report states that 42% of urban households will not be able to meet their cereal requirements this year, compared to approximately 30% for the same period in 2019 (World Food Programme Zimbabwe, 2021b). UNICEF's (2021) State of the World's Children noted at least 27% of young people in Zimbabwe aged 15–24 as suffering from depression, some of it caused by Covid-19. The UNICEF (2021) report lists Zimbabwe as one of the five leading countries, out of 21, whose young people suffer from depression. The UNICEF study had about 20,000 people aged 15–24 years and older people aged up to 40 years were part of the sampled population in the research conducted between February and June 2021 in Zimbabwe and 20 other countries (UNICEF, 2021).

In the analysis by World Food Programme Zimbabwe (2021a), despite continued official annual inflation rate decline, market prices continue to increase for some goods and services. According to World Food Programme Zimbabwe (2021a), parallel market exchange rates remain a key driver of high and increasing prices. Among other commodities, fuel prices increased by as much as 5%, with bread prices going up nearly 7% in late March 2021 (World Food Programme Zimbabwe, 2021a). Casual labour, livestock sales, cross-border and petty trade, remittances and other typical income-earning activities remain below normal, with most poor households' income below poverty lines. As of April and May 2021, the expectation was for improved household income across parts of the country from crop sales (Famine Early Warning Systems Network (FEWSNET), 2021).

Humanitarian needs continuously escalated from year 2020, triggered by the deepening economic crisis and the worsening impact of drought, floods, and the ongoing Covid-19 pandemic. In March 2020, the Humanitarian Response Plan (HRP) projected a total of 7 million people, including 3.2 million children, to be in urgent need of humanitarian assistance and protection. Covid-19 exacerbated urban hunger, and the WFP together with partners has supported the government of Zimbabwe to ring-fence developmental gains that have been so far achieved. Shrinking disposable income meant less money in people's pockets to buy food, while market and supply disruptions due to movement restrictions created challenges for accessing food (United Nations Zimbabwe Country Programme, 2021). Furthermore, a sharp decline in living standards is trending, with 83% across poor urban Zimbabwean communities now having below the cost of the minimum expected food items such as mealie meal, salt and cooking oil, compared to 76.8% in 2019 (World Food Programme Zimbabwe, 2021a).

On the basis of the analysis by the Zimbabwe Coalition on Debt and Development (ZIMCODD) (2021), youths are recognized as an important group and are accorded relevance to this end. Notably, out of a Z$426.1 billion budget for 2021, the youth ministry was only allocated Z$3.447 billion (0.8%) towards youth empowerment. There is, however, lack of clarity as to how much capital will go towards the Empower Bank and the National Venture Fund and on how the funds are to be disbursed to the youth (ZIMCODD, 2021).

On 1 May 2020, the Government of Zimbabwe announced a Z$18 billion economic recovery and stimulus package aimed at economic revival and relief to individuals whose businesses had been affected by the pandemic, coupled with a ZW$17 million Youth Relief Fund. On the same note, Makore-Ncube and Al-Maiyah (2021) outlined that like many other countries in Africa, as a result of the increased urbanization rates, Zimbabwe's urban areas have experienced drastic changes. This has been caused by complex rural-to-urban migration flows, socio-political tensions and extreme strain on basic services. Over the years, as a consequence of the dire socio-economic climate and state-led evictions, significant parts of urban Zimbabwe have been progressively forced into urban poverty and informality (Makore-Ncube & Al-Maiyah, 2021). Significantly, the cabinet approved the re-establishment of the National Youth Service (NYS) programme after it was suspended in 2018. The approval followed proposals presented to cabinet by Kirsty Coventry, the minister of Youth, Sport, Arts and Recreation, after consultations between her ministry and that of Defence and War Veterans Affairs (Machivenyika, 2021).

The Information, Publicity and Broadcasting Services' minister, Monica Mutsvangwa, stated that the NYS was an important youth development initiative crucial in nurturing youths to become responsible and resilient citizens with a clear sense of national identity and respect for national values (Machivenyika, 2021). The government also outlined how the NYS programme as a key youth empowerment strategy built on national, regional, continental and international frameworks guiding development to which Zimbabwe is signatory (Machivenyika, 2021).

Of note is the sharp decline in standards of living due to high poverty rates and an increasingly informal economy. According to the International Monetary Fund, Zimbabwe is the second most informalized economy in the world (after Bolivia). Poverty is more prevalent in rural areas where 68% of people live, and the majority of those people depend directly or indirectly on agriculture for employment and food security (Zimstat, 2015).

Nhunzvi (2020) asserts that before the onset of Covid-19, there was already a battle to contain an upsurge in substance abuse among youths and young adults. Many were, however, deriving livelihoods from the informal sector, including commuter omnibus touting. Because their lives were still stressful in a largely unsupportive environment, many saw substance abuse as a justified though maladaptive coping strategy (Nhunzvi, 2020). In the same vein, Crush and Tevera (2010) observe that Zimbabwe has become a far more significant exporter of migrant labour due to economic conditions deterioration. On the same note, various literature links structural poverty to the creation of inequalities between black and white due to Zimbabwe's colonial history. The bottlenecks for black Zimbabweans included unequal access to economic and natural resources, land, education and employment opportunities (United Nations Country Team (UNCT), 2014). Despite the government's attempts to redress the situation since independence in 1980, the consequences of systematic generation and sustenance of poverty in the colonial period continue to the present day (United Nations Country Team (UNCT), 2014). Of Zimbabwe's 13.06 million people, 52% are female and 48% are male, with 65% of households headed by men and 35% by women (Food and Agriculture Organization, 2017).

Undeniably, Zimbabwe's economy is natural resource dependent, and natural resource development is closely linked with economic growth potential (Akesson et al., 2016). Most areas of Zimbabwe experience a subtropical climate because of high altitude rather its geographical position (15 °35′ East and 220 °30′ South). The country also experiences a semi-arid climate, and average annual precipitation is estimated to be between 652 and 674.5 mm (Manzungu, 2014). The total number of Zimbabweans employed in agriculture, fisheries and forestry is 3 573 893, of which 45.4% are men and 54.6% are women. The percentage for women is high because they are mostly unpaid family workers. While men in Zimbabwe eclipse women in terms of ownership, decision-making and control of more valuable livestock, women's ownership of smaller livestock (like chickens) is greater (Food and Agriculture Organization, 2017). The land tenure policy allows households living on land designated as communal to operate under customary tenure, empowering them to occupy and use land within customary norms and practices. This tenure system does not provide for trading land and natural resource rights, limiting formal financial intermediaries' credit facilities for land development and agricultural financing (Food and Agriculture Organization, 2017). In Akesson et al.'s (2016) analysis, weak implementation and enforcement of existing legislation, poor institutional capacity and weak governance structures, including inadequate coordination, are some of the underlying causes of Zimbabwe's environmental challenges.

Zimbabwe's Fast-track Land Reform Programme (FTLRP) began to be implemented in 2000, under the pressure of occupations of white-owned farms by a war veteran-led movement. The FTLRP reversed the dualistic agrarian structure inherited at independence in 1980 (Mkodzongi, 2016).

Transformation of the rural authority structure was one of the major outcomes of the FTLRP (Mkodzongi, 2016). FTLRP's original objectives were the enhancement of the socio-economic well-being of low-income households (that is, the reduction of rural poverty), including their ability to feed themselves adequately (that is, achievement of food security) while at the same time earning a reasonable income from the sale of crops and livestock (Kinsey, 2010). Kinsey notes that these objectives were achieved through provision of a whole range of supporting services and facilities – health, markets, agricultural credit, veterinarians, housing loans and schools. Nevertheless, the government's economic blueprint, the National Development Strategy (NDS) 2021–2021 (Government of Zimbabwe, 2020), stipulates that several programmes, projects and interventions will be implemented for social protection to reduce extreme poverty and improve access to basic social services across the life cycle of vulnerable groups, as follows:

- Provision of food assistance, social cash transfers, health assistance and holistic education support including school feeding and provision of sanitary wear for female learners in schools
- Provision of discretionary assistance in funeral and transport assistance
- Support towards disaster preparedness and response programmes to build resilience in communities
- Strengthening social protection delivery systems inclusive of shock responsiveness. (Government of Zimbabwe, 2020)

Finally, The Zimbabwe Youth Policy is in line with the national constitution on the definition of youth. Section 20 is a component of Chapter 1 of the Constitution of Zimbabwe Amendment (No. 20) Act 2013 on Founding Provisions. Section 20 sets the youth's agenda for the rights of youths in Zimbabwe by stating that the state and its institutions and agencies at every level must take reasonable measures, including affirmative action, to ensure that youths:

- have access to education and training;
- have opportunities to associate and to be represented and participate in political, social, economic and other spheres of life;
- are afforded opportunities for employment and other avenues to economic empowerment;
- have opportunities for recreational activities and access to recreational facilities.

Conceptual Framework

The following section critiques the different conceptual underpinnings that are relied on when theorizing about youths. In Lintelo's (2012) observations, often organized around age but sometimes around alternative criteria, a bewildering range of definitions and working definitions are used for youth, hindering comparative research. Hodzi (2013) asserts youths are no homogeneous group, as socio-political and economic concerns differ among professionals, rural youth, urban youth, unemployed youth (rural or urban) and diaspora youth. Service delivery, access to financial loans and secure employment are the concerns of the majority of urban youth, with diaspora youth concerned about the state of the economy and their right to vote (Hodzi, 2013). On the same note, Honwana (2014) argues that youths' inability to access basic resources to be independent adults results in "waithood," a breakdown in the socio-economic system supposed to provide youths with the opportunities. Urban youth in Africa, according to Rashid (2020), have long been active interlocutors in global popular culture, utilizing images, clothing, music and language for their identities. Undoubtedly, proliferation of new communications technologies, especially the ubiquitous cell phone and numerous social media platforms, has greatly expanded this African youth engagement with global popular culture (Rashid, 2020).

Scoones' (2017) analysis highlights that youths are seen as a problem and admonished for not being committed to agriculture, creating a demographic "threat," a "youth bulge" of the unemployed, migrating to towns or abroad and becoming a societal burden through civil upheaval or even terrorism and thus are seen as potential sources of disruption. Scoones observed that many stylized assertions about rural African youths such as they cannot access land or credit, they do not want to farm, they are particularly innovative and that training promotes youth employment – are neither well-founded empirically nor sufficiently fine-grained to be policy relevant.

To add another conceptual dimension, Huijsmans, Ansell and Froere (2021) assert that sociological and anthropological conceptualizations of aspirations situate the production of aspiration as part of the social. This means that aspirations may manifest at the level of the individual but cannot be reduced to it. Drawing on the Bourdieusian concepts of doxa and habitus, Zipin et al., cited in Huijsmans et al. (2021), distinguish between doxic and habituated social logics. The former refer to aspirations rooted in discourse and practices that have acquired "a taken-for-granted status" but are in fact "grounded in populist-ideological mediations." Zipin et al. illustrate this with reference to the ethic of "If you work hard enough you can attain your dream." Youths are exposed to such doxic logics in the context of school but also through media, religion, popular culture and the market (Huijsmans et al., 2021), According to Moyo and Yeros (2005), profound socio-economic and political changes have been underway in the countrysides of the periphery in the last quarter century. Under the weight of structural adjustment programmes, peasants and workers have seen their conditions of social reproduction deteriorate, giving way to a desperate search for economic and political alternatives (Moyo & Yeros, 2005). Kabeer (2008) notes that "lack of livelihood opportunities" in rural areas, which is often stated as a reason for the rise of rural to urban migration, needs to be elaborated on in the context of the dominance of the neoliberal economic model.

Kabeer contends that rural impoverishment, which also inevitably leads to youths' exclusion, disenchantment and migration to urban centres, needs to be situated within the agricultural sector crisis. Kabeer asserts that decreased state investment in agriculture, rising takeover of smallholder farmers' lands by agribusinesses, small farmers' loss of income due to free-trade agreements in agriculture led by the World Trade Organization (WTO), land grabs, increasing landlessness and conflict are some of the key drivers.

Scholarly literature and policy documents indicate that the youth (and women) are among the most marginalized populations in terms of occupying political office and having access to economic opportunities (Jaji, 2020).

Younger and older people move for different reasons and in different ways in a mobile world. Pertinently, transnational mobilities shape distinct life phases of both the migrant and of those whose lives are linked and changed by these mobilities. More youths are projected to become mobile as the Global South will have a larger share of younger people compared to the Global North (Utrecht University, 2018).

Youth unemployment and underemployment constitute central challenges to Africa's development. As observed by the African Development Bank Group (2017), if youth unemployment rates remain unchanged in Africa, nearly 50% of youth – excluding students – will be unemployed, discouraged or economically inactive by 2025. Migration is not only a coping mechanism to escape poverty, but it is an opportunity for rural young people to feel a sense of pride and self-respect and to be viewed as leaders within their families and their broader community (Min-Harris, n.d.). Steffens (2018) notes that after a shock, most vulnerable people are unlikely to have resources to migrate, so it may not be an alternative that reaches those most in need. Given high migration costs, especially when through irregular channels, it is a privilege for those above a socio-economic threshold coupled with risks and conditions during transit and in the place of arrival all which aggravate vulnerabilities (Steffens, 2018).

Particularly with regard to African agriculture, youths' have become the centre of development debates. A poorly defined category of young people – maybe adults, sometimes children – youth are presented in relation to a dizzying array of policy narratives (Scoones, 2017). Pull factors attracting youths to the cities and towns rather than communal areas relate to the search for alternative economic opportunities. Banks (2016) comments that from a theoretical perspective, this implies youth ought to be the driving force behind agricultural production, particularly in communal areas, but realistically on the ground that they are moving *en masse* to urban areas (Banks, 2016). Young Africans are not finding that urban "promises" of dynamism and modernity and better access to education, wages and services are translating into better social and economic mobility for their generation. Increasing urban populations and shrinking formal employment opportunities have contributed to widespread urban poverty and insecurity across the continent (Banks, 2016).

Rural youths often have limited access to educational programmes addressing their specific situations and needs, resulting in high dropout rates at an early age. Curriculum is often geared more towards academic accomplishments and to urban-focused studies than to learning useful skills that enhance rural livelihoods (Min-Harris, n.d.). New arable land for cultivation shortages, inadequate training and extension services, low primary produce prices, poor markets and infra-structure, low technology levels and limited credit are obstacles for many rural youth wishing to remain on the land. Land pressure often results in marginal and unsuitable land being used for cultivation, leading to soil degradation and ero-sion, deforestation and other environmental problems for the region (Food and Agriculture Organization, n.d.).

While youth participation in policy processes has potential to channel their energy, passions and frustrations, it often turns out to be deficient, tokenistic or too episodic to be meaningful (Lintelo, 2012). Livelihood strategies evaluation among vulnerable groups, particularly the youth and women, is challenging and complex. As UN Environment (2018) observes, no continent will be as severely struck by climate change impacts than Africa, given its geographical position and vulnerability due to limited adaptive capacity, exacerbated by widespread pov-erty. Climate change is a particular threat to continued economic growth and to livelihoods of vulnerable populations.

Scope of Rural Development Programmes

The following section of this chapter outlines trends and dynamics of ongo-ing rural development programmes. Challenging macroeconomic conditions, including soaring inflation, income losses related to Covid-19 and back-to-back poor agricultural seasons, have eroded the livelihoods of millions across Zimbabwe and led to rising food insecurity (The Food and Agriculture Organi-zation of the United Nations (FAO), 2021). Drought is particularly a key threat to the agriculture sector composed of mostly rainfed farming systems and has caused water shortages, low production and food insecurity in recent years (The Food and Agriculture Organization of the United Nations (FAO), 2021). Henceforth, despite projections of a good 2020/2021 rainy season and improved crop production, yields are unlikely to rise above the five-year aver-age as farmers face challenges in accessing agricultural inputs, including qual-ity seeds and fertiliser (The Food and Agriculture Organization of the United Nations (FAO), 2021)

Nevertheless, it is laudable that government designed the Pfumvudza pro-gramme, a highly specified package involving the requirement to prepare two 39 x 16 m plots (0.06 ha) for grains (mostly maize, and some sorghum in some parts of the country) and a third plot for soya beans, sunflowers or another com-mercial crop for sale (Scoones, 2021). Pits of a certain depth and spacing are required to be dug and mulched, and seeds along with fertiliser (officially, Com-pound D and AN top dressing) are supplied by government (Scoones, 2021). According to Scoones (2021), the whole operation has been supported by more than 5,000 extension workers issues with new motorbikes, and ambitious targets have been set.

Ecology, land tenure and use, population density and land distribution strongly influence Zimbabwe's rural economy (Plan Afric, 2000). State land acquisition and disposal to provide for land subdivision and lease control and limiting the number of pieces of land any person can own is provided for by The Rural Land

Act [Chapter 20:18]. The Passage of the Traditional Leaders Act (TLA) in 1998 sought to make the old Ward and Village Development Committees (WAD-COs and VIDCOs) into elected committees of new structures – Ward and Village Assemblies (led by traditional leaders). The VIDCO functions remained as described in the Rural District Councils Act and those of the WADCO, previously undefined, were set out in the new TLA (Plan Afric, 2000). Zimbabwe lacks a clear, coordinated national rural development strategy. While there are several different policy strands influencing rural development, these have not resulted in an overall integrated and holistic rural development strategy.

Dynamics of Youth Development Programmes

Dzinotyiwei (2021) argues that Zimbabwe, though excluded from a number of international studies due to a lack of data, is arguably one of the most entrepreneurial countries in Africa. This cultivated "hustle" culture, Dzinotyiwei notes, could transcend into an ecosystem that produces the highest quality goods and services for the continent and the world.

Zimbabwe is signatory to the African Youth Charter adopted on 2 July 2006 by the Seventh Ordinary Session of the Assembly of the African Union. According to Hlungwani, Masuku and Magidi (2021), the Vocational Skills Development programme of the Ministry of Youth Development (MYD) uses a "Training for Enterprise" model. This capacitates youths with business start-up skills or for employment. Its 42 vocational training centres, spread across the country (10 of which are provincial training centres), offer a range of courses with certification levels ranging from National Foundation Certificate (NFC) and National Certificate (NC) to Trade Tested Worker Certificate (Journey Persons) (Hlungwani, Masuku and Magidi, 2021).

Hlungwani, Masuku and Magidi highlight that the MYD has facilitated establishment of youth micro-enterprises to reduce unemployment levels among the youth through introduction of the Training for Enterprise model in vocational training centres, with more than 17,500 youths empowered with skills and some supported with start-up kits (Government of Zimbabwe, 2016). The ministry created the Youth Empowerment Fund, supported by various banks, where youth were able to access up to USD 5,000 in short-term loans for entrepreneurial activities. Hlungwani, Masuku and Magidi (2021) aimed to probe experiences of street-level bureaucrats responsible for youth empowerment policies' implementation in rural Zimbabwe. Data were obtained from semi-structured key informant interviews that were undertaken between September 2017 and March 2018 in Mwenezi District of Masvingo province. The study was grounded in the sustainable livelihoods approach, which enabled an assessment of the degree to which institutions and policies can enhance socio-economic empowerment.

Hlungwani, Masuku and Magidi s (2021) study findings indicated that the failure to involve rural youth in the policy formulation process, as well as in the policy implementation stage, has adversely affected the effective implementation of such policies. Of the 25 youth respondents, 15 said that they did not know the contents of the National Youth Policy document. This evidence reinforces the argument that top-down, externally driven interventions are unable to meet the demand for socio-economic empowerment.

Government, church organizations and NGOs have collaborated in various programmes within Mwenezi District, in line with the idea of mainstreaming youth policies and ensuring that they engender socio-economic empowerment for the unemployed rural youth. The study found that the three key ministries were coordinating with Plan International, Care International, CAMFED and MDTC in the implementation of government programmes targeting youth in Mwenezi District. However, because the respective ministries had different focus areas for results, the emphasis and target or scope was varied. The major empowerment programmes offered to rural youths in Mwenezi involved:

- Training in various vocational skills (building, motor mechanic, welding, hotel and catering, tailoring, cosmetology, driving and agriculture);
- Entrepreneurship training with courses such as bookkeeping (record-keeping), stocktaking, marketing and finance sourcing;
- Funding of youth income generating projects;
- Registering youth clubs and associations, under the Zimbabwe Youth Council.

While the skills acquisition was in keeping with the promotion of sustainable livelihoods, youth were not adequately supported to implement their projects. This resulted in idle skills among the youth who, although equipped with cosmetology, motor mechanic and dressmaking skills, still lacked start-up capital to put their skills into practice. Literacy levels are noted by Hlungwani, Masuku and Magidi (2021) as impeding the implementation of entrepreneurial skills such as bookkeeping because of youths' limited comprehension of financial matters. The study observed that the main gap in the repertoire of interventions was projects' sustainability after the NGOs pulled out.

Pathways for Stemming Rural Youths' Migration

The following section of this chapter proposes strategies by which state and non-state actors can be more proactive in responding to rural youths' migration. Aspiration 6 of Agenda 2063 articulates "an Africa where Development is People Driven, Unleashing the Potential of its Women and Youth." Agenda 2063 also recognizes that "African women and youth shall play an important role as drivers of change." There has been an explosion of interest in youths' role in rural development. However, this tends to focus on the economic opportunity questions, not the complex, practical, lived, emotional realities of young people in challenging environments. The following section of this chapter enumerates robust interventions that can be expanded for the desired outcome of stemming rural youth migrations.

Youth Employment

To address youth employment challenges, more attention needs to be given to interventions that fall outside the conventional limits of training and other labour market programmes. However, the challenge of providing adequate, quality and decent employment provision for the majority of young people in the Southern African Development Community (SADC) region and particularly in Zimbabwe is certainly daunting and multifaceted.

A majority of jobs and self-employment, including household enterprises, are in the informal sector, and hence, access to finance specifically tailored to meet the needs of youths is pivotal. Meeting the youth employment challenge in all its demographic, economic and social dimensions, and understanding the forces that created the challenge, opens potential pathways towards a better life for youths. In many parts of the Global South, especially sub-Saharan Africa, agriculture employs more than 70% of the labour force and can be a source of employment for many youths. However, what is critical for the desired capacity building growth and value chain development prospects is generation of capacity to absorb the increasing numbers of unemployed youth (Kilimane, 2017). An integrated package bringing together relevant and quality skills training, labour market information, career guidance and employment services is an effective approach to facilitating the entry of young women and men into the labour market (ILO, 2018c).

Rural youths need financial services access for a range of productive (asset building, working capital) and protective (mitigating risk exposure, including health issues) purposes. This is to purchase stock, equipment and agricultural inputs; to maintain infrastructure; to contract labour for planting and harvesting; to transport goods to markets; to make and receive payments; to manage peak season incomes to cover expenses in the low season; to invest in education, shelter, health; or to deal with emergencies (ILO, n.d).

Green Jobs

As noted by the Humanist Institute for Cooperation with Developing Countries (HIVOS, 2018), an excellent way to tackle youth unemployment is green entrepreneurship which offers relatively low entry-level requirements for young women and men. And its technical aspects can provide an outlet for those interested in innovative business solutions – who are often young people. Additionally, new companies' creation allows equal access in terms of gender and is not limited to either rural or urban areas. Unfortunately, in practice, many young women still have to overcome extra hurdles to become entrepreneurs and stay and grow in their businesses (HIVOS, 2018).

Harnessing agribusiness entrepreneurship opportunities and innovations is critical in Africa as agriculture is an essential economic development driver for young people. To "green the economy" of Zimbabwe, the first step is to identify the availability of green jobs opportunities, assess the skills required to use such opportunities and then "green" vocational, technical and professional training institutions by introducing green curricula to produce skilled green collar workers. For employment creation outcomes among young women and men, an in-depth assessment provides recommendations and solutions for bridging a gap between the demand and the supply side of skills required to utilize green job opportunities in Zimbabwe.

With most of the world's young people living in areas where dependence on natural resources and persistent poverty intersect, climate change could pose a serious threat to youth livelihood patterns and economic stability (FAO, 2018). Adaptation and mitigation efforts are opening the door to a new category of employment – green jobs – across a multitude of sectors, and young people could be the segment of the labour market best positioned to access them (UN, 2013). Greening the rural economy is central to enhancing resource and labour productivity, boosting poverty eradication, increasing income opportunities and improving human well-being in rural areas. Rural populations often depend directly on the environment and natural resources for their livelihoods, such as in agriculture, forestry, mining and tourism (ILO, n.d.).

National Youth Policy Operationalization

National youth policies should not only remain robust on paper but through practical implementation modalities. Harnessing Africa's youth potential continues to be at the forefront of government and donor agendas (International Development Research Centre (IDRC), 2018). While this has galvanized political commitment and resources across the region, the youth employment challenge suggests that progress has been fragmented and slow. Innovative and inclusive approaches are required that can be scaled up for new jobs and economic opportunities for youth and prepare them for the future of work (IDRC, 2018). In post-independence Zimbabwe, the toxic and restrictive political environment has left many youths apathetic, hopeless and resigned. In spite of this environment, many young people in Zimbabwe as well as African youths in general still wiggle into the political field monopolized by older men locally referred to as "old *madala.*" Therefore, young men assert their presence in Zimbabwe's political terrain by devising strategies for performing masculinities that range from co-opting gerontocratic masculinities to subverting them (Jaji, 2020).

Policies and decisions should be based on sound rural economy evidence and knowledge with its particular opportunities, potential and constraints for youth employment. Policy coherence across sectors and enhanced dialogue among the different national and local levels stakeholders effectively promotes decent work in the rural economy (ILO, 2018a).

Knowledge Management

The vitality of robust knowledge management is of how it stimulates desired outcomes of rural youths' empowerment. Sumberg and Yeboah (2020) assert that not possessing basic education, including but not limited to literacy and numeracy skills, makes it hard to see how the pathways and outcomes of the next generation of youths will change for the better. In their analysis, Sumberg and Yeboah (2020) opine that, probably, the sense of disappointment expressed by many youths regarding their experiences of formal education highlights again the need to address both the quality of provision in rural areas and, just as importantly, the cash costs that put "free" education out of the reach of many rural children. Young women and men in the SADC, the ILO (2018) notes, can be powerful drivers of agricultural transformation and economic diversification of rural economies. Rural areas are diverse and youth are not a homogeneous group. Hence, sound diagnostics and multisectoral, integrated approaches and targeting strategies are needed (ILO, 2018b). Many SADC countries' rural economies have an often-overlooked potential to create decent and productive employment for youth and to contribute to food security, economic growth and sustainable development so as to ensure that no one is left behind (ILO, 2018). A sound rural economy knowledge base with its particular opportunities, potentials and constraints for youth employment that informs policies and decisions is needed. This will require upgraded labour market information systems, dedicated research and public–private dialogue systems that allow private sector and worker organizations to share their sectoral and value chain knowledge with policymakers (ILO, 2018b). As rightly outlined by Arslan et al. (2021), while the commercial potential of rural spaces has large impacts on welfare outcomes, their agricultural potential has no detectable impact. Further investments in market and informational connectivity will pay large dividends for rural youth (Arslan et al., 2021).

Encouraging and bolstering forums and avenues for authorities and stakeholders to discuss mobility, social cohesion, trade and planning issues is critical. Furthermore, creating and disseminating research synthesis (such as youth and rural development white papers), developing policy position statements or fact sheets and sharing information through media outlets (such as opinion editorials, press releases) is critical. Arslan et al. (2021) outline that productivity, connectivity and agency are central to youth's successful growth and launching into broader society and are interdependent and reinforce each other. With all the connections, Arsalan et al. (2021) argue that youths may not be able to harness information and techniques they have learnt if not connected to financial and social networks that provide them with access to financial capital, land and other productive assets.

Finally, Nhunzvi (2020) observed that parts of the strategies to manage the spread of Covid-19, including lockdowns, quarantines and isolation measures, have had adverse psychosocial impacts on youths. However, what is constant in all responses is that lives have been disrupted by the need to adjust, and unfortunately, many do not have the mental and economic resources to cope in adaptive ways (Nhunzvi, 2020). As Nhunzvi (2020) further opines, this is worse for the already marginalized, educated, unemployed, frustrated youths.

Conclusion

This chapter has identified how pervasive climate change, fear of mass unemployment and dominant survivalist and precarious livelihoods all drive undesirable outmigration of rural youths in Zimbabwe. The unprecedented restructuring of the Zimbabwean agrarian system since 2000 has seen more youths venturing into farming but migration out of rural areas has been inimical towards realization of youths robustly harnessing this natural resource. Climate change, lack of access to the value chain and intractable economic challenges have been noted in this chapter as key drivers for this. This chapter has explored some robust youth empowerment programmes currently underway in Zimbabwe that can stem rural youths' migration. This chapter concluded by advocating for increased application of evidence in policymaking and application for rural youth empowerment. This chapter also has shown that, despite migration out of rural areas due to exclusionary socio-economic policies continuing to marginalize youths, harnessing natural resources has become the basis for an imagined future of many youths. This is because life chances in formal employment after vocational or professional training have dwindled due to changes in the global economy.

References

Arslan, A., Tschirley, D. L., Di Nucci, C. and Winters, P. 2021. Youth inclusion in rural transformation, *Journals of Development Studies, 57*, 537–543.

African Development Bank Group. 2017, December 12. *Economic Transformation of Africa's Rural Areas Key to Curtailing Migration*. Available at: www.afdb.org: https://www.afdb.org/en/news-and-events/economic-transformation-of-africas-rural-areas-key-to-curtailing-migration-17696/

Akesson, U., Wingqvist, G. Ö., Ek, G., and César, E. 2016. *Environmental and Climate Change Policy Brief Zimbabwe*, Gothernburg, Sida's Helpdesk for Environment and Climate Change.

Banks, N. 2016. Youth poverty, employment and livelihoods: social and economic implications of living with insecurity in Arusha, Tanzania, *Environment and Urbanisation, 28*, 437–454.

Betcherman, G., Godfrey, M., Puerto, S., Rother, F. and Stavreska, A. 2007. *Global Inventory of Interventions to Support Young Workers: Synthesis Report*. Washington, World Bank.

Crush, J. and Tevera, J. 2010. Exiting Zimbabwe. In *Zimbabwe's Exodus Crisis, Migration and Survival*, Eds J. Crush and D. Tevera, pp. 1–52, Ottawa, International Development Research Centre.

Dzinotyiwei, C. 2021, March 12. *The Economic Reality of #BeingYoungInZim*. Available at: www.theindependent.co.zw/: https://www.theindependent.co.zw/2021/03/12/the-economic-reality-of-beingyounginzim/

Famine Early Warning Systems Network (FEWSNET). 2021. *Zimbabwe – Key Message Update: Wed, 2021-03-31*, Harare, FEWSNET.

FAO. 2018. *Youth Employment in Agriculture as a Solid Solution to Ending Hunger and Poverty in Africa*. Available at: www.decentjobsforyouth.org: https://www.decentjobsforyouth.org/event/38

Food and Agriculture Organization. 2017. *National Gender Profile of Agriculture and Rural Livelihoods – Zimbabwe: Country Gender Assessment*, Harare, FAO.

Food and Agriculture Organization (FAO). n.d. *Current Situation and Needs of Rural Youth*. Available at: www.fao.org: http://www.fao.org/docrep/x5636e/x5636e01.htm

Government of Zimbabwe. 2016. *Interim Poverty Reduction Strategy*, Harare, Government of Zimbabwe.

Government of Zimbabwe. 2020. *National Development Strategy 2021–2025*, Harare, Government of Zimbabwe.

Hlungwani, P., Masuku, S. and Magidi, M. 2021. Mainstreaming youth policy in Zimbabwe – what role for rural youth, *Cogent Social Sciences*, 7, 1–19.

Hodzi, O. 2013. *The Youth Factor in Zimbabwe's 2013 Harmonised Election*. Available at: from https://eisa.org.za/pdf/JAE13.2Hodzi.pdf [Accessed 10 September 2016].

Honwana, A. 2014. 'Waithood': youth transitions and social change. In *Development and Equity An Interdisciplinary Exploration by Ten Scholars from Africa, Asia and Latin America*, Ed. D. Foeken, pp. 28–40, Hague, Brill Publishers.

Huijsmans, R., Ansell, N. and Froere, P. 2021. Introduction: development, young people, and the social production of aspirations, *The European Journal of Development Research*, *33*, 1–15.

ILO. 2018a, April. *Call for Consultancy: An Assessment of Supply of and Demand for Technical and Vocational Skills to Support Green Jobs Opportunities for Young Women and Men in Zimbabwe*. Available at: www.ilo.org: https://www.ilo.org/wcmsp5/groups/public/---africa/---ro-addis_ababa/---sro-harare/documents/generic-document/wcms_625787.pdf

ILO. 2018b, August 23. *Promoting Decent Work Opportunities for Youth in Rural Areas of SADC Countries*. Available at: www.ilo.org/: https://www.ilo.org/addisababa/countries-covered/zimbabwe/WCMS_643741/lang--en/index.htm

ILO. 2018c, August 23. *Tripartite Workshop on Decent Work for Youth at the Centre of Rural Transformation in SADC Countries – Recommendations for Future Action*. Available at: www.ilo.org: https://www.ilo.org/wcmsp5/groups/public/---africa/---ro-addis_ababa/documents/meetingdocument/wcms_643744.pdf

ILO. n.d. *Developing the Rural Economy Through Financial Inclusion: The Role of Access to Finance*, Geneva, ILO.

International Development Research Centre (IDRC). 2018, September. *Boosting Decent Employment for Africa's Youth. Call for Concept Notes*, Ottawa, International Development Research Centre (IDRC).

International Humanist Institute for Cooperation with Developing Countries (HIVOS). 2018, February 13. *Green Entrepreneurship: Helping End Youth Unemployment*. Available at: www.hivos.org: https://www.hivos.org/opinion/green-entrepreneurship-helping-end-youth-unemployment/

Jaji, R. 2020. Youth masculinities in Zimbabwe's congested gerontocratic political space. *Africa Development*, *45*, 77–96.

Kilimane, N. 2017. Youth employment in developing economies: evidence on policies and interventions. *Institute of Development Studies (IDS University of Sussex) Bulletin*, *48*, 13–32.

Kinsey, B. 2010. *Poverty Dynamics in Rural Zimbabwe: The 30 Years (Lost) 'War Against Poverty'. Chronic Poverty Research Centre and the Brooks World Poverty Institute The University of Manchester*, Manchester, Brooks World Poverty Institute.

Lintelo, D. 2012. Young people in African (agricultural) policy processes? What national youth policies can tell us, *IDS Bulletin*, *43*, 90–103.

Machivenyika, F. 2021, April 14. *Youth Service Programme Re-Established*. Available at: www.herald.co.zw: https://www.herald.co.zw/youth-service-programme-re-established/

Makore-Ncube, B. C. and Al-Maiyah, S. 2021. Moving from the margins: towards an inclusive urban representation of older people in Zimbabwe's policy discourse, *Societies*, 11, 1–21.

Manzungu, E. 2014. *A Comprehensive Scoping and Assessment Study of Climate Smart Agricultural Policies in Zimbabwe*, Johannesburg, Food, Agriculture and Natural Resources Policy Analysis Network (FANRPAN).

Min-Harris, C. n.d. Youth migration and poverty in Sub-Saharan Africa: empowering the rural youth, *Topical Review Digest: Human rights in Sub-Saharan Africa, 6*, 159–186.

Mkodzongi, G. 2016. 'I am a paramount chief, this land belongs to my ancestors': the reconfiguration of rural authority after Zimbabwe's land reforms, *Review of African Political Economy, 43*(1), 99–114.

Moyo, S. and Yeros, P. 2005. The resurgence of rural movements under neoliberalism. In *Reclaiming the Land the Resurgence of Rural Movements in Africa, Asia and Latin America*, Eds S. Moyo and P. Yeros, pp. 8–64, London, Zed Books.

Nhunzvi, C. 2020, September. *COVID-19 and Its Impact on Substance Abuse*. Available at: www.//amari-africa.org/: https://amari-africa.org/newsevents/2020/9/17/impact-of-covid-19-on-substance-use

Plan Afric. 2000. *Local Strategic Planning and Sustainable Rural Livelihoods Rural District Planning in Zimbabwe: A Case Study*, Bulawayo, International Institute for Environment and Development.

Rashid, I. 2020. Introduction: African youth and globalisation, *Africa Development*, XLV, 1–5.

Reuters. 2021, March 3. *Zimbabwe Expects Maize Output to More Than Triple This Year*. Available at: www.reuters.com: https://www.reuters.com/article/uk-zimbabwe-grains-idUSKCN2AV0VO

Scoones, I. 2017, March 20. *Young People and Agriculture: Implications for Post-Land Reform Zimbabwe*. Available at: https://zimbabweland.wordpress.com: https://zimbabweland.wordpress.com/2017/03/20/young-people-and-agriculture-implications-for-post-land-reform-zimbabwe/

SNV. 2020. *Gender Action Research: Opportunities for Youth Employment (OYE), Zimbabwe*, Harare, SNV.

Steffens, I. 2018, August 6. *Migration and Social Protection in Crisis Contexts*. Available at: www.socialprotcetion.org: http://socialprotection.org/learn/blog/migration-and-social-protection-crisis-contexts

Sumberg, J. and Yeboah, T. 2020, May. *Hard Work and hazard: Youth Livelihoods in Rural Africa*. Available at: www.ids.ac.uk: https://www.ids.ac.uk/opinions/hard-work-and-hazard-youth-livelihoods-in-rural-africa/

The Food and Agriculture Organization of the United Nations (FAO). 2021. *Zimbabwe Humanitarian Response Plan 2021*, Rome, FAO.

UN Environment. 2018. *Responding to Climate Change*. Available at: www.unenvironment.org: https://www.unenvironment.org/regions/africa/regional-initiatives/responding-climate-change

UNICEF Zimbabwe. 2021. *Multihazard Situation Report # 1 February – 31 March 2021*, Harare, UNICEF.

United Nations. 2013. *World Youth Report*, New York, NY, United Nations Publications.

United Nations Country Team (UNCT). 2014. *Zimbabwe Country Analysis Working Document Final Draft – Information*. Available at: https://ims.undg.org/.../7e40fe82f edfcf6fb92306b459a8c1bdd0d13cc9ea8e9a18cadb [Accessed 12 May 2016].

United Nations Economic Commission for Africa (UNECA). 2021, March 2. *If COVID19 Impact Is Not Contained in 2021, 514 Million Africans May Fall Below Extreme Poverty Line*. Available at: www.uneca.org: https://www.uneca.org/stories/514-million-africans-risk-falling-below-extreme-poverty-line-in-2021-due-to-covid-19

United Nations Zimbabwe Country Programme. 2021. *Weekly UN in Zimbabwe Update Issue 40|26 Feb 2021*. Available at: https://zimbabwe.un.org/sites/default/files/2021-02/COVID-19%20Weekly%20Update-%20UNCT%20Zimbabwe%20-%2026%20 Feb%202021.pdf [Accessed 28 February 2021].

Utrecht University. 2018, August. *Call for Panel Proposals: "Life Phases Matter: New Imaginaries of Transnational Mobilities" Utrecht, 29-30 November*. Available at:

Canadian Anthropological Society: https://cas-sca.ca/call-for-papers/11355-call-for-panel-proposals-life-phases-matter-new-imaginaries-of-transnational-mobilities-utrecht-29-30-november

World Food Programme Zimbabwe. 2021a. *Hunger in Urban Zimbabwe Peaks as the Ripple Effect of COVID-19 Is Felt Across the Nation*, Harare, WFP

World Food Programme Zimbabwe. 2021b. *Market Monitoring Report Zimbabwe|February 2021 Issue No: 69*, Harare, WFP.

Zimbabwe Coalition on Debt and Development (ZIMCODD). 2021. *A Call to Establish a Youth Friendly Budgeting System in Zimbabwe – A Focus on 2021 Budget*, Harare, ZIMCODD.

Zimstat (Zimbabwe National Statistics Agency). 2015. *Multiple Indicator Cluster Survey*, Harare, Government of Zimbabwe.

Chapter Six

All-purpose Medicine: An Autoethnographic Reflection on Urban Market Solidarity and Dangerous Self-Integrative Medication in Child and Adolescent Care in Nigeria

Mofeyisara Oluwatoyin Omobowale and
Ayokunle Olumuyiwa Omobowale

Introduction

Provisioning of quality, accessible, inclusive and affordable health-care services is instrumental to youth development. Many public health policies and programmes regarding youth health have represented some failure, in formulation and implementation, at various governmental levels. The failure reflects in many layers on youth living conditions of poverty and marginalization, as reflected in their poor health-seeking behaviour, education and livelihoods (Agnes, 2010). Nigerian health policies and programmes are formulated and implemented in ways that often exclude groups in the lower socio-economic strata of the society. This often reflects the manifestation of inequalities and social exclusion in health care, which has, over the years, aided the continuous patronage and sustenance of "all-purpose medicine" (Kamorudeen, 2012). In contemporary Nigerian society, many adolescents and youth have limited or no access to adolescent or youth friendly health services, which had further encouraged the practice of dangerous integrative medicine even for reproductive health problems (Crawford et al., 2021; Odimegwu and Adewoyin, 2021). Autoethnography presents a unique strategy in social science and humanities research by allowing researchers to reflect on social issues based on personal experience gained over time in the course of research and practice. Autoethnography advances authors' deep reflective engagement with the contextual realities of social issues without neglecting epistemological, empirical and ontological facts. This is because an autoethnographic researcher deeply

Youth Exclusion and Empowerment in the Contemporary Global Order:
Existentialities in Migrations, Identity and the Digital Space, 85–95
Copyright © 2022 by Mofeyisara Oluwatoyin Omobowale and Ayokunle
Olumuyiwa Omobowale
Published under exclusive licence by Emerald Publishing Limited
doi:10.1108/978-1-80382-777-320221007

engages the realities that have been experientially accessed and assessed over time to generate personal reflections that advance contextual understanding of social and cultural issues (Lapadat, 2017; Pitard, 2018). Hence, in this research, we present a collaborative autoethnographic reflection (see Lapadat, 2017) on sociative[1] socialization and dangerous self-integrative medication in child and adolescent care in urban markets in Nigeria, based on empirical and experiential observations and knowledge we have gathered since about 2005 while studying market culture in South-western Nigeria. Self-integrative medication in child and adolescent care as used here refers to the practice of self-admixture of various modern medications and herbs in child and adolescent health management by nursing mothers and other caregivers within the family system. The practice is locally called *akanpo* (mixed), thus assumed to be an all-purpose medicine (*ogun gbogbonse*), especially in South-western Nigeria. Self-integrative medication in child and adolescent care is a practice that is commonplace among Nigerian mothers in the low socio-economic group, with dangerous implications for public health (Iribhogbe and Odoya, 2020, Oshikoya et al., 2007, 2008).

The diverse research we have conducted individually, jointly and in collaboration with other researchers on urban markets, traders and childhood and adolescent issues in Ibadan, Nigeria, has produced published works such as Olutayo and Omobowale (2007) on the production and marketing of cocoa; Omobowale (2011) on social capital and cooperative associations among working-class market traders; Babalola and Omobowale (2012) on the role of trust, innovation and knowledge management among micro-entrepreneurs; Ajala and Omobowale (2013) on the context of the use of alcoholic herbal mixtures among working-class traders, artisans and drivers; and Omobowale (2013a, 2013b) which partly discussed the organization of the second-hand market space and the context of consumer socialization that drives the market (see also A. O. Omobowale, 2008, 2012). Additionally, Omobowale and Omobowale (2019) examined market sociation and solidarity; Omobowale (2019) discussed class, gender, sexuality and leadership in the market space (see also M. O. Omobowale, 2012); Omobowale, Oyelade, et al. (2020) reflected on the impact of the Covid-19 pandemic on informal workers, many of whom are market traders; and Omobowale, Falase, et al. (2020) discussed responses to the Covid-19 prevention protocols partly in the market space and among the mass public.

Furthermore, Olutayo and Omobowale (2006) affirmed the impact of liberal reforms on the family, children and the youth; Oyom et al. (2016) discussed fatness, obesity and health among secondary school adolescents; and Omobowale (2018) examined Nigeria's child health policy historically. Also, Omobowale, Omobowale and Falase (2019) examined the context of children in Yoruba popular culture; Omobowale and Amodu (2019) discussed the local contexts of

---

[1]The concept "sociative" as used here refers to interactional and associational relations with embedded normative values and meanings that seek to enhance mutual advancement among interacting social actors, and in this case, market traders. Thus, the traders solidarize, even in competition (see Omobowale and Omobowale, 2019).

the social construction of childhood, livelihood and health; Omobowale, Akpabio and Amodu (2019) examined neighbourhood bullying among adolescents; Omobowale, Ademola and Amodu (2019) discussed malaria prevention measures used by parents of children under five years old; and Omobowale (2020) examined spirituality and child health in urban markets in Ibadan, Nigeria. Our experience (working individually and collaboratively) researching among and on working-class market traders, children and adolescents reflectively indicates and confirms contextualized sociative socialization processes aiming for community support and development, but also sometimes counter-productive, as in the case of self-integrative child and adolescent care among working-class nursing mothers and traders. Thus, sociative socialization and dangerous self-integrative child and adolescent care is the main focus of this autoethnographic chapter.

Again, scholarly research affirms the intellectual contributions of autoethnography to the global reservoir of knowledge. Writing on autoethnography, Doty (2010) emphasized the importance of bringing "self" into ethnographic writing. Researchers primarily want to dissociate self from their research in order to ensure an acceptable degree of value neutrality. Doty rightly notes:

> While I believe that the self is really always present in academic writing it is usually only present by virtue of its absence. A power inheres in this absence, a power that enables scholars to present their work as authoritative, objective, and neutral. Autoethnography shuns this power and makes it clear that writers are part of their work, part of the story they tell, they are connected. (2010, p. 1048)

Spry (2009) takes a step further to present "body as evidence" of performative autoethnography. Spry submits that the "performing body constitutes a praxis of evidence and analysis" (p. 603). Hence, Spry opines that in presenting a performance on sexual assault, the viewing audience must be able to see the performer's body as evidence of an assaulted body and visualize the context of the victim in the cultural environment that the assault has taken place. The principal method of enquiry of autoethnography is utilizing culture-bound personal experience and reflections for examining and recounting social issues (Boylorn, 2016; Lockford, 2014; McParland, 2012). Using principally personal experience has exposed autoethnography to critiques, and it has been dismissed by some authors as narcissistic, self-serving and self-indulging expressions lacking hard empirical grounding (Jackson and Mazzei, 2008; Winkler, 2018).

As much as the epistemological concerns that autoethnography relies on mere personal experiences cannot be entirely dismissed, it is important to also note that the use of autoethnography in the social sciences is predicated on personal and empirical experiences of the researcher on a subject matter over time. Hence, in writing this chapter, we support the submission of McParland (2012, p. 474) that: "Autoethnography is a blend of personal experience, socio-cultural values, and the investigative research process that are weaved together into artful motifs of the lived world." Autoethnography is thus not limited to presentations of personal experiences. Autoethnography in the interpretative social sciences also involves the infusion of personal and research experience in analytic interpretations of social issues and phenomena (Chang, 2013; Wall, 2016). It is impossible to totally detach one's experiences, values and norms from human-centred research, although a high degree of reflexivity helps in placing issues in the right perspectives. This research, therefore, does an autoethnographic examination of sociative socialization and market solidarity in the use of dangerous self-integrative medications in childcare in Nigeria. This section introduces this chapter. The next section presents the methodology; the third section discusses childcare, the Nigerian urban market space and sociative solidarity in context; the fourth section presents sociative socialization and dangerous self-integrative child and adolescent care; and the fifth section presents the conclusion and makes public health policy recommendations in relation to child and adolescent care in the market space.

Methodology

This chapter adopted a collaborative autoethnography approach with infusions of personal and research experiences for interpretive analytical presentation (Chang, 2013; Lapadat, 2017; Wall, 2016). This autoethnography reflects on the context of dangerous self-integrative medication in child and adolescent care especially among nursing mothers and traders in urban markets in Nigeria. The reflections are based on the authors' experiences and empirical findings from studies we carried out earlier individually and collaboratively cited and briefly described in the introduction. Many works have been done on child and adolescent care, and self-medication in Nigeria (see, for example, Iribhogbe and Odoya, 2020; Oshikoya et al., 2007, 2008). This research reflects particularly on the contextual values that propel and sustain dangerous self-integrative medication in child and adolescent care. Hence, the researchers primarily focus on sociative socialization and solidarity as value agents aimed as support system for child and adolescent survival, but which also led caregivers to use self-integrative medications oblivious of their imminent dangers. The research also reflects on some indigenous proverbs that contextually frame the sociative socialization and solidarity in the social relations of child and adolescent care. The reflections are presented and analysed through the autoethnographic approach.

Child and Adolescent Care and Sociative Solidarity in Context

Child and adolescent care remain matters of major concern in Nigeria's public health, especially with the widening inequality in the health service provisioning. Nigeria's fertility rate of 5.4 and under-five mortality rate of 117 per 1,000 live births in 2018 and 2019, respectively, remain among the highest in the world (World Bank, 2020a, 2020b). Nigeria's fertility rates indicate a preference for having children, yet the under-five mortality rates show significant number of those born do not survive the first five years of their lives as U-5 mortality rate increase from 128/1,000 live birth in 2013 to 132/1,000 live birth in 2018 (NPC and ICF, 2019). Thus, the likelihood of illness and eventual death of a newborn is continually ingrained in the social consciousness of the interacting public, to the extent that linguistic and ethnic groups across Nigeria have proverbial prayers and consolation on survival or death of a child. Among the Yoruba of South-western Nigeria, a common prayer for a newborn is *Olorun a daa si, Olorun a ka mo wa* (God will keep the child alive, God will count the child among us). This prayer contextually notes the potentiality of death and, thus, prays that the child survives and be counted among the living. Also, the consolation the interacting public gives relatives of a dead child (as for an adolescent or adult deceased) is that *Oluwa fifun ni, oluwa gbaa lo* (the Lord gives and takes). These sayings attribute the causes of death as destined and supernatural, thus dismissing the actual causes in the process of consolation (Omobowale, Omobowale and Falase, 2019; see also Adedini et al., 2015). The acceptance of the realities of child morbidity and mortality as described above is anchored in many layers of social, economic and health inequalities in the country (Ifeakachukwu, 2020).

Whereas high fertility and under-five mortality rates are not unconnected to poverty and dangerous cultural practices, it is important to note that the market space provides an escape from joblessness for many individuals without formal employment, and yet some child and adolescent care socialization processes in the market space which favour self-integrative medication endanger children's and adolescents' health and survival. The informal market is a major segment of the informal sector that absorbs about 70% of the Nigerian labour force (Omobowale, 2011; Omobowale, Oyelade, et al., 2020). The urban market system is structured, yet it allows ease of entry and exit within its laid down rules. Some of the major rules of the urban market system are that a new entrant must become a member of the trader's unit association and the general association of the market (Omobowale, 2019; Omobowale and Omobowale, 2019). The new member must pay all association dues and must be well behaved. The trader's behaviour is adjudged by the character they express in interactions with other traders and buyers in the market. Hence, a trader is normatively expected to be humane, accommodating and supportive of the progress of the market as a whole.

Some reflections of the indigenous social capital system that advances sociative solidarity still persist. Thus, the traders extend mutual support to one another, and the older, in particular, give advice to the younger on business management, investments, conduct and the care of their families and children. The guiding philosophy and principle is solidarity-in-competition (Omobowale and Omobowale, 2019). Though they are competitors, they solidarize to achieve mutual and universal progress. This is indeed a positive normative value in market management; however, self-integrative medication in child and adolescent care is a practice that has been passed down the generations of nursing mothers and other caregivers in urban markets (and among low socio-economic groups) with implications for children's and adolescents' health and survival. We do not claim that self-integrative medication in child and adolescent care is practised only in the market space. Indeed, many people would practise it in the confines of their homes. We have focused on the market due to our observations on the open practice of self-integrative medications in urban markets. A Yoruba proverb says: *Agba kii wa l'oja, k'ori omo tuntun wo* (which means, literally, a child's head cannot be twisted while an elder is in the market). This proverb generally describes the role of the older generation in socializing and instructing the younger. This normative value on the guiding role of the older generation penetrates most indigenous structures, especially where elders are accorded respect. Hence, in the market system, the older women who have nursed children play strategic roles advising and socializing younger women and one another regarding child and adolescent care practices. Unfortunately, self-integrative medication in child and adolescent care is a practice that is continuously passed down among traders with dangerous implications. The next section describes dangerous child and adolescent self-integrative medication.

The Market Space and Dangerous Self-Integrative Medication

The market, since time immemorial, is both an economic and a relational space, as exemplified among the Yoruba of South-western Nigeria. Fadipe (1970) in his ethnographic study of the Yoruba, aptly captured the sociative socialization spectrum of the Yoruba market and how such relations transcend economic transactions to extend to the social relations of health care.[2] Fadipe (1970, p. 163) noted that in the market space there is:

> Good-natured repartee, a rich fund of jokes, an occasional burst of confidence in which intimate matters are disclosed and discussed, advice and often prescriptions given for ailments, interest shown by one party on the other's child [health and well-being] ...

Fadipe's description above of the pre-colonial and early colonial market space reveals that self-prescription for ailments and communal care for children were major social practices in Yoruba urban market relations. The present situation is not entirely different from Fadipe's description. This is further confirmed by the proverb earlier cited above that *agba ki wa l'oja, ki ori omo titun wo*, which in practice means that, with the presence of elders in the market space, a newborn will be correctly cared for. The proverb simply depicts the sociocultural significance placed on the experiences of aged and older members of Yoruba and, by extension, African society. Childcare practice is a social process and young mothers are socialized into motherhood and childcare practices by the older generations around them. The socializing older generations are not limited to the immediate and extended family members but include all aged and older significant others

---

[2]Fadipe (1970) is the book publication of the author's PhD Thesis on the Sociology of the Yoruba, successfully completed at the University of London in 1930. The book aptly captures Yoruba culture and relations in pre-colonial and early colonial Nigeria.

around the new or young parents. Every older significant other, in the context of sociative interactionism, love and support, prescribes diverse medicines, both herbal and pharmaceutical, which they deemed had worked for them or others while nursing their children. These socializing agents in the market space draw from their experiences, advice young mothers on perceived cures for ailments and child and adolescent care practices. These socializing agents draw on myths, taboos and religious beliefs to make prescriptions and teach childcare practices, many of which endorse the use of self-integrative medications that they assume to be all-purpose medicine, that is, medicines that cure all ailments.

One of the major features of contemporary urban market spaces in South-western Nigeria is the presence of medicine men and women who claim to have remedies to numerous ailments through their medicines of *gbogbonise* (all purpose). These medicine peddlers move with the issues of the time as regards the advertising of their mixtures and claims about their efficacy for diverse ailments. For example, some of the medicines were advertised to be effective for the prevention and treatment of Ebola when Nigeria had cases of Ebola in 2014. The medicine peddlers also advertise their sales as effective for hypertension, diabetes, piles, erectile dysfunction, sickle-cell anaemia and, recently, Covid-19. The medicine peddlers also claim their mixtures treat health challenges locally associated with children such as convulsions, asthma, anaemia, anterior fontanelle and numerous viral, bacterial and worm infections, among others, which are locally believed to be resistant to pharmaceutical medications. Their presence and persuasive adverts are structured to suit the health desires and needs of the market public. Many nursing mothers and caregivers patronize all-purpose medicine peddlers in order to address assumed health issues of their children "diagnosed non-clinically" by their significant others. And even when health challenges have been clinically diagnosed, it is not uncommon for nursing mothers and caregivers to patronize all-purpose medicine peddlers to the detriment of the health of their children. A concern here is that these mixtures are either from herbs or combinations of herbs, and several pharmaceutical drugs are administered without proper controls, and the practice of all-purpose medicine is unregulated. All-purpose medicine is a crude integration of herbal and modern medicine which enjoys high patronage and poses grave dangers to child and adolescent health.

A nursing mother in the market space (and among many low socio-economic group families) is socialized to have an *ajogba omo* (baby medicine bowl). The *ajogba omo* serves as a first aid box. The bowl, however, usually contains herbs and pharmaceutical drugs that are considered effective for childcare and treatment. The *ajogba omo* is indigenously instituted in the Yoruba culture of childcare. It has survived to contemporary times. In the past, the *ajogba omo* was a calabash or aluminium bowl. In contemporary times, many nursing mothers use either a plastic bowl or fashionable trolley with four to six steps. The content of *ajogba omo* includes bathing materials such as soaps and powder; herbs such as camwood, leaves, barks, roots and honey, pile concoctions (*agbo jedi*), convulsion concoctions (*agbo ile tutu/giri*), pneumonia concoctions (*agbo otutu aya*) and anterior fontanelle concoction (*agbo oka ori*), among others; and pharmaceutical drugs such as paracetamol syrup and tablets, Nospamin, gripe water, multivitamins, teething power, Flagyl and antibiotics (usually Ampicillin or Cloxacillin based), among others. Mothers from previous studies of the market admitted that they were socialized into procurement and assemblage of *ajogba omo* for their children. The same socialization agents that recommend the patronage of all-purpose medicine peddlers to nursing mothers emphasize the need to have the baby medicine bowl (*ajogba omo*) and also prescribe its contents as well as the usage and dosage of the contents. Mothers and caregivers use these medicines and administer them to their children as prophylaxis or to cure perceived illnesses. The practice is not only crude but dangerous to the health of children and adolescents as the drugs can damage vital internal organs and other body parts of the children. Yet when death occurs, an autopsy is not usually done to determine the cause of death. The child is mourned and interred as another unfortunate child who was not fortunate to partake of the world for long.

Conclusion and Public Health Policy Recommendations

The persistent use of self-integrative medication in child and adolescent care among nursing mothers and caregivers in the urban markets has its strong roots in cultural traditions and has been passed down generations through the socialization process. This chapter does not undermine the importance of significant others in child and adolescent care, but the potential and real dangers of self-integrative medication in childcare that is passed down through the socialization process cannot be overlooked. This chapter opines that self-integrative medication in child and adolescent care that peddlers and partakers wrongly assume to be all-purpose medicine is a major contributor to high rates of morbidity and mortality, especially among children under five years in Nigeria. Unfortunately, when such human-induced child fatality happens, it is usually explained away in a construction of fatalism.

The market community in itself is a socializing agent and it thus builds its values and norms around sociation and socialization that cut across both socioeconomic and health well-being of traders and their children. It is, therefore, important to recommend a re-education and resocialization of the market community. Both nursing mothers and significant others, particularly older women in the market space, should be targeted for public re-education and resocialization to put an end to the practice of dangerous self-integrative medication in child and adolescent care. Enlightened messages should also be communicated to the market communities through market structures and networks such as the market leadership and associations. Nursing mothers should also be educated on the dangers associated with self-integrative medication for mother and child. The avenues for educating them should not be limited to ante-natal and post-natal clinics but should be taken to their doorsteps in market spaces through small group meetings, mass media and social media campaigns. Herbal medicine practice should be regulated and unscrupulous adverts and peddling of herbal and pharmaceutical mixtures as "all-purpose medicine" should be banned, and recalcitrant peddlers should be taken through a legal prosecution. The existence of all-purpose medicine is partly due to inequalities in society and in the national health system. It is vivid that youth are marginalized in many social and political spaces, due to the fact that children (up to 18 years) and even youths are culturally not involved in decision-making – they are to be directed, instructed and not heard (Okewumi and Akanle, 2021), even in health policies and programme formulation and implementations. This value system of exclusion from decision-making creates difficulties for youth in accessing health services that suit their needs, thus the increased patronage of all-purpose medicine.

References

Adedini, S. A., Odimegwu, C., Imasiku, E. N. and Ononokpono, D. N. 2015. Ethnic differentials in under-five mortality in Nigeria, *Ethnicity & Health*, *20*(2), 145–162.

Agnes, I. A. I. 2010. Youth unemployment in Nigeria: causes and related issues, *Canadian Social Science*, *6*(4), 231–237.

Ajala, A. S. and Omobowale, M. O. 2013. Paraga: socioeconomic context of the production and utilization of alcoholic herbal remedy in Ibadan, Nigeria, *Anthropos*, *108*, 149–162.

Babalola, S. S. and Omobowale, A. O. 2012. The role of trust, innovation and knowledge management in entrepreneurial survival strategies: a study of selected cybercafé micro-entrepreneurs in Ibadan, Nigeria. *Inkanyiso Journal of Humanities and Social Sciences*, *4*(2), 128–136.

Boylorn, R. M. 2016. On Being at home with myself: blackgirl autoethnography as research praxis. *International Review of Qualitative Research*, *9*(1), 44–58.

Chang, H. 2013. Individual and collaborative autoethnography as method. In *Handbook of autoethnography*, Eds S. Holman Jones, T. E. Adams and C. Ellis, pp. 107–122, Walnut Creek, CA, Left Coast Press.

Crawford, E. E., Atchison, C. J., Ajayi, Y. P. and Doyle, A. M. 2021. Modern contraceptive use among unmarried girls aged 15–19 years in South Western Nigeria: results from a cross-sectional baseline survey for the Adolescent 360 (A360) impact evaluation, *Reproductive Health*, *18*(1), 1–13.

Doty, R. L. 2010. Autoethnography – making human connections. *Review of International Studies*, *36*, 1047–1050. doi: 101 7IS026021051000118X

Fadipe, N. A. 1970. *The Sociology of the Yoruba*, Eds Francis Olu Okediyi and Oladeji O. Okediyi, Ibadan, Ibadan University Press.

Ifeakachukwu, N. P. 2020. Globalisation, economic growth and income inequality in Nigeria, *Indian Journal of Human Development*, *14*(2), 202–212.

Iribhogbe, O. I. and Odoya, E. M. 2020. Self-medication practice with antimalarials and the determinants of malaria treatment-seeking behavior among post-partum mothers in a rural community in Nigeria, *Pharmacoepidemiology and Drug Safety*. https://doi.org/10.1002/pds.5178

Jackson, A. Y. and Mazzei, L. A. 2008 Experience and "I" in autoethnography: a deconstruction, *International Review of Qualitative Research*, *1*(3), 299–318.

Kamorudeen, A. 2012. The dilemma of equity and social exclusion in health care delivery services in Nigeria. *Nigerian Journal of Sociology and Anthropology*, *11*, 56–68.

Lapadat, J. C. 2017. Ethics in autoethnography and collaborative autoethnography. *Qualitative Inquiry*, *23*(8), 589–603.

Lockford, L. 2014. Trusting the bridging power of autoethnography, *International Review of Qualitative Research*, *7*(3), 283–289.

McParland, S. 2012 Autoethnography: forging a new direction in feminist sport history, *Journal of Sport History*, *39*(3), 473–478.

NPC (National Population Commission) [Nigeria] and ICF. 2019. *Nigeria Demographic and Health Survey 2018 Key Indicators Report*, Rockville, MD, NPC and ICF.

Odimegwu, C. O. and Adewoyin, Y. 2021. Latent and under-explored determinants of contraceptive use in Nigeria, *Sexuality Research and Social Policy*, *18*(3), 715–725.

Okewumi, E. O. and Akanle, O. 2021. Children's participation in decision making within the family context of yoruba culture, *Child Indicators Research*, *15*, 1–13.

Olutayo, A. O. and Omobowale, A. O. 2006. The youth and the family in transition in Nigeria, *Review of Sociology of the Hungarian Sociological Association*, *12*, 1–11.

Olutayo, A. O. and Omobowale, A. O. 2007. Production, processing and marketing of export crops for rural development: the case of cocoa in Nigeria. In *African Development Perspectives Yearbook 2007*, Eds K. Wohlmuth, C. Eboue, A. Gutowski, A. Jerome, T. Knedlik, M. Meyn and T. Mama, Vol. *12*, pp. 295–316, Berlin, Lit Verlag.

Omobowale, A. O. 2008. The Tokunbo: a sociological examination of the imported second hand automobiles market in Nigeria. In *The Globetrotting Shopaholic: Consumer Spaces, Products, and their Cultural Places*, Eds T. E. Tunc and A. A. Babic, pp. 183–191, Newcastle upon Tyne, Cambridge Scholars Publishing.

Omobowale, A. O. 2011. Social capital and Ajo system among working class traders in Ibadan, Nigeria, *Working USA: The Journal of Labor and Society*, *14*(3), 333–346.

Omobowale, A. O. 2012. Global E-waste management and second-hand consumption in the third world: substandard context and Tokunbo phenomenon in Nigeria, *The Nigerian Journal of Sociology and Anthropology*, *10*, 88–99.

Omobowale, A. O. 2013a. *The Tokunbo Phenomenon and the Second-hand Economy in Nigeria*, Oxford, Peter Lang Publishing.

Omobowale, A. O. 2013b. Tokunbo ICT: symbolic-rationality of second-hand ICT utilization in Nigeria, *International Journal of Sociology and Social Policy*, *33*(7/8), 509–523.

Omobowale, A. O., Falase, O. S., Oyelade, O. K. and Omobowale, M. O. 2020. The COVID-19 pandemic and everyday life: the relations of lockdown, social distancing, face masking, discreet salutation and hand hygiene in Nigeria. *Sociološki Pregled/ Sociological Review (Journal of Serbian Sociological Association)*, *54*(3), 864–887. doi:10.5937/socpreg54-27155

Omobowale, A. O., Omobowale, M. O. and Falase, O. S. 2019. The context of children in yoruba popular culture. *Global Studies of Childhood*, *9*(1), 18–28. doi: 10.1177/2043610618815381

Omobowale, A. O., Oyelade, O. K., Omobowale, M. O. and Falase, O. S. 2020. Contextual reflections on COVID-19 and informal workers in Nigeria, *International Journal of Sociology and Social Policy*, *40*(9/10), 1041–1057. https://doi.org/10.1108/IJSSP-05-2020-0150

Omobowale, M. O. 2019. Class, gender, sexuality, and leadership in Bodija Market, Ibadan, Nigeria, *Journal of Anthropological Research*, *75*(2), 235–251.

Omobowale, M. O. 2020. "You will not mourn your children": spirituality and child health in Ibadan urban markets, *Journal of Religion and Health*. https://doi.org/10.1007/s10943-020-01032-5

Omobowale, M. O. 2012. The codification of sexuality in Bodija market space, Ibadan, Nigeria, *Journal of Environment and Culture*, *9*(1), 54–65.

Omobowale, M. O. 2018. Speak to the past and it shall teach thee: an appraisal of Child Health Policy in Nigeria, *The Nigerian Journal of Child and Adolescent Health (NJCAH)*, *1*(1), 22–34.

Omobowale, M. O., Ademola, S. A. and Amodu, O. K. 2019. Malaria preventive measures used by parents of under five years children in Ibadan urban markets, Nigeria, *Nigerian Journal of Child and Adolescent Health*, *2*(1), 6–11.

Omobowale, M. O., Akpabio, O. E. and Amodu, O. K. 2019. Masculinity and neighbour-hood bullying among adolescents in Ibadan, Nigeria – a research note, *Boyhood Studies Journal*, *12*(1), 1–16.

Omobowale, M. O. and Amodu, O. K. 2019. Omoboti and Omopako: social construction of childhood, livelihood and health in South-Western Nigeria. In *Rethinking Childhoods in Africa: an Anthology*, Eds Charles Quist-adade, De-Velera Botchway and Awo Abena Amoa Sarpong, pp. 1–14, Delaware, Vernon Press.

Omobowale, M. O. and Omobowale, A. O. 2019. *Oju* and *Inu*: Solidarity in the informal market space in Ibadan, Nigeria, *Journal of Black Studies*, *50*(4), 401–420.

Oshikoya, K. A., Njokanma, O. F., Bello, J. A. and Ayorinde, E. O. 2007. Family self-medication for children in an urban area of Nigeria, *Paediatric and Perinatal Drug Therapy*, *8*(3), 124–130.

Oshikoya, K. A., Senbanjo, I. O., Njokanma, O. F. and Soipe, A. 2008. Use of comple-mentary and alternative medicines for children with chronic health conditions in Lagos, Nigeria, *BMC Complementary and Alternative Medicine*, *8*(1), 66. https://doi.org/10.1186/1472-6882-8-66

Oyom, C. R., Omobowale, M. O., Orimadegun, A. E., Olumide, A. O. and Amodu, O. K. 2016 Central fatness among secondary school adolescents in Ibadan, Nigeria, *The Nigerian Journal of Sociology and Anthropology*, *14*(2), 1–16.

Pitard, J. 2018. A journey to the centre of self: positioning the researcher in autoethnog-raphy, *Forum Qualitative Sozialforschung/Forum: Qualitative Social Research*, *18*(3). http://dx.doi.org/10.17169/fqs-18.3.2764

Spry, T. 2009. Bodies of/as evidence in autoethnography, *International Review of Qualitative Research*, *1*(4), 603–610.

Wall, S. S. 2016. Toward a moderate autoethnography, *International Journal of Qualitative Methods*, *15*(1), 1–9. doi: 10.1177/1609406916674966

Winkler, I. 2018. Doing autoethnography: Facing challenges, taking choices, accepting responsibilities, *Qualitative Inquiry*, *24*(4), 236–247.

World Bank. 2020a. *Fertility Rate, Total (Births per Woman) – Nigeria*. Available at: https://data.worldbank.org/indicator/SP.DYN.TFRT.IN?locations=NG [Accessed 15 December 2020].

World Bank. 2020b. *Mortality Rate, Under-5 (per 1,000 Live Births) – Nigeria*. Available at: https://data.worldbank.org/indicator/SH.DYN.MORT?locations=NG [Accessed 15 December 2020].

Chapter Seven

Us and Them and After All – Cosmopolitanism in Identity-making and Integration of Muslim Migrant Youth

Shreya Bhardwaj

Introduction

Discourse on migration tends to locate migrants, including the migrant youth, within a transnational framework (Horst and Olsen, 2021), maintaining ties with their countries of origin and rooted in their national or ethnic identities. Such discursive iterations foreclose the inclusion of the youth in the cosmopolitan project, capable of a global outlook traditionally seen as the preserve of the white, Western elites. The present chapter engages an ethnographic study with Muslim migrant youth of the Czech Republic to show how the youth play an instrumental role in challenging such essentializing understanding of migrants. When Diogenes first declared himself as "a citizen of the world," it suggested an outlook of openness and tolerance. In *Regulating Aversion*, Brown observes that "tolerance as a political practice is always conferred by the dominant." Tolerance is a mark of the civilized Western communities, from which it follows that the communities which are intolerant are thus uncivilized and barbarians, becoming perfect receptacles of violence and aggression (Werbner, 2018). This discursive treatment of the West as the bastion of tolerant and open values has made cosmopolitanism the preserve of the Western elites, informed by the scholarship of philosophers such as Kant, Derrida and Hobbes, among others (Gani, 2017). As a departure from this traditional perspective, this chapter focuses on how the Muslim migrant youth in the Czech Republic are active stakeholders in the cosmopolitanism project.

Gilroy (2000, cited in Gikandi, 2002, p. 593), in his book *Against Race – Imagining Political Culture Beyond the Color Line*, argues the need for a cosmopolitan, humanistic approach that supersedes essentializing forms of racial identities wherein dwell and fester oppressive ideologies such as fascism.

Youth Exclusion and Empowerment in the Contemporary Global Order:
Existentialities in Migrations, Identity and the Digital Space, 97–111
Copyright © 2022 by Shreya Bhardwaj
Published under exclusive licence by Emerald Publishing Limited
doi:10.1108/978-1-80382-777-320221008

In recent years, researchers have debated such basic tenets of social sciences that take pride in a certain epistemological universalism of Western scholarship. In his seminal work, *Orientalism* (1978), Said challenged this notion of Western hegemony on knowledge production paving the way for entire schools of postcolonial thought, alongside subaltern studies, feminist epistemologies and decolonization theories. A key argument presented by the aforesaid schools of thought was the systematic exclusion of the sociocultural and historical context of scientific knowledge production; it is this dismissal that lent itself to the universal character of all knowledge produced in the West. In becoming truly global, social sciences have been called upon to shed the Western hegemonic garb and take into consideration the local, regional voices in scientific discourse. Therefore, Gilroy's well-meaning claim overlooks the paradox inherent in the conception of cosmopolitanism which, while universal in approach, remains inalienable from social categories such as race, gender, or class. Any attempt to subtract these social categories from the equation is reflective of an individual's privileged location (Calhoun, 2003; Gikandi, 2002). Of importance to the present study is Benhabib's (2004) contention regarding an individual's allegiances – across ethnicities, religions, languages and nationalities – that upset the definition of cosmopolitanism as one *polis*.

Thus, the present study aims to explore how migrant youth engagement with a multiplicity of cultures leads to their identity construction and integration in their country of settlement, thereby leading to a cosmopolitan outlook. What strategies and tools do the migrant youth have at their disposal to counter the inevitable antagonism in their host community surroundings of the Czech Republic? How do they bridge the gap of racial differences and create a cosmopolitan imaginary? Gilroy (1993b, p. 6, cited in Leurs, 2015, p. 47) offers that youth cultures, owing to their organization as age and generation-based cohorts, can position themselves as a formidable critique of "the logic of racial, national and ethnic essentialism." And while the state can institute policies to help tackle racism, youth cultures can additionally mobilize at the ground level and their everyday interactions with members of other communities or groups may help challenge nationalist and racist notions of "othering" by exhibiting "conviviality and cosmopolitanism" (Gilroy 1993b, cited in Leurs, 2015, p. 47). Based on ethnographic narratives of six Muslim migrant young women and men, the first two themes deal with how they mobilize tools such as media and personal experiences to bridge cultural differences in both virtual and real spaces. Lastly, the study shows how the migrant youth mobilize their cultural resources and assert themselves as different from the local Czech people and thus of equal value (Beck, 2004).

At this juncture, it is important to present a brief explanation of different paradigms of cosmopolitanism as they appear in the academic literature across disciplines such as philosophy, social science, political theory and so on. Moral cosmopolitanism, as proposed by Martha Nussbaum in her essay "Patriotism and cosmopolitanism," aimed at US educational system, argues for a universalist, tolerant and open outlook that supersedes national boundaries and ushers in a space of humanistic cooperation (Komulainen in Vila-Freyer and Özerim, 2020; see also Nussbaum, 1996). Political cosmopolitanism is informed by

Kantian ideology and espouses human rights on a global scale. Kant's conception of cosmopolitan right and the principle of hospitality was instrumental in bringing debates in the field of pure ethics into the realm of politics, informing ideas regarding citizenship, political agency, governance, and "probably the European Convention of Human Right" (Gani, 2017, p. 4). Cultural cosmopolitanism advocates for the diversity of cultures and the rejection of nationalistic pursuits. Kleingeld (2016) thus defines cosmopolitanism as a multiplicity of positions aiming for a conception of world citizenship, approached either in literal terms (as in through political cosmopolitanism) or in figurative terms (through cultural or moral cosmopolitanism). Alternatively, Delanty (2006, p. 27) understands cosmopolitanism as a "cultural medium of societal transformation," and a society cannot simply be labelled as being either cosmopolitan or not. It is an ever-evolving process founded upon the principle of openness. The term "cosmopolitanism" eludes a specific definition as it manifests across every and all levels of the society – from the everyday life of "bi-national families, [and] neighborhoods" to global conglomerates or corporations to international human rights groups, to name only a few (Beck and Sznaider, 2006, p. 3). This study uses the analytical framework of banal cosmopolitanism as proposed by Beck (2004). In congruence with the aim of the study, banal cosmopolitanism seeks to understand the everyday processes by which we integrate ourselves into a global phenomenon. Such a cosmopolitan sensibility emerges out of interaction with opposing cultures (Beck, 2004), wherein media becomes instrumental in its development.

Smets (2018), in their ethnographic work, has explored how the Kurdish youth in London understand their regional conflicts using the media. Espousing the framework of diasporic cosmopolitanism, the study concludes that the youth distance themselves from their regional media, which helps them engage with the regional conflicts better and to consolidate their ethnic identities. The researcher is particularly interested to see the manifestations of this cosmopolitan positioning in the basic, everyday levels of migrant youth living in the Czech Republic. Lamont and Aksartova (2002), in their article "Ordinary cosmopolitanism," have explored the strategies used by ordinary working-class black and white French and US workers to counteract racist rhetorics. The study, akin to the present one, aimed to see cosmopolitan imaginary in places where it is not traditionally sought, based on the origins of this concept as having already been defined in the first paragraph.

The Czech Republic, as a nation-state, presents a curious case for studying cosmopolitanism. The Czech Republic has remained largely insulated from contact with Islamic countries, save for a period of exposure to the Ottoman empire. The attacks of September 11, 2001, in the United States, which were attributed to Islamic groups, fuelled media outrage in the country against Islamic fundamentalism. This attitude carried forward to the general public's reaction in 2015, culminating in demonstrations against killings related to the Charlie Hebdo cartoon publications and mass migration. Slačálek and Svobodová (2018) have shown how this xenophobic reaction is a result of a collective need to preserve the liberal values upon which the Czech Republic is founded. However, cosmopolitan outreach is not completely unknown in the Czech Republic, as demonstrated through its strong ties and continuous support of Tibet. Hříbek (2015, cited in Cervinkova, 2015, p. 218) argues that

> in the continuous trajectory of Czech nationalist thought, an imaginary connection with the East has served to endow the Czech historical experience and national struggle with a universal – even transcendental – appeal.

Since the communist regime held pro-Arabic sentiments before 1989 (Slačálek and Svobodová, 2018), the "Middle East" could be said to have thus been excluded from the construction of this post-socialist consciousness.

Methodology

This chapter is part of a doctoral project aiming to understand the identity and integration processes of Muslim migrant youth in the Czech Republic. The researcher used a critical realist paradigm wherein the subjective experiences of an individual are informed by overarching mechanisms, structures, and events. For instance, right at the onset of this research, the researcher was confronted with the arbitrariness of labels accorded to displaced individuals ranging from "asylum-seekers" to "migrants" to "refugees." The larger bureaucratic structures affect such categorization, thereby potentially creating "real causal impacts" in the lives of individuals by determining their social and material worth (Iosifides, 2018). Using an ethnographic approach, the data were collected from 2019 to 2020. This chapter draws on findings from 26 semi-structured interviews and participant observations with migrant youth living in Prague and neighbouring cities. Muslim migration is still at its nascent stage in the Czech Republic – with the country hosting approximately 20,000 Muslim people and even fewer Muslim adolescents. This chapter presents the narratives of these participants.

Findings

Becoming a Virtual, Global Citizen

The youth in this research uses a variety of social media tools, from WhatsApp to Facebook to Instagram to TikTok. In a few families, television media is also consumed, where the participants, along with their parents and siblings, watch Arabic or Indian soap operas or films such as those from Bollywood (*Bilal, Usman*) or Turkish Netflix shows (*Jameela, Mikel*). Due to the small size and fragmentation of the Muslim diaspora in the Czech Republic, such regional media, through its depiction of shared, moral values, lends a sense of community and proximity with the region of origin (Georgiou, 2012). However, for the most part, the youth limit their media usage to the Internet. On the Internet, the youth come to engage with and inhabit a cosmopolitan space:

Bilal[1]: In Africa, you can guess by looking at them that they really don't have food, they are poor. This makes me sad because some have got millions, billions, I don't know these numbers, and there in Africa, people are starving. Here in the Middle East people are killing each other. And people in South America are selling drugs.

Me: Where do you get all this information?

Bilal: Internet, Google. Like I don't want to read them but when I am scrolling, I see an ad or I see a page. If I am interested, I go inside and I read it. (Bilal, 19, Interview 2)

Here, Bilal describes a typical day he spends on the Internet which is marked by, besides his regular social media usage, ads and news pieces on events across the globe. He describes the differing plights of people from Africa, South America and the Middle East. The Internet, in this way, becomes a preliminary introduction to alternative experiences, of people inhabiting "other" worlds. An increased visibility of the day-to-day experiences of individuals on social media has tapped into the visceral emotions of the consumers, while also lending itself to cultivating an environment of empathy. As Beck (2004, p. 152) argues,

> People experience themselves as part of a fragmented, endangered civilization and civil society, whose characteristic feature is the simultaneity of events and knowledge of this simultaneity everywhere in the world.

Such a cosmopolitan outlook also comes to be sustained through active engagement on social media, as Bilal exemplifies in the following exchange:

Me: (…) you wanted to show the mean memes.

Bilal: Oh they are basically jokes about religion, personality. Like some people get offended. They even have in their bio that if you get offended, don't follow this page. I don't get offended as I told you, I learned not to care. I learned to laugh. Sometimes if I get offended I just scroll, I don't comment.

Me: Oh, do you comment on memes?

Bilal: Yes sometimes. I think I have a screenshot of a comment.

Me: Which got many likes or something?

---

[1]All names have been anonymized.

Bilal: Yeah … why would I screenshot it if it doesn't have likes? I commented about this guy's hair because I found it funny and many people agreed with me. But many people got offended. Some even texted me that it's normal, you know.

Me: How did you handle those comments?

Bilal: I just told them "fuck you!" No … I just gave them a like or a heart-reaction to their comment. I mean they just got triggered from one comment. I got a comment that I insulted the whole culture and I understood it after that guy told me how it is normal for black people. So sorry … I didn't know. (Bilal, 19, Interview 2)

Bilal demonstrates how the migrant youth negotiate this "digital thrownto-getherness in a progressive way." His engagement on social media is preconditioned by a general awareness of its functionality – there is offensive content, there are offense-takers and one can stay on the sidelines by not commenting and simply scrolling past. In the vignette presented above, Bilal recalls his Instagram exchange with fellow virtual users wherein they pointed out his inadvertent racism and the learning outcome which resulted. This contributes to the cultivation of what Leurs (2015) labels "hypertextualselves," which essentially refers to the dividends of multiculturalism that enable the migrant youth to relate to regional and transnational as well as global contexts. Being constantly bombarded by news bits, events or entertainment from different sociocultural locations forces the migrant youth to confront the differences. This results in the construction of identity with multiple affiliations – be they cultural, ethnic, gender, religious. Usman (Yemen) posts on Facebook about his experiences of playing a multiplayer video game such as PUBG. Faiza (Syria) recounts her love of the singers Adele, from the United Kingdom, and Fayrouz, from Iran. Shirin (Iran) watches videos of Italian TikTokkers explaining complex nuances of sexuality: "You basically can educate yourself from the media if you know how to use it" (Shirin). Such multiple affiliations help sustain the cosmopolitan outlook (Leurs, 2015).

Cosmopolitanism in Everyday Interactions

While the context of social media provides noteworthy insight into the development of cosmopolitan imagination, another equally potent space to observe this identity construction is the everyday interactions of migrant youth. Such quotidian socialization remains bereft of the media and political frenzy that stir debates and anxieties about communal inclusion (Noble, in Wise and Velayutham, 2009), especially crucial in the context of the Czech Republic (Georgiou and Zaborowski, 2017; Kovář, 2019; Meciar, 2016), and thus provide a more practical glimpse into how the migrant youth negotiate the differences and broker inclusion at the grassroots. An important feature of Beck's cosmopolitanism, which distinguishes it from nationalism, is the coexistence of people with different lifestyles which compels one to reflect upon "the otherness of others."

Due to a paucity of people from the same regional background in their age group, the migrant youth in the Czech Republic is inevitably called upon to socialize across racial and ethnic boundaries.

Me: Who are your friends?

Usman: Jagar, he was at my birthday party.

Me: Jagar, who spoke in Hindi? From Kurdistan?

Usman: Kurdistan, yes.

Me: How old is he?

Usman: Now he is 18 (…) he is crazy. He is not crazy crazy. But he goes to work directly after school every day. After work, he comes back home. And then again, directly to work. He has to make a lot of money. Because he has to go to Kurdistan and it's difficult for him. (Usman, 19, Interview 1)

Since his arrival in the Czech Republic from Egypt, Usman (originally from Yemen) has lived in the Foreign Children's facility, sharing the "home" with children from other nationalities. It was during his time in the facility that Usman met people from different backgrounds. In the above conversation, he shared about the friendships he has cultivated in the Czech Republic. He immediately delved into the life circumstances of his friend, stating the latter's dire need for money which justified his strenuous routine. Since displacement is a common denominator, friendships come to be predicated on life circumstances, wherein Usman began to empathize with someone from a different ethnic background who was nevertheless sharing his monetary hardships. Delanty (2012) posits that cosmopolitan relationships can manifest in a variety of ways, including an awareness of other people's vulnerabilities. Similarly, Jameela empathized with her Russian classmate, citing racial discrimination when her instructor at her medical school allegedly failed both of them in a course subject. Such interactions challenge particularistic notions of marginalization and deprivation of the migrant youth by putting into perspective their own experiences in relation to those of individuals from different backgrounds. However, the interactions of migrant youth are not limited to their own or other migrant youth. As all of the participants are either school or college students, they attend educational institutions with a majority Czech population. This inevitable intermingling causes the migrant youth and their classmates to confront and reflect upon certain preconceived notions about one another. Below, Mikel recounts one such development:

Me: So tell me, how do you think the Czech society perceives the Muslim migrants?

Mikel: Living here in the Czech republic? Basically what I see is that they're scared, they're scared of the migrants. I don't think they have so much of a problem with those already here, living here. The ones who came individually and not en masse but they're very scared of this mass migration and having many of them or all of them come in at once. They're scared and should be, honestly, from what I have been hearing about the migrants in Turkey. In Turkey, nearly the whole country was happy to let the migrants in. They said okay let's greet our brothers and you know … around 2 million Syrian migrants are in turkey right now. But what happened was that they started to cause problems.

Me: What kind of problems?

Mikel: You know like gangs, like form gangs. Another thing they would do is they would not work, they would just get the resources from the government. It's not a great attitude given that you are in a different country that is helping you. Many attacks, littering, and these kinds of things. So many people in Turkey don't want them anymore, those that wanted them at the beginning. That's what they're scared of. They already have a minority of … don't know how you … Gypsies! Couldn't find the English word. They have only had bad experiences, mostly bad experiences with them from what I know, from what I see they are … I have not seen nearly any integration from their side. They don't usually go to school, you usually see them smoking, the father just gets the money for children and buys himself things and leaves the children alone. So they don't … that affects how they perceive potential migrants. (Mikel, 19, Interview 2)

In this exchange, Mikel describes the issues he perceives that the local Czech people may have with the Muslim migrants. This perception has been built upon what he has heard from his teachers at school and the experiences of his classmates (for example, "My friend got punched by a young Gypsy girl and his nose broke"). He makes a distinction between the Muslims already living in the Czech Republic, who came individually, and the ones migrating en masse. Accordingly, the already residing migrants are not the cause of the problem whereas the new migrants may be a potential cause of problems, as he finds from the Turkish example. In his ethnographic work with Polish migrants in Norway, Pawlak (2015, cited in Cervinkova, 2015, p. 31) shows how the cosmopolitan migrants, who interact with the host society, can distance themselves from migrants of their national cohort, especially the ones they perceive to be not making any efforts at integrating, such as the mass migrants in Turkey responsible for "many attacks, littering and these kinds of things." In the present exchange, the researcher framed the question as "issues with Muslim migrants" and not migrants of a specific nationality to reflect the diasporic nature of Muslim religiosity.

The migrant youth of this study occupy certain social positions that enable their cosmopolitan outlook. Of the six participants with whom the researcher worked for one year, five of them had some kind of connection with the Czech Republic, while all of them had certain kinship networks in other European countries such as Germany. The youth hail from middle or upper-middle-class backgrounds, equipping them with capital to enable transnational mobility for education or employment. Based on cultural traditions, the similar class backgrounds make it incumbent upon the young people to pursue certain predetermined career paths, albeit gendered, such as medicine for girls and business or economics-based higher education for boys. Western countries such as the United Kingdom, United States, and Canada have relaxed migration legislation to attract such highly skilled professionals as medical doctors and business managers (Habti, 2012), thus further ensuring their global mobility. However, due to strict migration policies and relatively underdeveloped institutional infrastructure in the Czech Republic, labour retention within the country presents a noteworthy issue that can potentially result in the drainage of personnel with cosmopolitan imaginaries. All of the participants of this study have shown an inclination to pursue careers outside the Czech Republic, foreshadowed in thorough deliberations over which additional language needs to be chosen as a school subject such that it yields appropriate results in the future. This was evident in the study about intra-European Union (EU) migration of highly skilled professionals from central and eastern European countries to Germany owing to better standards of living, career opportunities and economic conditions in the latter (Pavel et al., 2014; Teney, 2019).

Yallah,[2] Cosmopolitanism

The migrant youth in this research construct a cosmopolitan outlook through virtual and real-life interactions, deploying core cosmopolitan practices of tolerance, openness and bridging racial differences through an outlook of empathy and understanding. Further, these successive experiences with the "Other" and otherness engage the critical and reflective faculties of the youth, leading them to evaluate their own value in relation to that of the Others. This boundary between oneself and the Other contributes to upholding a plurality of ideas, otherwise at risk of erasure in societies where migrants are mandated to assimilate into the host culture, gradually bringing the cosmopolitan vision into sharp relief. In an anthropological study by Skovgaard-Smith and Poulfelt (2017), transnational workers similarly reiterated their cultural and national attributes to achieve "commonality in difference." The migrant youth of this project demonstrate such reiterations across different spheres of their lives:

Me: What is this dress called?

Usman: (showing pictures on his phone) This is a *thawb*. I think, for this knife. And this is a *shaal*, 22 countries speak Arabic ... so *shaal* is better.

---

[2] *Yallah* is Arabic slang meaning "let's go" or "come on."

Me: *Shaal* is like a shawl. They have it in English now, they took the word. What do you call it in Yemeni?

Usman: *Guthra.* This is the knife.

Me: Why did your mother give you this knife?

Usman: Because of the tradition of Yemen. For us it is normal. In Yemen, when I wear it, I don't take it out. Only here. We say, for example, when you take it out, you have to put blood on it. So you can't take it out. Only if you have a problem, or someone wants to take something from you. You have to take it out. Only men in Yemen have it every day. When I was in Yemen, I also had it. (Usman, 19, Interview 1)

The first time the researcher met Usman was in the Children's Facility for Foreign Nationals where he had been living since March 2018. Originally from Yemen, his family of 14 siblings, along with his parents and a stepmother, relocated to Egypt in 2015 when the war broke out in their country of origin. Ostensibly hailing from the upper-middle class, his father being an important political figure, Usman shared his experience of studying in a modern school where he shares educational spaces with members of the opposite sex and becomes knowledgeable in the English language as he "was left with American people." Noble (in Wise and Velayutham, 2009) asserts that everyday cosmopolitanism should not only be studied through the narrow confines of ethnic and cultural differences but also a host of relations commonly seen in an ordinary school setting – between males and females, teachers and students, among friends, and so on – which can forge an outlook of openness and tolerance. Like Usman, all the participants showed excellent command of the English language, which additionally eased them into a multicultural sphere (Haque, 2020). In 2018, Usman's entire family moved to Europe – albeit to different countries including the Netherlands, Sweden, Slovakia, the Czech Republic – dispersed owing to what Usman cited as a "problem with visas." He came to the Czech Republic along with his older brother who lives in another city. Being a minor, Usman was housed in the Children's Facility which is where the researcher met him for the first time on his birthday. The house hosts minors from several countries. The birthday invitation was extended to a social worker from a Czech non-governmental organization (NGO) who asked me to accompany her. This way the researcher could meet Usman and talk to him about the possibility of participating in this research. While waiting for Usman and his friend, the researcher initiated conversations with the facility coordinators who recounted how they had hosted two boys from the Middle East thus far, including Usman, and how the boys had displayed exemplary conduct. This challenges the discursive dehumanization of Muslim migrants, especially young men, in the media (Szczepanik, 2016), while at the same time burdening these young adults with carrying the mantle for acceptable racial and ethnic conduct. Usman and his friend arrived with what they call a falafel cake. At one point, the attendees queued up to approach Usman and congratulate him on his birthday as per Czech traditions. Usman also changed into a *thawb*, traditional Yemeni attire, with a holster for a dagger. He described the tradition as mentioned above.

Beck (2002) argues that cosmopolitanism can have both "roots" and "wings," which implies that a cosmopolitan identity is not predicated upon erosion of self-rooted in one's local culture. The youth reassert their cultural values and present them on par with the others. While certain cultural representations are occasioned by special events such as birthdays, remaining invisible for the most part, as was the case with Usman, other symbols find perpetual visibility, as in the case of Faiza, who continued to wear the hijab and observe basic Islamic tenets such as conducting daily prayer (*salat*) and undertaking month-long fasting (*Ramzan*).

This cosmopolitan identity is reified and reinforced across various settings which youth frequent the most, such as school and workplace, or while pursuing recreational activities such as going out with peers or playing sports.

> I also say, you know what is *yallah* in Arabic – come on, come on – *yallah*. every time we play some sport in school I say *yallah yallah*, everyone caught that word from me and they even say it. Even the teacher, you know, the teacher. (Bilal, 19, Interview 5)

This particular instance proved to be an important milestone in Bilal's journey as a migrant in the Czech Republic. Having been bullied on account of his ethnic and racial identity by his classmates and peers during his initial years, Bilal has now reached a stage wherein his cultural traits have not only come to be accepted but also adopted by his peers while he plays football with his schoolmates. The literature on political engagement of Czech youth is quite scarce, but according to a multinational report (Kucharczyk, Łada and Schöler, 2017), 61% of the Czech youth see Islamic fundamentalism and terrorism as the biggest threat facing the EU, closely followed by refugee migration. In order to bridge this racial gap and rectify imagined notions about others, sports (especially football) provide a viable avenue for developing cosmopolitan thinking. In the context of football, Giulianotti and Robertson (2009) understand what they term "thin cosmopolitanism" as an "equal-but-different" approach to other cultures which also involves learning and incorporating said learning from the former in order to enrich one's own culture. This viewpoint is notably altered in present research wherein the migrant youth agentially arrive at the juncture where they consider themselves "equal-but-different" to their teammates, but the dividends of this reflection are distributed back to the same team. In this manner, convenient regional colloquialisms such as *yallah* or certain sports manoeuvres come to be employed in the games played in the host community. Usman, who played for a local team at the time of the research, hoped to play for the Czech professional football club, Slavia, and represent the country in their international games. Mikel, hailing from a multicultural background, actively chose his allegiance based on his love for football:

> I was around six or seven. I don't know exactly. And Italy was playing. I don't know if it was the World Cup at the time. I think it was the World Cup. And I think my father was watching it. And

you know, I was born in Italy. So it was or it must have been a semi-final or something. And I always, when I was younger, used to say I'm Italian. I'm not British. I'm not Czech. I'm not Somali. I'm Italian. Because I had this connection since I was young, to Italy. I had a nice feeling when I was there (...) And my father was an Arsenal fan (...) and we were playing against Barcelona and there I started supporting Arsenal and since then it's been Arsenal till I die and since then I've learned all the chants and everything about the history and all. (Mikel, 19, Interview 3)

Discussion of Findings

Migration discourse presents a rather myopic view of migrants by placing them within a transnational frame wherein the migrants are posited to remain firmly rooted in their ethnic and national identities, thereby preventing them from integrating into liberal, Western societies supported by universalist, cosmopolitan notions (Moosavi, 2015, in Horst and Olsen, 2021). In this chapter, the researcher argues that by mobilizing everyday resources such as social media and interactions in quotidian settings, the migrant youth go beyond this transnational mould by assuming a cosmopolitan imaginary.

The study highlights the ways in which a post-migration life issues the youth into everyday practices of cosmopolitan envisioning, using the theoretical framework provided by Beck's banal cosmopolitan, which seeks to look at these very same everyday processes to understand how a cosmopolitan viewpoint emerges. The three registers along which the youth develop a cosmopolitan outlook include the virtual spaces of the Internet where they navigate the reality of "digital throwntogetherness," which equips the youth to understand regional, national and global contexts by virtue of being constantly fed information on the same across social media platforms. This is followed by an exploration of how a cosmopolitan imaginary is created in non-virtual, physical spaces where abstract ideas of cosmopolitan understanding come to be tested in quotidian spaces such as schools. What strategies and tools do the migrant youth use to counter racist ideas? The youth remain aware of the general stereotypes and prejudices surrounding Muslims in virtual and real spaces. They show an awareness of how to operate and function on social media platforms. In face of opposing beliefs, the youth either chooses to engage in a healthy manner or withhold comment and continue to educate themselves. Subsequently, along with the third register, the youth themselves become active stakeholders in the cosmopolitan project by reflecting upon their value and creating spaces for themselves in their host community.

Conclusion

This chapter has explored how the migrant youth's interactions with multiple cultures contribute to their identities and the integration process leading to a cosmopolitan outlook. Using the analytical framework of banal cosmopolitanism advanced by Beck (2002), the study has inquired into how everyday processes help the migrant youth integrate into Czech society and larger global phenomena, thereby challenging the discursive notion in migrant literature which stations migrants as transnational entities fixated in their ethnic and national roots and unable to imagine themselves as a part of a global whole.

The study serves a two-pronged purpose: first, to upset the discursive treatment of the Western milieu as a bulwark for cosmopolitan values of tolerance and openness; second, to acknowledge the role of social categories such as race and ethnicity in cosmopolitan imaginary, based on arguments developed by Calhoun and Benhabib. However, most importantly, since research studies on migrant integration have largely remained focused on its structural and practical aspects, taking, as Korac (2003) called it, a "top-down" approach, these findings make salient the role of youth in upsetting the status quo of migrant discourse centred around transnationalism, by introducing narratives of identity and integration created by the youth at the grassroots, facilitating a cosmopolitan approach.

References

Beck, U. 2002. The cosmopolitan society and its enemies, *Theory, Culture & Society*, *19*(1–2), 17–44. https://doi.org/10.1177/026327640201900101

Beck, U. 2004. Cosmopolitical realism: on the distinction between cosmopolitanism in philosophy and the social sciences, *Global Networks*, *4*(2), 131–156. https://doi.org/10.1111/j.1471-0374.2004.00084.x

Beck, U. and Sznaider, N. 2006. Unpacking cosmopolitanism for the social sciences: a research agenda, *The British Journal of Sociology*, *57*(1), 1–23. https://doi.org/10.1111/j.1468-4446.2006.00091.x

Benhabib, S. 2004. *The Rights of Others: Aliens, Residents, and Citizens*, Vol. 5, Cambridge, Cambridge University Press.

Calhoun, C. 2003. 'Belonging' in the cosmopolitan imaginary, *Ethnicities*, *3*(4), 531–553. https://doi.org/10.1177/1468796803003004005

Cervinkova, H. Ed 2015. *Rethinking Ethnography in Central Europe*, New York, NY, Springer.

Delanty, G. 2006. The cosmopolitan imagination: critical cosmopolitanism and social theory, *The British Journal of Sociology*, *57*(1), 25–47. https://doi.org/10.1111/j.1468-4446.2006.00092.x

Delanty, G. 2012. The idea of critical cosmopolitanism. In *Routledge International Handbook of Cosmopolitan Studies*, pp. 38–46, London, Routledge.

Gani, J. K. 2017. The erasure of race: cosmopolitanism and the illusion of Kantian hospitality, *Millennium: Journal of International Studies*, *45*(3), 425–446. https://doi.org/10.1177/0305829817714064

Georgiou, M. 2012. Media, diaspora and the transnational context: cosmopolitanizing cross-national comparative research? In *The Handbook of Global Media Research*, pp. 365–380, Oxford, Wiley-Blackwell.

Georgiou, M. and Zaborowski, R. 2017. *Media Coverage of the "Refugee Crisis": A Cross-European Perspective*, Strasbourg, Council of Europe.

Gikandi, S. 2002. Race and cosmopolitanism. American Literary History, *14*(3), 593–615. http://www.jstor.org/stable/3054587

Giulianotti, R. and Robertson, R. 2009. *Globalization and Football*, London, Sage.
Habti, D. 2012. *Highly Skilled Mobility and Migration from MENA Region to Finland: A Socio-analytic Approach*, Kuopio, Itä-Suomen yliopisto.
Haque, S. 2020. Language use and Islamic practices in multilingual Europe, *Signs and Society*, *8*(3), 401–425. https://doi.org/10.1086/710157
Horst, C. and Olsen, T. V. 2021. Transnational citizens, cosmopolitan outlooks? Migration as a route to cosmopolitanism, *Nordic Journal of Migration Research*, *11*(1), 4–19. http://doi.org/10.33134/njmr.337
Hříbek, M. 2015. Dalai-Lamaism: an orientalist construction of postsocialist consciousness. In *Rethinking Ethnography in Central Europe*, pp. 217–239, New York, NY, Palgrave Macmillan.
Iosifides, T. 2018. Epistemological issues in qualitative migration research: self-reflexivity, objectivity and subjectivity, In R. Zapata-Barrero & E. Yalaz (Eds.), *Qualitative Research in European Migration Studies* , (pp. 93–109). https://doi.org/10.1007/978-3-319-76861-8_6
Kleingeld, P. 2016. Cosmopolitanism. In *International Encyclopedia of Ethics*, pp. 1–10, Hoboken, NJ, John Wiley & Sons, Ltd. https://doi.org/10.1002/9781444367072.wbiee629.pub2
Komulainen, S. 2020. A case for cosmopolitan, pragmatic sociology in the context of migrant youth integration. In *Young Migration. Vulnerabilities, Boundaries, Protection and Integration*, pp. 173–176, London, Transnational Press.
Kovář, J. 2019. A security threat or an economic consequence? An analysis of the news framing of the European Union's refugee crisis, *International Communication Gazette*, *82*(6), 564–587. https://doi.org/10.1177/1748048519832778
Korac, M. 2003. The lack of integration policy and experiences of settlement: a case study of refugees in Rome, *Journal of Refugee Studies*, *16*(4), 398–421. https://doi.org/10.1093/jrs/16.4.398
Kucharczyk, J., Łada, A. and Schöler, G. 2017. *Exit, Voice or Loyalty. Young People on Europe and Democracy. Case Studies From Austria, the Czech Republic, Germany, Hungary, Poland and Slovakia*, pp. 127–137.
Lamont, M. and Aksartova, S. 2002. Ordinary cosmopolitanisms: strategies for bridging racial boundaries among working-class men, *Theory, Culture & Society*, *19*(4), 1–25. https://doi.org/10.1177/026327640201900448
Leurs, K. 2015. *Digital Passages: Migrant Youth 2.0: Diaspora, Gender and Youth Cultural Intersections (MediaMatters)*, 1st ed., Amsterdam, Amsterdam University Press.
Meciar, M. 2016. Immigration discourses in the Czech Republic from the perspective of the current refugee crisis, *Beykent Üniversitesi Sosyal Bilimler Dergisi*, *9*(1), 148–161.
Nussbaum, M. 1996. Patriotism and cosmopolitanism, In *For love of country: Debating the limits of patriotism*, Ed. J. Cohen, pp. 3–17, Beacon Press.
Pavel, C., Cech, V. E., Hradecna, P., Holikova, K., Jelinkova, M., Rozumek, M. and Rozumkova, P. 2014. Foreign workers in the labour market in Czech Republic and in selected European countries, Prague, Association for Integration and Migration Organization for Aid to Refugees and Multicultural Center Prague. Retrieved February, 19, 2020.
Pawlak, M. 2015. Othering the self: national identity and social class in mobile lives. In *Rethinking Ethnography in Central Europe*, pp. 23–40, New York, NY, Palgrave Macmillan.
Said, E. 1978. *Orientalism: Western Concepts of the Orient*, New York, NY, Pantheon.
Skovgaard-Smith, I. and Poulfelt, F. 2017. Imagining 'non-nationality': cosmopolitanism as a source of identity and belonging, *Human Relations*, *71*(2), 129–154. https://doi.org/10.1177/0018726717714042

Slačálek, O. and Svobodová, E. 2018. The Czech Islamophobic movement: beyond 'populism'? *Patterns of Prejudice*, *52*(5), 479–495. https://doi.org/10.1080/00313 22x.2018.1495377

Smets, K. 2018. Ethnic identity without ethnic media? Diasporic cosmopolitanism, (social) media and distant conflict among young Kurds in London, *International Communication Gazette*, *80*(7), 603–619. https://doi.org/10.1177/1748048518802204

Szczepanik, M. 2016. The 'good' and 'bad' refugees? imagined refugeehood (s) in the media coverage of the migration crisis, *Journal of Identity & Migration Studies*, *10*(2).

Teney, C. 2019. Immigration of highly skilled European professionals to Germany: intra-EU brain gain or brain circulation? *Innovation: The European Journal of Social Science Research*, *34*(1), 69–92. https://doi.org/10.1080/13511610.2019.1578197

Vila-Freyer, A. and Özerim, M. G. 2020. *Young Migrants: Vulnerabilities, Boundaries, Protection and Integration*, London, Transnational Press.

Werbner, P. 2018. De-orientalising vernacular cosmopolitanism: towards a local cosmopolitan ethics. In *Beyond Cosmopolitanism*, pp. 275–295, Singapore, Palgrave Macmillan.

Wise, A. and Velayutham, S. 2009. *Everyday Multiculturalism*. Palgrave Macmillan UK. https://books.google.cz/books?id=Eo9_DAAAQBAJ.

Chapter Eight

Youth Migration After the Arab Spring: Single Women Migrants as Agents of Change

Amani El Naggare

Introduction and Background

Following the peak of youth political engagement during the Arab uprisings, youth faced repression, polarization and social and political marginalization. As a result, some youth envisaged ways to exit. This chapter examines migration as an exit for Arab youth after the Arab Spring. Single Arab women are only a subset of the Arab migrants who fled their countries during the uprisings. Despite their increasing numbers, single women are an under-researched population (Lesch and van der Watt, 2018). There is a gap in research on the migration trajectories of single Arab women; little is known about their migration motivations and the many obstacles they have faced in their home and host countries.

Furthermore, little attention has been devoted to their single marital status and its impact on their migration choice to identify whether this was a factor for easy or difficult integration or settlement in the host nation and the Arab diaspora.

This chapter aims to give voice to Arab single women who chose to migrate to Europe, Canada, the United Kingdom and the United States after the Arab uprising by highlighting the macro- and micro-factors that influenced their various motivations for migration, as well as the obstacles they faced before and during their migration as single Arab migrants.

This chapter highlights the intersection of three research areas: migration, activism and singlehood. It addresses the extent to which the various political, social and cultural pressures faced by single women in their home countries drive them to migrate. It also examines the hopes that single migrant women have for change in their home and host countries. This chapter explores single women's views on their migration journey by examining their perspectives on the dynamics of inclusion in and exclusion from the host society. It will also enhance our understanding of the social dynamics that Arab single women have with their

Youth Exclusion and Empowerment in the Contemporary Global Order:
Existentialities in Migrations, Identity and the Digital Space, 113–129
Copyright © 2022 by Amani El Naggare
Published under exclusive licence by Emerald Publishing Limited
doi:10.1108/978-1-80382-777-320221009

families in the home country around their new position as single migrants, on the one hand, and with the host society and diaspora networks, on the other.

Single Women Migration in the Literature

For decades, migration literature neglected the migration of single women. In the 1970s, women's migration was studied by categorizing migrant women into two groups: first, as part of family reunification, where a woman was expected to follow and be financially dependent on her husband or a male relative, and second, as migrant domestic workers (Toma, 2016). According to Cortes (2016), women were considered passive in the migration process since they were wives, daughters and relatives of male migrants. Women were considered invisible and unproductive migrants. With labour migration, the image of women's passivity changed, but they were still considered not active enough, working mainly in the domestic sphere. The limited representation of Arab migrant women aligns with research on women's migration (Killian, Olmsted and Doyle, 2012). Arab migrant women were represented in two groups: first, as "tied movers," partners or family members (Flynn and Kofman, 2004). They follow their fathers or spouses to areas where the latter can pursue their careers or educational goals. In this context, some literature has been devoted to the perspectives and attitudes of Arab women in the diaspora (such as Cainkar, 1996, 2004; Foroutan, 2009; Read, 2004; Read and Oselin, 2008). Second, in the period after the Arab Spring, women have been studied as migrants forced to flee their home countries and cross borders in precarious situations, facing various threats (Al Gharaibeh and O'Sullivan, 2021).

A less explored research area is the increase in individual and voluntary migration of Arab single women. Few studies have examined women's agency in deciding to move for educational and employment reasons and how they continue to do so in the face of various impediments that may influence their migration decisions (Duda-Mikulin, 2017; Killian, Olmsted and Doyle, 2012). There has been much silence on single women who are "free mobile agents" (Duda-Mikulin, 2017) and agents of their decisions and choices who decide to relocate and travel overseas to explore new horizons and learn new things.

Methodology

For this research, the hermeneutic phenomenological approach to data collection and analysis was adopted to gain a deeper understanding of the lived experiences (Renn, 2018) of single migrant women by giving them the space to articulate and share their experiences as single migrants. Hermeneutic phenomenology, or interpretive phenomenology, can be traced back to the work of Martin Heidegger. For Heidegger, individuals are actors and not merely knowers of phenomena (Neubauer, Witkop and Varpio, 2019). However, hermeneutic phenomenology goes beyond describing the phenomenon and interprets it (Neubauer, Witkop and Varpio, 2019). As described by Bynum and Varpio (2017), hermeneutic phenomenology seeks to define the meaning of a phenomenon and understand the contextual factors that shape it. It also enables understanding of the deep layers of human experience that are hidden and how the individual's lifeworld, or the world as he or she pre-reflexively perceives it, influences his or her experiences.

Hermeneutic phenomenology involves exploring the historical, social and political processes that shape and organize experiences to illuminate issues of power, privilege and injustice. By exploring their experiences, hermeneutic phenomenology seeks to give voice to people who may be marginalized or who are not part of privileged groups (Lopez and Willis, 2004, p. 729; Zschomler, 2017). Furthermore, while the idea of phenomenology states that each individual perceives a phenomenon individually, it acknowledges the social division of lived experiences (Lesch and van der Watt, 2018). Accordingly, singlehood is experienced not only between different identities but also as a social group. The emphasis is on shared single experiences rather than individual variations (Lesch and van der Watt, 2018).

In hermeneutic phenomenology, the researcher's prior experiences and knowledge are appraised as valuable guides for research by admitting that the researcher's knowledge and expertise lead him or her to consider a phenomenon or experience worthy of investigation. Furthermore, hermeneutic phenomenology acknowledges that the researcher and the research subject cannot detach themselves from their lifeworld (Neubauer, Witkop and Varpio, 2019; Van Manen, Higgins and Van der Riet, 2016). According to Williams (2020, p. 66),

> Researchers become aware of their own experiences, beliefs, assumptions and judgment, not so that they could set them aside to focus on the research but to consider how their own experience might relate to the experience that is being researched.

Additionally, hermeneutic phenomenology encourages researchers to recognize their own experiences and knowledge, which is a fundamental part of the interpretative process (Bynum and Varpio, 2017; Renn, 2018).

The interpretive process of hermeneutic phenomenology does not reduce itself to a particular set of rule-bound analytical procedures but is an interpretive process that involves the interaction of various analytical activities. According to Bynum and Varpio (2017), the analysis process first recognizes an intriguing phenomenon that draws researchers' attention to a lived experience. The research team then explores the experience as it is lived rather than conceived, mainly focusing on the key phenomenological themes that define the participant's encounter with the phenomena while also reflecting on their own experience. Second, researchers put down their thoughts and then reflect and write again, resulting in continual, iterative cycles for developing increasingly vital and advanced insights. Across the analysis, researchers must have a strong focus on the phenomena under investigation and pay attention to the relationships between the parts and the whole. The last step, known as the hermeneutic cycle, emphasizes assessing how the facts (the parts) contribute to the developing knowledge of the phenomena (the whole) and how they enhance the understanding of the other (Bynum and Varpio, 2017).

The requirement that the researcher approaches data without preconceptions is incompatible with the philosophical origins of hermeneutic phenomenology.

Instead, researchers working in this tradition should openly admit their biases and consider how their subjectivity plays a role in the analysis process (Neubauer, Witkop and Varpio, 2019). Adopting an interpretive lens involves researchers reflecting on their assumptions and identifying and integrating theories (Miller, Chan and Farmer, 2018; Renn, 2018).

In this chapter, hermeneutic phenomenology is employed to examine the migration journey, motives and views on singlehood of Arab single women who migrated exclusively to Europe, Canada, the United Kingdom and the United States following the Arab Spring. The principal author conducted semi-structured interviews for five months between February 2019 and June 2019 with 14 women who met four criteria: They were between 25 and 45 years old at the time of the interview; had at least tertiary qualifications; had never been married and had no children; and had migrated to Europe, Canada, the United Kingdom and the United States in the period following the Arab Spring.

Participants were selected using the snowball method through the primary author's network by asking friends, colleagues and acquaintances to suggest single women in their circles who fitted the criteria cited above. After taking part in the interview, some research participants voluntarily suggested that other participants from their networks participate in this research. Interviews were candid, reflective and lasted between one and three hours. All interviews were conducted virtually via Skype. To ensure that participants were able to express themselves in the language in which they felt most comfortable, they were given a choice to choose one of three languages which the primary author was also fluent in (Arabic, French and English). With the participants' consent, all interviews were recorded and transcribed in the language they were conducted in. The quotes from the interviews were translated into English by the author.

As the principal researcher of this study, it is crucial to note that sharing four standard parameters (single status, age, cultural-religious similarity, migrant status) with participants contributed to developing a rapport. First, using the hermeneutic phenomenological approach allowed me to draw on my own experience as a single migrant woman in her mid-30s to better understand and relate to the participants' various encounters with their activism, singlehood and migration journey. Participants felt more comfortable sharing and expressing their opinions and feelings about sensitive topics (Glassner and Loughlin, 1987). Second, it allowed me to notice various aspects that the participants did not express explicitly during the interviews, such as silent moments when they reflected on traumas they had developed during their period of activism back home; the way women participants articulated emotions related to important events they had experienced in migration; or the sensitivity of some participants to sharing their experiences of being single.

Interviews were analysed using the thematic analysis of Van Manen (2017). First, the transcribed interviews were reviewed in their entirety to get a sense of the phenomenon as a whole (Wertz, 2005). Second, the transcripts were reviewed and reread, which supplied a perspective on the overall context of the interviews and allowed for a better understanding of the context of each interview (Lesch and van der Watt, 2018). Third, the units of meaning were examined. They refer to the participants' experiences, feelings, reactions and the expressions and metaphors they used. Each participant's meaning units were then clustered into themes – or meaning units – within the holistic aspect of the interview (Groenewald, 2004; Lesch and van der Watt, 2018), and those with similar content were placed into preliminary themes. This allowed for a more abstract level of analysis. The preliminary themes were constantly compared to the transcripts to ensure they were based on participants' narratives. Some prototypical themes were discarded, others were summarized and new ones were developed. Data from all participants were analysed independently. In the final phase, the participants' experiences were synthesized into a whole. Seven themes were developed for this study that reflected the participants' experiences as single immigrant women.

Ethical Considerations. A reflective journal was kept during the research journey to note any prior information, ideas and feelings about the phenomena. Moreover, the reflective journal helped me maintain my critical self-awareness, reflection and reflexivity about the phenomena through data collection and data interpretation by highlighting the participants' thoughts and meanings. To increase the trustworthiness of the interpretation (Jones et al., 2012), two researchers who were not involved in the process were invited to double-check the interpretation of each interview and the data analysis.

Findings and Discussion

Demographics of the 14 Participants

Fourteen participants were interviewed virtually via Skype between February and June 2019. At the beginning of their migration journey, participants were aged 24–39 years old and the majority started their migration at 28 years or older. The year of relocation for all participants ranged from 2011 to 2016, emphasizing 2012 and 2015. These two dates relate to the post-Arab Spring period, during which youth faced political and societal exclusion in their home countries. The sample of participants originates from various Arab countries which were strongly or slightly affected by the Arab uprising. Four participants are from Egypt and two participants each from Jordan, Lebanon, Morocco, Tunisia and Yemen. The host countries they have chosen were mainly Europe (nine participants), the United Kingdom (three participants) and North America (two participants). All participants have a tertiary education (six with BA and eight with MA degrees). Regarding their occupations in the host country, they formed a diverse sample including PhD students, scientific researchers, political analysts, artists, doctors, engineers and teachers. Women participants were still single in their early 30s to mid-40s at the time of the interview. The majority were single at 31 years old or older.

The experiences of single women migrants are diverse and varied. This section will expose the seven themes that emerged through analysis of the transcripts. Direct quotations from interview transcripts are presented to emphasize the main themes. The identities of participants are not revealed in order to protect their anonymity. The themes were divided into two periods: pre-migration and post-migration phases.

The Pre-migration Phase.

Individual Migration, a Negotiated Path?.   Gender dynamics play a role in influencing women's migration before and after migration (Boyd and Grieco, 2003). Autonomy in migrating is usually influenced by cultural values and gender roles (Comoe, 2013). Gender norms and social norms in some cultures are shown to determine who is allowed to migrate, how and with whom (Toma, 2016). Structural opportunities may also facilitate or limit women's agency in migration (Duda-Mikulin, 2017). Various dynamics shape the pre-migration phase: individual, familial and societal (Boyd and Grieco, 2003). Most participants confirmed that deciding on an individual migration path was incredibly challenging before it became a challenge for their families as well. They chose to migrate in their late 20s and early 30s, which in Arab society is considered a time to settle down and start a family. In some cultural contexts, single Arab women are expected to stay with their parents until they marry.

Participants added that, to migrate, they needed fundamental reasons to convince their parents. They went through conflicting feelings when deciding to migrate. They were looking forward to exploring overseas but had concerns about leaving their parents alone, especially those who lived with their parents since their siblings were married and had their own households. This finding is similar to what Duda-Mikulin (2017) has found in her study of Polish migrant women: Women feel obliged to provide care for their parents as long as they are not married. Women respondents also pointed out that their decision to migrate would not have been possible without their families' support and knew that they had not left their parents alone. Although gender norms in Arab societies make it difficult for women to emigrate alone under certain circumstances, several participants revealed that they did not experience any pressure from their parents, who supported their plans.

The Arab Spring and the Intersecting Motivations for Migration.   When discussing Arab women's migration decisions, traditional reasons for migration such as political, educational and employment opportunities can be seen as limiting, as reasons for migration are constantly changing due to global, societal and personal conditions (Killian, Olmsted and Doyle, 2012). Before the political upheaval of 2011, half of the participants stated that they had never considered leaving their home country. Many were intimidated by the prospect of leaving everything behind and building a new life abroad. The other half of the participants had always hoped to emigrate but had been waiting for the right time. Surprisingly, all participants shared that the so-called Arab Spring was the deciding factor for considering migration. Some respondents saw it as an excellent opportunity to position themselves in society and in the family and make autonomous life choices. For others, the Arab Spring was the event that interrupted their daily routine and inspired them to consider a fresh start in a foreign country.

Most participants belonged to the upper-middle class and were active in civil society in their home countries; some had small projects. Others were preparing to start their master's studies abroad, but when the upheaval occurred, they chose to stay in their country and join the youth in the squares. They became politically involved, whether by participating in demonstrations or joining new youth political parties. One participant added:

> As a young woman who participated in and witnessed the Tahrir Days, I believe that this experience has changed my life and the lives of other Egyptians positively and negatively; everything has changed since January 2011, my identity and my thoughts, including my circle of friends. I was reborn in Tahrir Square. (Interview 14)

Participants said they were particularly influential and engaged in their home country's political, economic and social development. After a period of euphoria and hope, participants claimed that former regimes had prevented the change desired by the youth from occurring. Furthermore, some participants said that after the Arab uprisings and the increasing political and social polarization, they started a kind of "fictional migration" or "migration from home," as they called it. This is described as living at a distance or in isolation from the outside world (family, friends, circle of colleagues) before leaving their home countries.

The concept of living in a "bubble" they constructed was a meaningful way to escape social and political constraints, especially in times of political closures. Six participants recounted their experiences of "fictional migration," which they began after being harassed and oppressed for their political involvement. As a result, they decided to withdraw politically and avoid any activities that reminded them of their engagement time. They also withdrew from political and social life for fear of harming themselves and their families. Another group of respondents explained that as political and social divisions increased among different youth groups, many felt social exclusion because they lost close friends or networks as it became difficult to have fruitful discussions in a shrinking political and social space. According to Etling, Backeberg and Tholen (2018), young people have reached a point of disengagement from politics as the political arena is closed and exit should be the preferred possibility in unresponsive political regimes. Young people frustrated by existing conditions have found a way out of the political setting and into a new place where they can speak and interact freely. Participants said they migrated to escape political and social constraints. When asked about their feelings before migrating, participants emphasized the feeling of being "deceived."

Participants viewed migration in various ways. In the first group, migration was initially seen as distancing them from where women participants had been engaged and where they believed their lives would improve, but their efforts to change were arbitrarily interrupted. By migrating, they hoped to escape the sense of deception and dissatisfaction prevalent among young people such as them and recover from the despair and trauma they experienced after Arab Spring. The second group consisted of women who were politically active in civil society. They explained that, after the ban on non-governmental organizations (NGOs) in their home country, they refused to remain in a place where they could not engage in civil society because advocacy and participation in society were part of their daily lives. They found it challenging to give up their collective social and human resources and their civil society experiences. A participant expressed her opinion on migration:

> Sometimes it is difficult to understand why some activists fled the country and others did not. Some youth were dissatisfied with being forced not to discuss politics and decided to leave the country. Others could not cope with political censorship but were unable to leave the country for various reasons. There is also a third group that could live with being silenced. I could not stand being passive as a feminist activist, so I decided to leave the country; I decided to have a voice. (Interview 12)

Youth who returned to their home countries after the Arab Spring to participate in political and social change following the collapse of some authoritarian governments require further attention but are not the subject of this study. For example, one Egyptian interviewee expressed a desire to return to Egypt after the 25 January Revolution because she believed that youth would significantly affect political and social life. Two years after her return, she wanted to leave Egypt again since she could no longer bear the political stalemate. Therefore, she was forced to move to another place where she could be politically active. Most participants said they were not directly pressured to leave their home country but could make this life-changing decision themselves. In this context, agency refers to "the ability of social actors to think on their position, create strategies, and act to accomplish their aspirations" (Bakewell, 2010). Women participants also revealed that migrating to Europe, Canada or the United States is a strategic option because they want to secure citizenship which offers them more opportunities, such as mobility and security. According to Etling, Backeberg and Tholen (2018, p. 5), "political migration occurs on a continuum of forced and voluntary migration." It is important to note that under certain circumstances, women who chose to study abroad intended to return to their home country after completing their studies. However, when the political situation in their home country deteriorated, they were forced to remain in migration, and a return plan was no longer feasible. In the interviews, several female respondents explained that it was difficult to accept the change from voluntary to forced migration, as it significantly affected their future plans.

The decision to stay away from the political tensions in their home countries did not deter participants from re-engaging in the causes of their home countries. About one third of the respondents have coordinated or took part in political activities related to the political situation of their home countries. Three of the respondents work as researchers in think tanks dealing with security issues in their home countries. They added that being from the Middle East and North Africa (MENA) region has helped them understand the problems and difficulties they face in diverse ways. They also mentioned that, as experts in think tanks, they are looking for ways to influence Western policies and strategies towards their countries. Although they described themselves as politically disengaged, participants still follow their country's political news and debates on social media platforms.

Post-migration.

Between the Excitement of Settlement and Moments of Discrimination. Migration is a challenging life decision in every sense of the word, as it involves a change in a person's opportunities in terms of language acquisition, educational attainment, job opportunities and social status (Rumbaut, 2002). Participants emphasized that they were eager to live independently in another country and took early action, such as finding a job or contacting universities to apply for master's or doctoral programmes. The thought of starting a new life in their 30s triggered conflicting feelings of excitement and anxiety; participants thought they were too old to make this decision. In terms of the type of neighbourhood sought by single women in the host country, half of the participants indicated that they preferred to live in areas that would be more frequented by host country residents, as they did not want to be observed or asked whether or not they lived alone by people from the same cultural background. The other half of the participants had not considered these factors, and the only important criterion was adequate housing. Some of them found housing in areas familiar to migrants. Participants were initially relieved as they did not feel distant from their homeland, but they also accepted some inconveniences. Others found it easy to adjust to their new living situation, as it was a microcosm of what they had left behind in their homeland, and they focused on the positive elements of the situation (such as the opportunity to shop in nearby oriental stores and often hear Arabic music in the street).

One of the difficulties participants face when talking about their journey to host countries is racism and bigotry. Discrimination is not a one-time event, but rather a consequence of age, time and social environment. Discrimination and responses to discrimination might alter over the length of a person's life (Gee, Walsemann and Brondolo, 2012). It is important to note that respondents' opinions on racism varied. Respondents who chose Germany and Switzerland as destinations were more likely to report being discriminated against than women who chose Canada, the United Kingdom and the United States. One respondent said she received letters from a neighbour warning her that she was a loud person and should not live in that area. She was perplexed because she had never hosted a party or played loud music. She thought she could not feel comfortable in that neighbourhood because she was an immigrant, specifically an Arab. She went on to say that her friends had similar problems with housing in different strata.

Discrimination was not limited to housing problems, nor to challenges at work or at university; participants were inadvertently pushed to correct some preconceptions about women from the Middle East or Muslim backgrounds at the start of their careers or studies. One participant is a graphic designer; she described her first week at work as a nightmare as her colleagues were shocked that an Arab woman could operate a computer and work as a graphic designer. Moreover, women who had been to Europe and took part in language courses stated that learning a language should be fun. However, their perception was the opposite: it was an arduous journey since their language professors had preconceived notions that Arab women lacked the ability to learn and think critically. Other interviewees, however, found no racism or prejudice in their workplaces or classrooms. When they learned about the unpleasant discriminatory incidents their friends had experienced, they were grateful that they had not been exposed to such. Participants added that the migration experience helped them reflect on themselves and be aware of their strengths and weaknesses.

Migration had enabled them to be more autonomous, courageous, and accurate in their decisions. Despite random instances of discrimination, participants said they had learned to cope with times of fear and exposure in moments of intimidation.

Being a single woman in migration is a common characteristic of participants. It is essential to highlight how participants viewed their singlehood in migration and how it was also perceived by their families and close circles back home and how it was seen in the host country.

Being a Single Woman in Migration.   Despite the increase in the number of single women in the Arab world, they continue to face discrimination and social segregation as they break with social expectations based on the belief that adulthood is associated with marriage (Hamilton et al., 2006). The number of people who are not married and do not intend to marry is increasing (Sharp and Ganong, 2011). As DePaulo and Morris (2005) denote, single people face a form of bias called "singlism," which is based on the belief that everyone wants to and will get married, and that married couples lead happy and satisfying lives, as opposed to single people, who are considered unhappy and unfulfilled (Adamczyk, 2016; Lesch and van der Watt, 2018). Singlism is a pervasive marital and family philosophy that manifests itself in daily thoughts, experiences, rules and social policies that favour couples over singles. In addition, deviation from societal norms can put greater pressure on women (Sharp and Ganong, 2011). Participants experienced two types of discrimination. First, they faced discrimination in their home country due to their single status. Five participants emphasized that they migrated because they were still unmarried in their early 30s, the age at which women are expected to start a family. Second, as single women migrants with Arab and Muslim identities, they experienced prejudice and discrimination in the host country and within the Arab diaspora as well.

Migration, an Escape for Single Women?.   Van der Watt (2015) describes being a single woman as not being in a relationship with a male, and being single in the Arab world implies not being married. All participants had one thing in common: they were all single women from different Arab nations who had faced some of the same societal pressures because of their position as single women. They believed they had broken familial and cultural norms by not marrying before the age of 30. Participants viewed the age of 30 as a pivotal point in their lives, consistent with research on singleness in various settings (Azmawati, Mohd Hashim and Endut, 2015; Byrne, 2000; Lesch and van der Watt, 2018). In addition, the age of 30 is highlighted as women's surrender acts as a reminder to women that they do not conform to traditional ideals of marriage and motherhood (Byrne, 2000; Sharp and Ganong, 2011). Surprisingly, most respondents felt pressure to marry not from their parents or siblings but from their extended families and relatives or even married friends. Some participants wondered why it was already so important for women to marry before the age of 30. One participant added:

> There is no right or wrong time to get engaged, it depends on a woman's circumstances, and people should stop reminding us of our biological clock; we are more aware of our bodies than they are. (Interview 3)

Eight participants added that one of the main reasons they chose to migrate was to escape societal pressures by finding a job or completing their studies abroad. Participants also indicated that they were relieved when they left their home country and moved to another country as they believed that people would not regularly ask them about their single status.

Single Migrant Women: Being too Picky and Demanding.   According to participants, the perception of single women in society remains unfavourable, whether in their home countries or host communities. They were alarmed to find that the pressures they had left behind in their home country prevailed in the host country as well on some occasions. Many people do not consider being single a real and realistic option for a woman. There is an assumption that there is something wrong with these women, and they are often criticized for their single status (Ntoimo and Isiugo-Abanihe, 2014). Seven respondents stated that women who rejected possible relationships were often accused of being man-haters, being less feminine, being lesbian or having a problem that needed to be dealt with (Hamilton et al., 2006). As expressed by a participant:

> Single women in our community are under a lot of pressure, especially if they are in their mid-thirties and still living alone. People start wondering what the problem is, and they keep asking you why you have not married yet. Do you have an aversion to men? They wanted me to doubt myself, my personality or my looks so that I could find an explanation for being a single woman in my mid-thirties, but I never did. (Interview 7)

Some participants reported that they were uncomfortable interacting with married women in the host country because they were the only single person in the group, which gave them high visibility in a closed network (Sharp and Ganong, 2011). One participant described her experience at a social gathering organized by a group of married women from her home country:

> Since this was my first time moving to this region, everyone was married, and some were younger than me. They were friendly, but they were concerned about my marital status and asked me some personal questions, such as why have not you gotten married yet? Do not you want to have children? No, not yet was my answer. Then some ladies expressed their concern about my age and how I managed to leave my family and come here alone at the age of 33 to do my master's degree. (Interview 6)

Another participant added,

> Married women do not openly criticise you for being single on
> such occasions. Instead, they make you feel inadequate or look at
> you pityingly. A married acquaintance once advised me that I was
> a successful and courageous woman but that I would be lonely
> without a partner and children if I did not marry as soon as pos-
> sible as I was approaching forty. She expressed the fear that no
> one would take care of me if I became ill and that I would need
> someone by my side since I am in a foreign country far from home.
> (Interview 11)

Participants emphasized that married women often criticized them for being
selfish, prioritizing work over marriage and motherhood. They were also seen
as overly picky as they had set multiple criteria for their ideal partner (Budgeon, 2015). It is imperative to stress that marital status is an important factor for
accessing some of the home communities in the host country. Some participants
added that they were not invited to social events because they were not married.
Marital status can be the gateway to certain diaspora societies.

Some respondents indicated that they were rarely asked about their marital status in their contacts with the host community, which was seen as positive as they
did not feel obliged to justify their decision. On the other hand, four respondents
said that on certain occasions, such as in a language course, their first day at work
or a job interview, they were asked to introduce themselves and say that they were
single and were shocked by the comments they heard such as "Amazing that you
managed to come to Europe alone; how could your family not prevent you from
travelling because you are a single woman?" or "As a woman of Arab and Muslim
origin, we assumed you had more than three children" (Interviews 1, 7, 9).

Single by choice?.   Previous studies have shown that the change in women's
marriage habits is due to education and income, giving women more autonomy
and higher socio-economic status (Azmawati, Mohd Hashim and Endut, 2015;
Frazier et al., 1996; Manning and Smock, 2002; Stolk, 1981). Respondents were
consistent about their experiences of being single in their early or mid-30s but
held different views about their migration path and their status as single women.
For the first group of women, migration allowed them to gain independence and
increase their chances of finding the partner of their choice. They emphasized
that they could not find a suitable partner who shared their beliefs and views in
their home country. Ten of the 14 respondents were previously in a partnership or
officially engaged but had dissolved their relationship for various reasons before
migration (such as incompatibilities between partners, misunderstandings in the
family and conflicts over the marriage budget).

Initially, respondents expressed enthusiasm about finding a partner in the new
destination country that met their criteria. A few years later, after they had set-
tled, one group of women interviewed concluded that marriage in migration was
more difficult than marriage in the home country for various reasons. The women
often found it difficult to sustain relationships when they became involved with

men from different socio-economic and cultural backgrounds. A second group of women reported being content with their single status and expressed no desire to marry at the moment. Based on their experiences with marriages within their family or circle of friends, they were more comfortable with their singleness and saw it as an advantage in migration. One of the interviewees shared her thoughts about being a single Arab woman. She explained:

> The increasing number of single women in our Arab countries can be explained by the fact that there are more women than men in society or that high youth unemployment means that few young people are willing to get married. However, I believe that people are unwilling to acknowledge that women nowadays tend to be overly cautious when choosing their partners. Many of my female friends are content with their single status; many have foregone the social and family pressures. (Interview 14)

Participants added that they sought three kinds of fulfilment in their relationships (intellectual, emotional and physical) and were unwilling to give up any of them. This selectivity included the desire to choose a partner based on equally important characteristics such as educational level, professional ambitions and financial status (Ahuvia and Adelman, 1992). When asked about their experience of loneliness during migration, most respondents indicated that they were not afraid of loneliness if they did not marry, as they believed that a couple could also feel lonely. Most of the respondents said that they had plans and hectic schedules that kept them busy all the time. Those who experienced loneliness indicated that it had been difficult for them to cope with loneliness without support at the beginning of their migration journey, but they managed to handle it over time.

In terms of motherhood, participants expressed that they wanted to be mothers and have children; for this reason, choosing a good father for their children was crucial. One participant added,

> People keep telling me that I need to be more flexible in my choice of a partner if I want to have a child. However, I am not willing to choose the wrong spouse to be a mother. I think it is a form of selfishness. (Interview 5)

Some of the women interviewed were convinced that once they reached a certain age where they could no longer have children, they would consider adopting a child and raising them independently. Some interviewees felt that society should focus less on single women and more on the rising divorce rate, which means that people rush to form partnerships and families only to divorce again after a short time.

Conclusion

Considering the lack of literature on Arab single women migrants in the aftermath of the Arab Spring, this chapter brought a new perspective to the broader literature on Arab youth migration post-Arab Spring by focusing on political activism and singlehood as motives for migration.

According to the findings of this chapter, shrinking political and social space in the period after the Arab Spring prompted single Arab women to seek an exit to overcome the political and social marginalization they faced in their home countries. Migration had distinct implications for them. First, it helped single women migrants slightly to overcome the depression and disappointment that many young people experienced after the Arab Spring. Second, it allowed them to escape the social pressures faced by single women in their late 20s and mid-30s. In terms of migration, single women proved agency by making this life-changing decision independently and with the support of their parents and siblings, who showed a high degree of understanding. The voluntary migration might also be viewed as an implicitly forced exodus by women who could not endure their home country's political and social isolation. The study's notable findings are that women participants did not cease to be politically engaged even while away from home. They also dispel some stereotypes about Arab women, especially single women, who are seen as vulnerable or lacking agency by both the host society and the Arab diaspora. Despite the challenges posed by their migratory experiences, single women's ability to act and make decisions is enhanced. As single migrant women, they had the opportunity to become more autonomous, determined and assertive. Single women migrants claimed that the fact that they had not yet married does not imply hostility to marriage. They were opposed to social pressures that compel women to compromise on the criteria and expectations they have for future partners.

This chapter contributes to the literature on youth exclusion and youth migration by addressing the topic of women's singlehood migration and offering insights into the political and societal pressures that single women faced before migration and the various forms of inclusions and exclusions they experienced post-migration. However, this chapter cannot cover all aspects of a single migrant woman's life. This study is limited in scope since it focuses on the experiences of 14 single female migrants who are highly educated and financially independent and come from a social milieu that supports their migration aspirations.

Future studies should be conducted with single women migrants who come from diverse social milieus and socio-economic positions. Particular attention should also be paid to women who have experienced a change in marital status from married to divorced in migration, to women who have experienced a change in migration status from voluntary to forced migration due to increasing political instability in their home country, and the impacts that single migrant women may face.

References

Adamczyk, K. 2016. Voluntary and involuntary singlehood and young adults' mental health: an investigation of mediating role of romantic loneliness, *Current Psychology*, *35*(1), 1–17.

Ahuvia, A. and Adelman, M. 1992. Formal intermediaries in the marriage market: a typology and review, *Journal of Marriage and Family*, *54*(2), 452–463. https://doi.org/10.2307/353076

Al Gharaibeh, F. and O'Sullivan, J. 2021. The impact of war followed by forced displacement on women and children: how Syrian mothers perceive their experiences, *International Journal of Sociology and Social Policy*. https://doi.org/10.1108/ijssp-11-2020-0508

Azmawati, A. A., Mohd Hashim, I. H. and Endut, N. 2015. "Do not Marry, Be Happy!" – how single women in Malaysia view marriage, *SHS Web of Conferences*, 18.

Bakewell, O. 2010. Some reflections on structure and agency in migration theory, *Journal of Ethnic and Migration Studies*, *36*(10), 1689–1708. https://doi.org/10.1080/1369183x.2010.489382

Boyd, M. and Grieco, E. 2003. Women and migration: incorporating gender into international migration theory. *Migration Information Source*, 1–7. Available at: http://migrationinformation.org/feature/print.cfm?ID=10

Budgeon, S. 2015. The "problem" with single women. *Journal of Social and Personal Relationships*, *33*(3), 401–418. https://doi.org/10.1177/0265407515607647

Bynum, W. and Varpio, L. 2017. When I say ... hermeneutic phenomenology. *Medical Education*, *52*(3), 252–253. https://doi.org/10.1111/medu.13414

Byrne, A. 2000. Single's women's identities in contemporary Irish society. Unpublished PhD theses, Department of Government and Society, University of Limerick, Ireland.

Cainkar, L. 1996. Immigrant Palestinian women evaluate their lives. In *Family and Gender Among American Muslims: Issues Facing Middle Eastern Immigrants and Their Descendants*, Ed. B. C. Aswad and B. Bilge, pp. 41–58, Philadelphia, PA, Temple University Press.

Cainkar, L., Abunimah, A. and Raei, L. 2004. Migration as a method of coping with turbulence among Palestinians, *Journal of Comparative Family Studies*, *35*(2), 229–240. https://doi.org/10.3138/jcfs.35.2.229

Comoc, E. F. 2013. Femmes et migration en Côte d'Ivoire: le mythe de l'autonomie, *African Population Studies*, *20*(1). https://doi.org/10.11564/20-1-389

Cortes, G. 2016. Women and migrations: those who stay. *EchoGéo*, 37. https://doi.org/10.4000/echogeo.14892

DePaulo, B. M. and Morris, W. L. 2005. Singles in society and in science. *Psychological Inquiry*, *16*(2–3), 57–83. https://doi.org/10.1207/s15327965pli162&3_01

Duda-Mikulin, E. A. 2017. Should I stay or should I go now? Exploring Polish women's returns "home." *International Migration*, *56*(4), 140–153. https://doi.org/10.1111/imig.12420

Etling, A., Backeberg, L. and Tholen, J. 2018. The political dimension of young people's migration intentions: evidence from the Arab Mediterranean region, *Journal of Ethnic and Migration Studies*, *46*(2020), 1388–1404. https://doi.org/10.1080/1369183X.2018.1485093

Flynn, D. and Kofman, E. 2004. Women, trade, and migration, *Gender and Development*, *12*(2), 66–72. http://www.jstor.org/stable/4030616

Foroutan, Y. 2009. Migration and gender roles: the typical work pattern of the MENA women, *International Migration Review*, *43*(4), 974–992. https://doi.org/10.1111/j.1747-7379.2009.00791.x

Frazier, P., Arikian, N., Benson, S., Losoff, A. and Maurer, S. 1996. Desire for marriage and life satisfaction among unmarried heterosexual adults, *Journal of Social and Personal Relationships*, *13*(2), 225–239. https://doi.org/10.1177/0265407596132004

Gee, G. C., Walsemann, K. M. and Brondolo, E. 2012. A life-course perspective on how racism may be related to health inequities, *American Journal of Public Health*, *102*, 967–974. https://doi.org/10.2105/AJPH.2012.300666

Glassner, B. and Loughlin, J. 1987. *Drugs in Adolescent Worlds: Burnouts to Straights*, New York, NY, Springer.

Groenewald, T. 2004. A phenomenological research design illustrated, *International Journal of Qualitative Methods*, *3*(1), 42–55. https://doi.org/10.1177/160940690400300104

Hamilton, M. C. Anderson, D., Broaddus, M. and Young, K. 2006. Gender stereotyping and under-representation of female characters in 200 popular children's picture books: a twenty-first century update, *Sex Roles*, *55*(11–12), 757–765. https://doi.org/10.1007/s11199-006-9128-6

Jones, F., Rodger, S., Ziviani, J. and Boyd, R. 2012. Application of a hermeneutic phenomenologically orientated approach to a qualitative study, *International Journal of Therapy and Rehabilitation*, *19*(7), 370–378. https://doi.org/10.12968/ijtr.2012.19.7.370

Killian, C., Olmsted, J. and Doyle, A. 2012. Motivated migrants: (re)framing Arab women's experiences. *Women's Studies International Forum*, *35*(6), 432–446. https://doi.org/10.1016/j.wsif.2012.09.006

Lesch, E. and van der Watt, A. S. 2018. Living single: a phenomenological study of a group of South African single women, *Feminism & Psychology*, *28*(3), 390–408. https://doi.org/10.1177/0959353517731435

Lopez, K. A. and Willis, D. G. 2004. Descriptive versus interpretive phenomenology: their contributions to nursing knowledge, *Qualitative Health Research*, *14*(5), 726–735. https://doi.org/10.1177/1049732304263638

Manning, W. D. and Smock, P. J. 2002. First comes cohabitation and then comes marriage? A research note. *Journal of Family Issues*, *23*(8), 1065–1087. https://doi.org/10.1177/019251302237303

Miller, R. M., Chan, C. D. and Farmer, L. B. 2018. Interpretative phenomenological analysis: a contemporary qualitative approach. *Counselor Education and Supervision*, *57*(4), 240–254. https://doi.org/10.1002/ceas.12114

Neubauer, B. E., Witkop, C. T. and Varpio, L. 2019. How phenomenology can help us learn from the experiences of others, *Perspectives on Medical Education*, *8*(2), 90–97. https://doi.org/10.1007/s40037-019-0509-2

Ntoimo, L. F. C. and Isiugo-Abanihe, U. 2013. Patriarchy and singlehood among women in Lagos, Nigeria, *Journal of Family Issues*, *35*(14), 1980–2008. https://doi.org/10.1177/0192513x13511249

Read, J. G. 2004. Cultural influences on immigrant women's labor force participation: the Arab-American case, *International Migration Review*, *38*(1), 52–77. https://doi.org/10.1111/j.1747-7379.2004.tb00188.x

Read, J. G. and Oselin, S. 2008. Gender and the education-employment paradox in ethnic and religious contexts: the case of Arab Americans, *American Sociological Review*, *73*(2), 296–313. https://doi.org/10.1177/000312240807300206

Renn, J. (2018). Makroanalytische Tiefenhermeneutik Qualitative Sinnrekonstruktion als Gesellschaftsanalyse. In S. Müller & J. Zimmermann (Eds.), Milieu – Revisited: Forschungsstrategien der qualitativen Milieuanalyse (pp. 157–246). Wiesbaden Springer Fachmedien Wiesbaden Gmbh Springer Vs.

Rumbaut, R. G. 2002. Severed or sustained attachments? Language, identity, and imagined communities in the post-immigrant generation. In *The Changing Face of Home: The Transnational Lives of the Second Generation*, Ed. M. C. Waters, pp. 43–95, New York, NY, Russell Sage Foundation.

Sharp, E. A. and Ganong, L. 2011. "I'm a loser, I'm not married, let's just all look at me": ever-single women's perceptions of their social environment, *Journal of Family Issues*, *32*(7), 956–980. https://doi.org/10.1177/0192513x10392537

Stolk, Y. 1981. The spinster stereotype: a demographic refutation? *Australian Journal of Social Issues*, *16*(3), 187–201. https://doi.org/10.1002/j.1839-4655.1981.tb00709.x

Toma, S. 2016. Putting social capital in (a family) perspective: determinants of labour market outcomes among Senegalese women in Europe, *International Journal of Comparative Sociology*, *57*(3), 127–150. https://doi.org/10.1177/0020715216653998

Van der Watt, A. S. J. 2015. *Women's Experience of Being Single*, p. 374, MSc thesis. Available at: https://core.ac.uk/download/pdf/37439791.pdf

Van Manen, M. 2017. *Researching Lived Experience: Human Science for an Action Sensitive Pedagogy*, London, Routledge, Taylor & Francis Group.

Van Manen, M., Higgins, I. and van der Riet, P. 2016. A conversation with Max van Manen on phenomenology in its original sense, *Nursing & Health Sciences, 18*(1), 4–7. https://doi.org/10.1111/nhs.12274

Wertz, F. J. (2005). Phenomenological research methods for counseling psychology, *Journal of Counseling Psychology, 52*(2), 167–177. https://doi.org/10.1037/0022-0167.52.2.167

Williams, S. 2020. *Respectful Relationships: A Phenomenological Study on the Lived Experience of Respect for Second-Generation Korean Canadian Pastors within the Korean Church Context*, p. 174. PhD thesis. Available at: https://scholars.wlu.ca/etd/2257

Zschomler, S. 2017. *A Critical Hermeneutic Phenomenology of Adult Migrant Language Learners' Experience of Social Class in London: Struggles for Value and Values and the Potential Transformative Impact of the Language Classroom*, p. 92. MSc thesis. Available at: https://www.teachingenglish.org.uk/sites/teacheng/files/mda2017_university_of_cambridge_silke_zschomler.pdf

Chapter Nine

Youthful Sexuality and Human Rights in the Era of Social Media in Nigeria: Emerging Themes and Insights

Kafayat Aminu and Jimoh Amzat

Introduction

Social life is becoming digitized due to technological advancement, especially the Internet and social media, which have changed interaction, communication and the trajectories of human relationships. Access to the Internet and social media have practically altered the extent of youth inclusion in or exclusion from social, cultural, political and economic activities. Similar to the experience in many developing nations, the majority of Nigerian youth have unequal access to resources, rights and opportunities compared to their counterparts in economically advanced nations due to different norms, values, beliefs, ideologies, institutions and behavioural patterns. The experience of social exclusion negatively impacts their sense of belonging and expressly triggers social vices (Hilker and Fraser, 2009). However, the extent to which the Internet and social media have shaped youth exclusion/inclusion in Nigerian social life is vague. This chapter explores how social media norms of engagement have influenced youth social exclusion/inclusion, particularly in social discourse around sexuality and human rights, by tracing the historical development and implications of youth participation in digital interaction on society.

The origin of social media is linked to the history of the Internet, which began in the twenty-first century. According to Edosomwan et al. (2011), the Internet was inaugurated through the invention of ARPANET, known as the "early network of time-sharing computers ...," that was developed by the United States Advanced Research Projects Agency (ARPA) in 1969. Decades later, Six Degrees, the first known social media site, was launched in 1997 (Edosomwan et al., 2011). Facebook was launched in 2004 and its current website became active in 2005, although the public only gained access to it in 2006. The popular video blogging

Youth Exclusion and Empowerment in the Contemporary Global Order: Existentialities in Migrations, Identity and the Digital Space, 131–145
Copyright © 2022 by Kafayat Aminu and Jimoh Amzat
Published under exclusive licence by Emerald Publishing Limited
doi:10.1108/978-1-80382-777-320221010

site, YouTube, was activated in 2005, followed by Twitter in 2006 (Edosomwan et al., 2011). Subsequently, these and many other social media platforms have become popular across the globe, Nigeria included. Some of the platforms that Nigerians use widely, in no particular order, include ToGo, WhatsApp, Telegram, TikTok, Snapchat, Instagram, MySpace, Quora, Reddit, LinkedIn, Pinterest and, lately, Clubhouse.

The social media is a subset of the mass media, a prominent agent of socialization. Since its innovation, the social media has revolutionized and become intrinsic to our daily functionality. Social media is multifunctional, as it plays both manifest and latent roles in human interactions globally. It presents opportunities for symbolic communication and social construction, thus serving spheres external to it. It allows users to communicate with a large audience and still retains the intimacy found in face-to-face communication. Social media intersects multiple areas of human endeavour and affects everyone directly or indirectly irrespective of age, gender and social status, among others. However, the younger generation is more influenced.

Communication on social media transcends all forms of communication barriers, enabling the creation of virtual communities. As a digital community, the social media has its norms, values and acceptable interaction culture and communication mechanisms appealing to a subset of the audience within its ambience. This is not to disregard the significance of sociocultural norms and values in the real world, which inform the operational rules, norms, regulations and sanctions on various media platforms. Social media norms reflect what society holds in high esteem or value. These norms define acceptable and obnoxious online behaviours, which are rewarded through positive sanctions (such as likes, shares and approving comments) and negative sanctions (dislike, disapproving or derogatory comments, blocking, unfollowing and unfriending). The symbolism of social media has crept into and altered the patterns of social interaction in society off the Internet. It has become an extension of the real world, where people discuss topics affecting them in the offline world and vice versa. Moreover, most social media notions have logical equivalents in real-life social processes, thereby having a direct and indirect bearing on all spheres of social life.

Its impacts include extensive reach plus a direct connection to a large transnational audience, consequently creating an improved opportunity for collaboration. By supplementing the existing communication channels, social media has created an opportunity for seamless social networking, communication and social interaction. It likewise plays hedonic (entertaining), educative and cathartic roles and has utilitarian value (Van Oosten, 2021). Furthermore, social media promotes cross-fertilization of ideas as users are exposed to their immediate cultural contexts and remote locations whose culture may be at variance with theirs. Regardless of its many positive impacts on society, the proliferation of Western civilization and pop culture, often disseminated via social media platforms, has irreversibly transformed the psyche of youths around the world. The internalization of and attention paid to social media messages or contents by adolescents and young adults impact their self-perception, social expectations and attitudes towards others. The younger generation uses social media to create and explore "possible selves" alongside their self-identity. Hence, users' social media identity affects their self-concept in real life (Van Oosten, 2021). Moreover, the virtualization of social media has incontrovertibly altered the process of building new relationships by removing political, social and geographic barriers. This is what Matook and Butler (2015) considered as a significant impact social media has on organizations and society.

Interaction on social media, even though it is virtual, goes beyond the online world to influence offline behaviours. Since it became a part of our daily interactions, social media has altered the quality and depth of offline interactions and relationships, both individually and for groups. It has redefined the entire system of socialization in general and sexual socialization specifically. It influences self-identification, individual construction of gender and femininity construction among female users and self-expectations of sexuality (Davis, 2018). These are evident in the changing sexual culture and understanding of sexual rights among Nigerian youths, which has evolved with their increasing access to various social media channels. The cumulative interaction with social media has eased the accessibility of sexualized items (images, videos and animations) to young, under-age users, which has undesirable implications for their attitudes, personhood, sexual orientation and behaviour. However, the consequences are seemingly more deleterious for young girls than boys (Davis, 2018; Van Oosten, 2021).

Its differential impacts on male and female users may be attributed to the polysemic nature of media messages or content, implying that they could be interpreted differently, depending on the user's immediate context (Haralambos, Holborn and Heald, 2004). Moreover, an individual's interpretation of media information or messages is dependent on their age, level of education, life experience, social environment, family background and peer influence. Other determinants are beliefs, attitudes and the functionality of users' intellect in shaping, interpreting and internalizing online interaction.

The prominence of the social media as a popular channel of communication in our environment has increased dramatically over the last couple of years. This latest development is occupying the centre stage in academic discourse and public opinion. The popularity of social media and its virtual-facelessness is of particular concern for many reasons, such as moral, ethical and human rights concerns. These concerns matter due to the role of the social media in triggering sensitive or heated debate and uprisings in real life. Consequently, it could be a threat not only to individuals but to society at large. Some behavioural scientists have further observed other inherent risks associated with its use. According to Matook and Butler (2015), social media breeds "homophily" in society, as relationships have become more homogeneous. This may hinder real-life interactions and mental and emotional development, especially among the young users who tend to adopt it as a substitute for offline relationships.

In Nigeria, as in other countries, the social media has transformed communication and social relationships. The country has witnessed an exponential surge in the number of social media users in recent times. The latest estimate put the rate at nearly 33 million active users (mostly youth) as of January 2021. Among the accessible social media platforms, WhatsApp was said to be the most widespread, with more than 90 percent of social media users (Statista, 2021). Therefore, we examine the role of social media comments, depictions and reportage of sexual orientation, sex scandals, sexual rights and body image, with a view to understand the emerging themes and insights in the Nigerian context.

Youth participation in digital interaction in Nigeria is a vital sociological issue which has not received much deliberation in scientific literature. This chapter documents how social media interaction has modified the trajectories of human relationships, both online and offline. It depicts how youth participation in digital communication can determine their social exclusion or inclusion, as the case may be, depending on which social norms get violated in their attempt to participate in interactive engagements online. This is a significant addition to sociological discourse of communication on social media. The authors have introduced new ideas which are relevant to researchers of contemporary issues affecting youth in our time, especially at a time when the control of social media usage is driving debates on human rights violations and youth exclusion from digital communication in a democratic dispensation.

Methodology

This is a review based on case studies. Therefore, this chapter relies on case studies in Africa aligning with the objective of this chapter. Cases in Nigeria, as well as some related cases that attracted global attention in Ghana and South Africa, were identified through a media search. These are discussed in relation to relevant literature and existing reality. Trends and implications for social interaction online and in the larger Nigerian community were then highlighted. Topics of interest were searched for on Twitter due to the peculiarity of its algorithm, which allows for tracking old tweets and comments using the hashtag feature. Cases on each topic were selected based on the extent of the social response and attention they received or generated, both online and offline. Another criterion for inclusion was the ease of recovering the topic and its social relevance. The cases were explored to reveal how much social media usage and the new norms it has introduced into social interaction have impacted human relations in our environment. Only significant cases involving celebrities and incidents which attracted public reactions have been selected as cases for interpretative analysis.

Social Media, the Individual and Society

The media effects model provides the theoretical underpinning for this chapter. The model explains the mutual effects which the media and society have on one another. According to this model, exposure to the social media may have either direct (individual) or indirect (social) effects. Proponents of the direct media effect borrow from the idea of the hypodermic model, which states that the media is like a drug to which people can get addicted. According to Borah (2016), "moral panic" is of grave concern to these exponents.

"Moral panic" is the fear of possible negative effects of deviant behaviours such as human rights violations and cyberbullying on social media users. It is the feeling that such deviant behaviours may get out of control and become a threat to the moral order or individual well-being. How the media presents a particular social phenomenon affects human perception and behaviour. By contrast, exposure to media representation of a specific social phenomenon such as sexuality has consequences for the audience or users since it shapes their opinions, attitudes and behaviour.

It is noteworthy that media effects on the audience could be significant or minimal. The media offers impetuses that may indirectly strengthen users' predilections momentarily. It could also have substantial, aggregate and direct consequences (on behaviour) for an extended period. The model is associated with the constructivist perspective, which argues that the media do more reality construction. At the same time, users have the agency to align with the media's perspectives or other available options based on the shared cultural experience (Borah, 2016).

Protagonists of the indirect media effect believe that, rather than having direct effects on individual users, the social media, along with the users' environments, needs or desires, prejudiced philosophies about society and the media, shared reality construction and real-life experiences have combined effects on the community and its members. They believe that users' consumption and interaction with specific social media contents are based on their agency, because no user interacts with media messages or contents with "a blank mind." Human beings possess "cognitive structures" or "schemata" used for actively interpreting the world around them. Hence, the influence of the social environment on how users interact with the media is unavoidable. Also, the media is constantly contending with other forms of communicative stimuli, such as interpersonal communication with family, peers and school (Borah, 2016). Fig. 9.1 shows the interconnectedness of social media and society and the individuals at the receiving end.

Emerging Themes and Insights

Socialization and Sexual and Human Rights Issues

Social media functions are multidimensional. As Zilli and his colleague rightly noted, the social media serves as a platform for "the exercise and expression of sexuality, exchange of sexual knowledge, which includes information on sexual rights and sexual health, as well as issues of sexual expression ..." (Zilli and Sívori, 2013). Since it became popular, social media has been providing easy access to unvetted information about sexual rights and human rights in general. It likewise promotes freedom of expression, including sexual expression, through the empowerment it offers, particularly to those whose voices may otherwise not be heard in society. The social media ecosystem provides complete freedom of expression to young adults and adolescents, without the parental restrictions and controls obtainable in the offline world. Social media users have the opportunity of limiting interference from significant others because the social media allows users to stage-manage their audience or network or to select folks they are comfortable sharing their media contents with. In addition, there is the possibility of

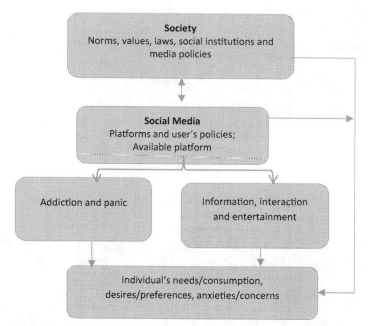

Fig. 9.1.   Media Effects Model. *Source*: Developed by the authors.

changing online identity and remaining anonymous, if desired, thereby ensuring the users' rights to privacy.

Notwithstanding, human rights infringements such as hackers' intrusion on some users' privacy, which generates moral panic in the online social milieu, are widespread. A recent example is the release of a Nigerian business mogul's partially unclad picture by his estranged girlfriend, which spawned public outrage. Although the current law against revenge porn in Nigeria has not been effective as many cases go unreported, lessons from other countries suggest that laws against such a crime may be inadequate in preventing prospective offenders from perpetrating the same (Arimoro, 2015). There is also the controversy around the right to report certain social media accounts perceived as threatening to others. Similarly, the "screen grab" features on most smartphones, along with the ubiquity of new face-swap applications, hint that personal information shared on social media may not remain private for too long. As it stands, strangers can easily access personal information online and manipulate it for selfish gain. Fig. 9.2 depicts the emerging themes on social media and youth sexuality in our environment. Discourse on body image, intimacy on social media and offline intimacy, the sexual infodemic and other topics are obstinately controversial.

As Schaefer (2008) rightly observed, the social media has become a significant source of information and ideas about sex as its influence is far stronger than that of parents, peers and the school combined. It is gradually eroding the African style of parenting or socialization, which is highly conservative and characterized

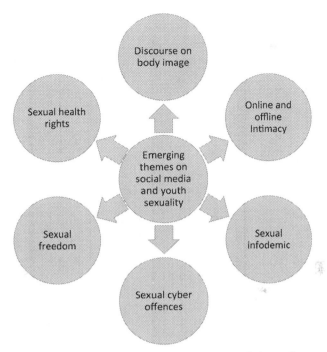

Fig. 9.2.   Emerging Themes on Social Media and Youth Sexuality.
Source: Developed by the authors.

by leaving adolescents and young adults to figure sexuality out independently. Parent–child conversations are traditionally restricted to few topics, while sexually related subjects were forbidden, until lately. Globally, teaching, learning and discussions centred on sexuality and sexual-rights issues have been transformed by social media interactions. Hence, the emerging patterns of sexual socialization of adolescents and young adults, especially through unhindered exposure to porn videos, racy images, sexist comments and other immoralities that accessibility to social media offers, despite the censorship. Many young social media users share erotic images, sexist comments and details about their personal sexual life on social media with flagrant disregard for consequences. The psychological development of adolescents and young adults is particularly threatened, since they are more attached to the social media, thus seemingly tying their self-esteem to social media validation. The psychological pressure on adolescents and young adults is generally higher, as their mental capabilities are still developing. Moreover, their emotional intelligence and life skills are still fragile and may be easily swayed by the social media pressure. Additionally, not all users are media literate enough to discern helpful and harmful information or contents.

Among Africans, sexuality and sexual-rights issues have been creeping into the public domain due to social media accessibility. Social media provides some kind of sanctuary for exploring sexual experiences that are otherwise forbidden from the daily reality of clients' offline interactions. Moreover, certain public matters that are prohibited, circumscribed or regulated offline are freely conversed about online (Zilli and Sívori, 2013). In many cultures, sexuality is a sensitive issue with widespread myths, preconceptions and beliefs associated with the subject. It has remained a personal and controversial topic even on social media (Schaefer, 2008), where it often causes a massive wave of reactions. Despite being personal, sharing sexual content and erotic images regularly takes centre stage in online interactions, thus raising concerns about the ubiquity of perverse individuals who may be lurking around to prey on the weak or vulnerable (women, children and youths) (Zilli and Sívori, 2013).

Influence of Social Media on Sexual Orientation

Many young people depend on the Internet and social media to learn about biological changes in their bodies at puberty when they get more curious about their sexuality and physical appearance. The likelihood of striving for independence at this stage, which ushers them into adulthood, is high. They tend to seek knowledge independently, since the trope that sex-related topics are discussed in a hush tone is rooted in Africanism. Therefore, social media affords them ample opportunity to learn about the shared norms, values and other rules that dictate the forms of sexuality that are seemingly supported or repressed by society. Sexuality is anything that has sexual reference and is linked to gender roles (Van Oosten, 2021), including sexual orientation. Free expression of sexual orientation on social media justifies the moral panic expressed by concerned scholars. Moral panic is described as concerns associated with excessive explicit depiction of homosexuality, male and female sexuality, sexism and levels of intimacy shared on social media, including other sensitive topics such as the sexual lessons that parents shy away from (Haralambos, Holborn and Heald, 2004).

The functions which social media fulfils for each user are different. For some, it is for learning, while for others, it is for expressing sexuality and sexual identity. People such as Idris Okuneye, also known as Bobrisky, who was shot into the limelight through social media, was able to express her sexuality with minimal social sanctions. She and other cross-dressers also try hard to fit into culturally acceptable body standards by constantly attempting to prove their sexuality and show off their newly feminine appearance. Even though homosexuality remains outlawed in Nigeria, Bobrisky's escapades as a cross-dresser and her recent claims of having undergone gender affirmation surgery as well as having sexual relationship with other men have seemingly rubbed off directly on others in the sexual minority category, who have become emboldened and encouraged to reveal their sexual orientation. This they have done with little or no sanction on the social media, which has provided them with freedom and controversial fame. Compared to the offline life, there is some form of acceptability of cross-dressers on social media, considering the number of their followers and the amount of attention they receive from bloggers and some other online news platforms. Nevertheless, the expression of sexual orientation in the media ecosystem is not without consequences. Bobrisky and people like her who do not fit into a conventional sexual category or stereotype are often cyberbullied and stigmatized online.

Depiction of Body Image on Social Media

A postmodernist, Jean Baudrillard, underscored the difficulty of separating media images from reality since media images have become part of our new social experience (Haralambos, Holborn and Heald, 2004). As Haralambos, Holborn and Heald (2004) rightly observed, since the invention of television, the media has been portraying the ideal male and female body features, separately, using models from each gender as standards. There is a high proliferation of these images in magazines, on television and billboards, and lately on social media.

It is to be expected that behaviours and content that promote self-objectification, or adopting and valuing a third-person perspective of self, are common on social media (Salomon and Brown, 2018). The intensity of the exposure to such behaviours and contents has prompted the internalization of culturally acceptable body standards by the audience (Salomon and Brown, 2018). Hence, the portrayal of specific images believed to be culturally acceptable on social media is now common among users. This explains why embracing a "positive body image" by young users has become synonymous with and interpreted as posting sexually suggestive images, selfies and videos online. However, this stands at variance with the African culture of modesty, which is considered more graceful, especially for women.

The internalization of culturally acceptable physical features for both genders has provoked a surge in bullying and body-shaming of persons perceived as having un-ideal body features. This primarily affects women, although men may also be targets of body-shaming. Women are often bullied for having certain un-ideal body features such as stretch marks, saggy breasts and big tummies and for their complexion, weight and height. On the other hand, men are sometimes bullied for their lack of muscle, short stature and so on. For instance, the famous singers, Teni and Wande Coal, were once body-shamed on a podcast by some people who considered their body weights as un-ideal and not befitting pop artists.

It is worth noting that the supposed ideal physical appearance equally magnetizes sexualization from the public, making the social media more sexist and misogynistic. The case of another famous Nigerian singer, Tems, comes to mind, given the numerous sexist comments she received from male followers, bloggers and commenters who sexualized her body after she posted her pictures. Similarly, to attract traffic and increase audience engagement for likes and shares on their platforms, social media influencers and celebrities sometimes place sexist, erotic and other sex-related topics and images at the heart of their media content. Some other reasons for sharing sexualized messages include the need for self-validation, to increase followership, get feedback or comments and attract attention. Some, however, do so to create an identity or promote their person or brand and for self-documentation (Van Oosten, 2021).

Sexualization refers to a situation where

> a person's value comes only from his or her sexual appeal or behaviour, to the exclusion of other characteristics; a person is held to a standard that equates physical attractiveness (narrowly defined) with being sexy. (Schick, 2014)

The sexualization of a woman's body and the internalization of the ideal body image may have contributed to a surge in cosmetic surgery, which has become the norm among celebrities in the developed world. Some Nigerian female celebrities such as Tonto Dike have equally embraced the trend. This affirms Solomon and Brown's idea that some people engage in high self-monitoring; that is, they are more sensitive to social cues and more willing to change their behaviour based on their interpretation of such cases. By comparison, some individuals value a third-person perspective on their person or looks. Since modern body standards (for example, thinness and a curvy shape for girls and muscularity for boys) are impossible for most people to achieve naturally, they attract body-shaming online. Hence, some resort to cosmetic surgery to enhance their body shape (Salomon and Brown, 2018).

The sexualization and objectification of a woman's body explicates why many unsuspecting men still fall victim to Internet fraudsters who use sexy images of women as bait to attract unsuspecting victims through dating websites. Public reaction to body image on social media differs from one platform and user to another. Women who dress in a certain way may be judged either positively or negatively by the audience. A picture may receive positive feedback or get bullied or slut-shamed on the same or different social media platform as each has its norms and rules of engagement.

Counter-Messaging

The extent to which young girls can resist, build resilience to and critique the "stereotypical messages or sexualised media content" through the same medium is contentious (Van Oosten, 2021). In most climes, the rate of sexualization resistance by women is somewhat low. The Feminists Coalition of Nigeria have, however, been condemning sexist comments, sexualized content, misogynous comments, objectification of women and stereotypical messages online, and this is equally gaining offline support. They have been countering content – skits – centred on rape or promoting rape culture and those that objectify women. However, the coalition and other Nigerian female social media users are often challenged by their male counterparts for an inconsistent and duplicitous stance. The female users are often blamed for their bias and critique of males who share such content. By contrast, women who share such erotic images or sexualized messages are regarded as being body positive or confident. A notable instance is the #shedibalabalachallenge, which involved dancing to music that used slurs and derogatory words about women's body parts. Scores of women took up this challenge without condemning the lyrics. Hence, many find it challenging to balance being body positive and objectifying or sexualizing women. This has engendered controversies about who between the two genders has the right to use sexually explicit words or sexualized images.

The Interface of Online and Offline Interaction

Real-world social norms and rules define normal and abnormal social behaviours. They also dictate online social regulations (Zilli and Sívori, 2013). This is why

Nigeria, like other countries, officially passed its Cybercrimes Act of Nigeria into law in 2015 to address cases of extortion, blackmail and revenge pornography or image-based sexual violence in every guise (Aborisade, 2021). Given the complexity of human relationships, the social media footprint has real-life consequences because the "liberty" of online expression has bounds. There are instances where some people have been sanctioned. This is worth commenting on here as we are not free of judgement and who we portray ourselves to be online may affect our lives offline. For instance, a landlady denied a potential tenant access to her apartment after finding out about her sexual orientation and identity online.

Similarly, an actress, Tonto Dike, received a backlash for her choice of dress and body tattoo when she announced her ambassadorship with Nigeria's Christian Pilgrimage Board. Subsequently, many social media handles trended a hashtag online to protest against her purported appointment by the Board for her "indecent dressing" and "unchristian like" appearance. The board later refuted Tonto's claim as its ambassador.

Also in Ghana, actress Akuapem Poloo, was jailed for 90 days for posing nude with her son during a photo session posted on her Instagram page. A Nigerian family corporally punished a young lady for sharing her nude image on social media; the punishment was recorded and shared online to shame her. These prove that behaviours divergent from traditional, offline-approved behaviours may attract rewards (likes, shares) or sanctions (bullying, negative comments, assault) both offline and online. The similarity of social responses to these events shows that people tend to have a moral opinion about private affairs and others' sexuality and rights.

The intersection of offline and online interaction may also have negative consequences for mental well-being. Sadly, people have been using social media to document their struggles with depression by writing suicide notes or suicidal intentions online. Some may have learned about suicide or copy suicide acts from social media. For instance, Sniper® is a notorious suicidal substance in Nigeria as it is what many victims reportedly used to take their own lives. A Unified Tertiary Matriculation Examination (UTME) candidate recently live-streamed his suicide on Twitter due to poor performance. Live streaming suicide is not common in Nigeria; perhaps he learned the act through exposure to foreign social media handles.

Reportage of Rape and Other Sex Scandals

Digital communication has changed patterns of self-expression, considering the rate at which victims of rape and other forms of sexual harassment have been coming forward to share their stories in recent years. The considerable increase in transnational feminism, which encouraged sex-scandal reportage, is unprecedented before the communication revolution occasioned by the social media and the Internet. The social media is instrumental to such laudable activism as the #MeToo campaign, which received international recognition and generated reactions against online and offline sexual abuse. In Nigeria, the campaign influenced women from the northern region, where women are culturally forbidden from speaking up in public. These women started the #ArewaMeToo campaign to share their experiences of sexual abuse and create awareness about the rape culture in the country. Sharing these sensitive stories on the Internet empowered them to own their narratives and get the needed emotional support. Unfortunately, some ladies have misused the medium to make false allegations against targeted persons. The rate of false rape allegations has since increased on social media due to the popularity and influence of the social media court of law. This became a trend without regard for the accused's feelings and possible negative emotional consequences. Some false rape accusations on social media include that of a famous young doctor, Olufunmilayo Ogunsanya, falsely accused of rape in London by a female friend. Another example which resulted in a campaign tagged #JusticeforIzu trended online after the late fashion designer, Legend Izu Madubueze, committed suicide in response to a wrongful accusation of sexual abuse by a lady, Nachini Anese.

Impacts of Social Media on Health

In spite of the many benefits of the social media, cases of poor adjustment to communication and social interaction within the cyberspace are ubiquitous. Some cyberbully cases highlight a significant failing in social media control and the unintended consequences of its usage. One of the common indications of social media impacts on life is mental well-being. Many research findings have revealed a significant relationship between cyberbullying and emotional complications such as depression, anxiety, severe isolation and poor self-esteem among persons who experience bullying (Cookingham and Ryan, 2015). Many cyberbullies engage in a guise to look petty or funny to others, not minding the pain their slurs may cause others. Cyberbullies usually target people who share a different opinion about a topic. Sometimes, they ridicule others' sexual orientation and physical appearance and body-shame some for not conforming to modern standards of beauty.

Another emerging trend is the issue of "fandom," which involves celebrities having an army of followers who bully others or pass insensitive remarks about them at every opportunity. In such exchanges, some "fans" and celebrities have been found to encourage suicide. Sometimes, they wish serious harm on others by asking them to "kill yourself." Online abuse has become a regular daily occurrence in the Nigerian social media space, where it is easy to disrespect others through minor sanctions. Since there is no teaching on how to deal with the emotions, an individual's ability to cope with negativity in the social media milieu is dependent on some social and individual factors. Some may find it challenging to get over an abuse, while others may remain unfazed, despite numerous condemnations or bullying and derogatory comments. A prominent example of the latter is Florence Otedola (DJ Cuppy), a DJ and music artist who regularly gets bullied for her dressing and musical talent.

Cyberbullying and other online vices are dangerous to health because an emotionally distraught person could be triggered into depression or even suicide. An example is Ubi Franklin, a music record label owner, who once said in an interview that he had contemplated suicide some years back due to cyberbullying. This indicates that cyberbullying could have long-term emotional effects on victims. This may have contributed to the suicide rate in Nigeria, which is believed to be the highest in Africa and the sixth highest in the global community (Akinremi, 2019). Although numerous authors have expressed grave concerns about cyberbullying, other social media-induced vices, such as the hyper-sexualization of women, may also have health implications, especially among young users. The internalization of women's sexualization has been linked to depression, self-objectification and a fall in self-esteem and body satisfaction (Van Oosten, 2021). Online sexual victimization, such as revenge pornography, also has adverse psychological effects on victims and their loved ones. This has been attributed to the general attitude towards gender and sexuality that has normalized such behaviour. Other contributory factors are victim-blaming, sexual objectification, slut-shaming, trivializing rape and the culture of silence (Aborisade, 2021).

Conclusion

This chapter examined themes and issues emerging from the use of social media for sexuality and human rights-related interactions. Cases discussed prove that a safe and responsible use of social media is crucial for a healthy online and offline social interaction and well-being. Since it is relatively easy to get into the trap of online behaviour, protecting private information is also crucial as online and offline actions have consequences. Although social media provides access to free expression, navigating the free world of the Internet may not be without implications in offline reality, as individuals and society are both at the receiving end if this technology is not put to a reasonable use. All users have the agency to discern appropriate and inappropriate online behaviour and make informed decisions. The social media and the Internet represent a safe hiding place for the good, the bad and the ugly that lurk behind the screen to attack victims and perpetrate an agenda.

The safety of social media, therefore, lies in the acknowledgement of digital rights as human rights. Through this, social media can be an indispensable tool for youth inclusion. In essence, social media can be used to either tackle social exclusion or be a threat to social inclusion. Given its global interconnectivity, social media primarily serves as a platform for social inclusion by bringing people of different beliefs and cultures together. Participation in social media interaction has provided access to educational resources and employment opportunities for many youths around the world. This has helped them to achieve economic independence. As shown in this chapter, social media promotes awareness of human rights and it has likewise granted adolescents and young adults' access to sexuality education which empowers them for decision-making, especially on issues relating to their rights and well-being, thereby promoting their social inclusion.

By contrast, due to their socio-economic exclusion from the larger society, some youths are experiencing digital exclusion as they still do not own a smartphone or have a social media profile required for their inclusion in social media interaction. Even in the face of digital inclusion, participation in social media interaction can work against youth's survival within the institutional frameworks and traditional norms which may be at odds with the global standards. Being the largest creators and consumers of social media content, some users in Africa are currently encountering a certain level of exclusion from social, political and economic opportunities owing to their previous activities online which contradict predominant norms, values and practices in their communities.

Just as it can serve as an emotional outlet for people with mental illness and disability who often experience discrimination in society, social media can equally trigger or worsen mental illness as it is filled with offensive posts, slurs, abuses, harmful remarks, targeted harassment and digital punishment. The internalization of acceptable body image on social media has further excluded some youth from digital interaction. The failure of some users to attain the expectations set by social media has resulted in feelings of isolation and worsening of mental health conditions. At the same time, social media has enhanced social inclusion of many who believe they fit into the expected norms. Female social media users are significantly more disadvantaged and often predisposed to the emergent ills from social media misuse which can lead to their social exclusion. This is due to the inequities in African traditional norms which are supposedly meant to promote gender-appropriate roles and behaviour, but which, in fact, encourage subjugating women and mansplaining.

Although the female users are not in any way free from unconscionable acts in the social media space, African philosophy about gender-appropriate behaviour is still complicit as it kindles the culture of silence among women, which the social media also seemingly approves to some extent. As it stands, men dominate online sex-related interaction because certain elements in our philosophy promote male dominance in sexual discourse. This chapter thus acknowledges the fact that the social media has and is still changing the status quo with respect to sexuality, parenting, social relationships and social inclusion in an African context. Social media is a medium for learning and unlearning behaviours and subculture; validation-seeking online is a major influence that social media currently has on its users. This is the new norm, which has become ingrained in the consciousness of adolescents and young adults in our environment. Nevertheless, social media interaction can be safe for youth social inclusion if users are mindful of their actions and inactions and their possible consequences.

References

Aborisade, R. A. 2021. Image-based sexual abuse in a culturally conservative Nigerian society: female victims' narratives of psychosocial costs, *Sexuality Research and Social Policy, 19*, 220–232. doi: 10.1007/s13178-021-00536-3.
Akinremi, R. 2019. Nigeria has highest suicide rate in Africa, Sixth globally | international centre for investigative reporting. Available at: https://www.icirnigeria.org/nigeria-has-highest-suicide-rate-in-africa-sixth-globally/ [Accessed 23 June 2021].
Arimoro, A. E. 2015. Applying the law to tackle the menace of revenge porn in Nigeria: Lessons from the United Kingdom, *Law and Social Media, 20*(10), 75–80.

Borah, P. 2016. Media effects theory. In *The International Encyclopedia of Political Communication*, Ed. G. Mazzoleni, 1st ed., pp. 1–12. Atlanta, GA, American Cancer Society.

Cookingham, L. M. and Ryan, G. L. 2015. The impact of social media on the sexual and social wellness of adolescents, *Journal of Pediatric and Adolescent Gynecology*, *28*(1), 2–5. doi: 10.1016/j.jpag.2014.03.001

Davis, S. E. 2018. Objectification, sexualization, and misrepresentation: social media and the college experience, *Social Media + Society*, 4. doi: 10.1177/2056305118786727

Edosomwan, S., Prakasan, S. K., Kouame, D., Watson, J. and Seymour, T. 2011. The history of social media and its impact on business, *The Journal of Applied Management and Entrepreneurship*, *16*(3), 13.

Haralambos, M., Holborn, M. and Heald, R. 2004. *Sociology: Themes and Perspectives*, Ed J. Messenger, 6th ed., London, HarperCollins Publishers Limited.

Hilker, L. M. and Fraser, E. 2009. Youth exclusion, violence, conflict and fragile states. Report prepared for DFID's equity and rights team, *Social Development Direct*, 50.

Matook, S. and Butler B. S. 2015. Social media and relationships. In *The International Encyclopedia of Digital Communication and Society*, Eds P. H. Ang and R. Mansell, 1st ed., pp. 1–12. New York, NY, Willey.

Salomon, I. and Brown, C. S. 2018. The selfie generation: examining the relationship between social media use and early adolescent body image. *The Journal of Early Adolescence*, *39*(4), 539–560. doi: 10.1177/0272431618770809

Schaefer, R. T. 2008. *Sociology*, 11th ed., New York, NY, McGraw-Hill.

Schick, L. 2014. Hit me baby: from Britney Spears to the socialization of sexual objectification of girls in a middle school drama program, *Sexuality & Culture*, *18*, 39–55. doi: https://doi.org/10.1007/s12119-013-9172-7.

Statista. 2021. Nigeria: active social media users 2021. Statista. Available at: https://www.statista.com/statistics/1176096/number-of-social-media-users-nigeria/ [Accessed 25 May 2021].

Van Oosten, J. M. F. 2021. Adolescent girls' use of social media for challenging sexualization, *Gender, Technology and Development*, *25*(1), 22–42. doi: 10.1080/09718524.2021.1880039

Zilli, B. and Sivori, H. 2013. Sexuality and the Internet. In *Global Information Society Watch 2013: Women's Rights, Gender and ICTs*, Ed. A. Finlay, Hague, APC and Hivos.

Chapter Ten

Youth Exclusion and Empowerment in China and the United States of America

Ọláyínká Àkànle and Damola Toyosi Olaniyi

Introduction

This chapter engages youth exclusion and inclusion in the circumstances of China and the United States. The importance of youths as veritable tools for the development of nations cannot be overemphasized. It is suicidal for any society to neglect its youths in the scheme of things, and in its quest for developmental goals which consist of social, economic, health and political developments. The youths are the bedrock and the foundation on which every nation builds upon in its pursuit of development and improved standards of living. The basis for positive or negative images of society rests largely on the youth as the backbone and the building block of society. Their creativities, energies, resourcefulness and dispositions define the rates at which nations are developed. Whatever noticeable strides that any nation might have recorded over time, economically, socially and/or politically, cannot be excluded from the efforts of the youths (*The Nation Newspaper*, 2017). Hence, they play essential roles and serve as important tools for national development. Interestingly, the evolution of any society from one generation to another is crucial to its formative and developmental aspiration. A society that prepares its youths for the sake of future aspiration will not only secure its future but equip its next set of leaders with the abilities to meet future challenges of national development ((Idike and Eme, 2015). If youths are excluded or included in the issues that are germane to the fabric of the society, such society will either experience underdevelopment and disaster or experience development, peace and progress.

There are several countries in the world where youths are confronted with a plethora of barriers that hinder them from fully taking part in the nations' social, economic and political life. This marginalization, discrimination of a sort, may hinge on the legal system, customs or cultural structure of the societies, thereby preventing the youths from thriving. No matter how highly rated a nation may

Youth Exclusion and Empowerment in the Contemporary Global Order:
Existentialities in Migrations, Identity and the Digital Space, 147–157
Copyright © 2022 by Ọláyínká Àkànle and Damola Toyosi Olaniyi
Published under exclusive licence by Emerald Publishing Limited
doi:10.1108/978-1-80382-777-320221011

be among the comity of nations, there is a possibility that such a nation may not practise total youth inclusiveness which fully entrenches the young ones in the fabrics of the society or into its developmental processes. Development and youth involvement are like a conjoined twin that is difficult to separate; they each contribute to the growth of the other. If one is separated from the other, the survival rates for a better tomorrow of a country become difficult and sometimes unattainable. It is to this end that this chapter will discuss, among other things, the implications of exclusion and empowerment for sustainable development and global youth competitiveness, youth exclusion and empowerment in politics, education, economy, health and so on in China and the United States.

Youth Population Discourse: Focus on China and the United States

China is located in the eastern part of the Asian continent and is presently the most populous nation in the world. According to the global population statistics from the United Nations (UN) in 2019, China has a population of 1.43 billion inhabitants, which amounts to 19% of the world population; these figures excluded Hong Kong and Macau's population (UN, 2019). In 2021, the National Bureau of Statistics in China published the total population and put it at 1.41 billion (National Bureau of Statistics of China, 2021). This shows a decline in the population of China. The United States, on the other hand, is the third most populous nation in the world, with a population of 329 million inhabitants (UN, 2019) and located in the North American continent. China has a population growth of 0.57% (National Bureau of Statistics of China, 2021). and 149.8 people per square metre, while the United States has 0.58% population growth rate and 94 people per square metre (United States Population, 2021). The population of China is expected to further reduce over the years due to the fertility rate in China, which is limited to one childbirth per lifetime (Statista, 2021).

There are different perspectives on the age of youths all over the world. Specifically, various nations and fields of study define the age of young people differently. Some group the youth age bracket as those from 10 to 24 years of age, some 15–29 years of age, while some regard 15–35 years of age as a youth. Likewise, some reports group adolescents and youth together under the same age bracket, some only tagged some age brackets as youth with specific age limits. Some even consider youth to be from 40 years of age down to 15 years. Hence, there is no generally acceptable age group for the youths. However, since there is no generally accepted standard for youth age grouping, in this context, this chapter will relate to and possibly make use of all of the age groups stated above in its discussion.

The number of young people around the world who were between the ages of 10 and 24 years, according to the United Nations Population Funds (UNFPA), in 2014 was 1.8 billion (Gupta et al., 2014). In another report published by the World Future Council in 2019, Samia and Ingrid explain that the world youth population was estimated to be 1.8 billion between the ages of 15 and 35 years. This is one quarter of the world population which is the largest world youth population that has ever been recorded in history (Samia and Ingrid, 2019). It was important to note that some of the people within this demographic status are still grappling with needs that are specific to their youthfulness and with several challenges hindering their aspirations for the desired future. India has the highest youth population globally, according to the UNFPA report (2014). Without a doubt, apart from India, China and the United States have a large youth population, possibly more than any other country in the world, as both are in the category of the most populous nations in the world. The National Bureau of Statistics of China, in its 2021 census report, put the population of people between the ages of 15 and 59 years at 894.38 million billion (Gupta et al., 2014). This does not specifically address the youth population in China. However, the 2014 UNFPA report, as further reiterated by Gupta et al., puts the population of youths in China and the United States at 269 million and 65 million, respectively.

China has a small youth population relative to its general population. This may be because of the one-child policy which was introduced in the country in 1979. In another report on China's youth population, JieyingXi and Yan Xia and China's National Bureau of Statistics report on the fifth census in China in the year 2000, which put the total figure of youth (between the ages of 15 and 29) in mainland China at 315 million, which is around 26% of the total population (Xi and Xia, 2006). Again, in another report on the United States youth population, the statistic reveals that the number of young people between the ages of 14 and 24 was around 47 million from 2000 until 2010 (Statista, 2019). With all these population figures in these countries, how fair are these nations to their youth population? To what extent are these youths involved in or excluded from politics, education, economy and health care, to mention just a few in China and the United States? How empowered are the youths of China and the United States? It is against this backdrop that the chapter analyses inclusion and exclusion or empowerment of youths in China and the United States. What are the implication of exclusion and empowerment for sustainable development and global youth competitiveness of the two countries?

Youth Exclusion/Empowerment in China and the United States of America

Social exclusion as a concept originated in France in the 1960s and was broadly used in the European nations and is now incorporated into the European Union's official lexicon (Parent and Lewis, 2003). It was first coined by Red Lenior in the 1970s and later became a widely used concept in discussing marginalization, discrimination, inequalities and inadequate access to social amenities for individuals or groups excluded from the social fabrics of the society they belong to, irrespective of their socio-economic background (Ogundairo and Ijimakinwa, 2020; Silver, 2019). Parent and Lewis (2003) defined social exclusion as the process and consequential conditions where entities are fully or partially denied acquisition of basic needs of life. They further explained that social exclusion is a product of a social system. It has multiple dimensions and is dynamic in time and space. In the context of our discussion, youth exclusion and empowerment are like opposite words used to explain the discrimination against or inclusion of young people in the fabrics of their society. Conversely, a socially inclusive society, as posited by Northway (1997), is a society that allows diversities and creates opportunities for people to belong and express themselves. Such societies create platforms and opportunities for self-fulfillment and actualisations.

Youth inclusiveness into the fabric of the society of any country is a demographic dividend. Any nation with a large youth population will experience exponential growth provided they make use of it to their advantage, protect the youths' rights and invest in youths' education and their general well-being. Youths are catalysts of change because they possess huge prospects to revolutionize the future, and several countries of the world are better for it. The former executive director of UNFPA, Dr Babatunde Osotimehin, pointed out that young people possess powers of innovation and creativity and power to build and lead and to transform the future (Osotimehin, 2014). The caveat, according to Osotimehin, is that if in life, youth have skills, health, decision-making ability and ability to make real choices, transformation of the future will then be inevitable for any country that makes these available for them. Society's involvement in the life of young people will help them be what the future hold for them. It is costly not to invest or to under-invest in the future of young people. It was reported that 9 in 10 young people in the world reside in developing countries (Osotimehin, 2014) where, practically, their future is uncertain and possibly without any hope for a better tomorrow. From such nations, young people migrate *en mass* to the developed nations where they believe there is a better tomorrow for them, and the developed nation will reap the benefits of these cohorts in the future at the expense of their home countries. Because of the developing state of the developing countries, they cannot often make provisions for social services and thereby fail to harness the benefits of engaging this youthful dynamic workforce.

In the 1950s and 1960s, several East Asian countries, which consist of China, Hong Kong, Japan, North and South Korea, Mongolia, Taiwan and Macaus, made it a duty to invest in young people (Osotimehin, 2014). This transformed the economy of these nations and gave them extraordinary growth economically. This unprecedented growth in the economy culminated in what they are enjoying till today. We can make bold to say that youth inclusiveness in the years past in this region where China belongs also helps China to be one of the superpower nations of the world, as they are perceived today. The growth of China in the 1950s was strategic and youth took a considerable part in it. Historically and throughout the world, youth have been a driving force behind social change and also ignited social movements. The actualization of independence by several colonized nations was made possible through the efforts of the young people's brilliant minds and doggedness to liberate their countries from colonial dominations. Several leaders at the forefront of the liberation struggle were little more than 30 and 40 years of age.

However, today, youths hardly participate in politics. They are excluded from political participation. Martin Chungong, the Secretary-General of the Inter-Parliamentary Union (IPU) in Samia and Ingrid (2019) states that the youth population of those below 30 years of age is half of the world's population and out of it, only 2% are members of parliament (MPs) (Samia and Ingrid, 2019).

Without the action of the youth, the world would have been dull and unattractive. Young people have always been said to be the leaders of tomorrow, but how included are they in the political arena? Excluding them from political leadership negates that truism. Institutions, either political or economic, that continue to marginalize the youth from engaging with the public or civic duties, is not only killing the tomorrow of that nation but drawing such nation back to the precipice of underdevelopment. Youth involvement in public life impacts greatly on the political, cultural and economic states of nations. There is a positive synergy from young people's participation in political processes in the country at national, regional and local levels.

The United States, over the years, has been the superpower nation and the world pacesetter. Now, China is becoming one of the superpower nations, if not the most dreadful one with its speed of development competing strongly with the likes of the United States. Wherever China steps her foot, the United States wants to know what is going on there, be it health, technology, politics, education, economy, trades or what have you. These two nations have been at each other's throats several times and recently, over one policy or the other, or to move one ahead of the other. When Covid-19 broke out in Wuhan, China, China received series of knocks from the United States. The most developed nations of the world doubled their efforts to be the first to produce Covid-19 vaccines ahead of China. It would be right to say that the name of countries gets on the world map as nations of great power, substance and influence because the young population in these countries, in the past, were empowered, included and taken care of. Today, they are the ones to keep pushing the countries to their greater heights. To what extent today are youths of China and the United States marginalized or empowered or have a "right to belong" – in the words of Ruth Northway – in governance, economy, education, family, health, religion and other fabrics of their countries? And to what extent are the youths' involvements in politics in these societies?

It is a fact that the United States is one of the developed nations of the world; in fact, the president of the United States is like the president of the world. Meanwhile, China, with its recent development, is still not yet classified as a developed nation but the society is becoming well-off in all forms of development. The income balance is the major yardstick for measuring how developed a nation is according to the World Bank and the UN. China is the largest developing nation in the world (World Bank, 2017). In the United States, 273.98 million people (that is, 82.8% of the population) live in urban areas out of 333.84 million people (United States Population, 2021). This suggests that fewer than 50 million people are in the rural areas (that is, one seventh of the population). Therefore, one seventh of the youth population of 64 million in the United States, which is about 9 million, are in rural areas. Out of the 1.4 billion people in China, about 902 million people are living in urban areas, while 510 million live in rural areas (Statista, 2018).

In other words, rural areas in China contain one third of its entire population. This can also be interpreted that one third of the youth population in China, which is about 100 million youths out of 315 million, are in the rural areas – which are perhaps places where social amenities are not quite feasible and where the youths are excluded from social realities and from making meaningful contributions to the development of the nation. Youth exclusion by virtue of location may not be unique to China; the United States does have its share, but the fact remains that there are youths in both countries facing difficulties in participating fully in their society, possibly because of lack of or inadequate resources and enabling environments to thrive. Nevertheless, concerning the breakdown in China, the level which the United States has reached in terms of development is glaring for all to see, and one will want to agree that it will be easy for the United States to empower its young ones both in the urban and the rural areas.

It was said that education is the bedrock of development in any society almost immediately after the formation of the People's Republic of China on 1 October 1949 by the then communist leader, Mao Zedong. The government of China took education and also the quality of life of the Chinese as a major priority. Hence, the literacy rate improved and the quality of life in China also improved from that period till now. The number of students enrolled in various schools increased greatly, with the help of the educational policies. At the heels of this reformation, and going forward, compulsory elementary education was instituted across the country with about 91% compliance, and about 99% of children of school age were enrolled. The rate of illiteracy and dropout rates among the youths declined considerably to less than 7% (Asianinfo.org, 2021; Yeoh and Chu, 2012; Zhou and Yang, 2016). Education for the young people and employment for them will help to harness growth opportunities in terms of the economy. This, we think, was the point in the minds of the leaders of China when the country became a republic. On the other hand, one of the foremost presidents of the United States – JF Kennedy – made a statement concerning education for the American youth, according to William Lawrence Breese in 1986, that: "Civilization, it was once said, is a race between education and catastrophe'-and we mean to win the race for education" (Longview Foundation, 2021). The United States seeks to empower youths who will be equipped to understand the global perspective on issues that relate to political, social and environmental spheres, both nationally and globally. This is done through the support given to the teachers and academic facilitators, in initiatives engineered by the state in coalition with the stakeholders to initiate innovative programmes on youth education.

Globalization and technology in contemporary times have linked people with diverse cultural backgrounds and geographical locations together for common good. However, currently, there is a massive disconnect among the majority of the youths in China. Normal social interaction and other vital ingredients of development are not as important to them as being indoor and online all day. A lot of Chinese youths dedicate almost all their time on a daily basis to social media, computers and Internet-related events (Serpentza, 2019). It is perceived that the willingness of the youths' to be included in some aspect of society has gone down. Family income disparities are one of the factors affecting student enrolments in schools in the United States, especially those moving from high schools to colleges. A large percentage of the high school graduates who came from wealthy families enrolled in colleges immediately after graduation as against those from low-income homes (Serpentza, 2019). This inequality in attaining education at the right time may, in some instances, derail the youth in this category and thereby lead them to engage in any other available endeavours that appeal to them, irrespective of whether it is legitimate or not.

As noted earlier, China has a small youth population relative to its general population. This may be because of the one-child birth policy in the country. Currently, there is a reduction in the birth rate, especially among the youths in China, owing to economic reasons as compared to what is obtainable in the United States. The economy and the childbirth policies in the United States seem to be quite suitable for the young population to have children – at least, policy on childbirth in the states supports the family. Any child born in the states has some privileges. That is why we see several people across the world, mostly from developing countries, crossing over to the United States to give birth to their babies. There is the privilege of the babies becoming American citizens, which will also allow the parents to stay in the United States, and come along with several other advantages. However, generally, the young Chinese believe that people lose more than they gain by bearing children. The current crop of youths in China, the "Generation Z" or "millennials" as they are occasionally referred to, believe that childbirth imposes more financial burdens on them because the economic policy of the country does not encourage them to do so. This has contributed to low fertility rates in China and also a population reduction. For some of the youths, raising kids in the urban areas of China and having a good life at the same time is somehow difficult and unaffordable (*South China Morning Post*, 12 May 2021). The attitude of Chinese youth towards childbirth and marriage has changed. In the past, in the 1950s and the 1960s, people give birth to as many children as they wanted, sometimes more than four children per family. Later, China's policy pegged childbirth to one child per family. Now, in 2016, that has been reviewed to allow two children per family. Yet youths are not so interested in having kids, mainly because of the economic demands of raising a child.

To youths in China, it is economically demanding to raise children in Chinese cities. In a study conducted by the Shanghai Academy of Social Sciences, as reported by the *South China Post*, it was revealed that raising a child from birth to junior high school in a city such as Shanghai would cost, on average, about US$124,000 (Y800,000). Similarly, on average, according to another study published by Sina Education in 2017 and reported by the *South China Post* in 2021, 26% of family annual income caters for child education in preschool, 21% for the one in primary and secondary and 29% for the one in the college (*South China Morning Post*, 12 May 2021). The implication of the lack of interest in childbearing among the youths in China is that, in the future, there will be more aged people than younger ones, which will translate into a more dependent population than the independent or working population. Hence, those that will push the economic and the political strength of China will no longer be able to do so. Therefore, China as a superpower of today may become an underdog nation tomorrow, knowing that, presently, the population of China is one of their major strengths and it is part of what gives them an edge on other nations of the world. At least, they have the largest army in the world today and the largest workforce to push up their economy.

Exclusion/Empowerment: Implications for Sustainable Development and Global Youth Competitiveness

What are the implication of exclusion or empowerment for sustainable development and global youth competitiveness of the two countries? The concept of sustainable development was explained by the 1987 United Nations Brundtland Commission report as that which has the capacity of meeting the needs of the present without compromising the ability of the future generation in meeting their own needs – the kind of development that is sustainable now and in the future without jeopardizing the future of the now young generation and generations that are yet to come. Sustainable development is the process or pathways to be used to achieve sustainability (UNESCO, 2015). The Sustainable Development Goals (SDGs), as initiated by the UN in 2015 with the agenda to last till 2030, were substituted for the Millennium Development Goals (MDGs). Sustainable development is categorized into four dimensions focusing on the society, environment, culture and economy. It was then streamlined into 17 goals that cut across issues relating to poverty, health and good life, education, economy, infrastructure and innovation, reduction of inequality, climate issues, peace and justice, sustainable community and others.

The fundamental principle and pledge behind the SDGs is not to leave anyone behind – the inclusiveness of all and sundry, the privileged and the underserved in the world, the youths and the aged. China and the United States have domesticated these agendas in their domains so as not to be in the back seat in the global arena. China is the highest gross domestic product (GDP) contributor and the biggest economy in the world. It has also become a force to reckon with among the Organization for Economy Co-operation and Development (OECD) countries. The country has a plan that, by 2050, it will become a well-developed nation which will also enable it to achieve the agenda of the UN on SDGs. In terms of economic development for the youth, China fosters skills through education and training to enhance labour market prospects of the young people, creating supporting platforms for small- and medium-sized enterprises (SMEs) to strengthen and develop local skills (OECD, 2017). This helps the country to explore collaborations for high-quality jobs, income distribution, social security and middle-class income.

Health and well-being is the third goal of the SDGs; it is believed that a healthy society is a wealthy society. Sport is one of the components that are believed to promote good health. The SDGs recognize sports and physical activities as an important tool that can be used to facilitate and promote health and well-being among people. Studies show that regular participation in sport and physical activities helps social, physical and mental well-being (UN, 2003). Both China and the United States are championing this cause among young people. The Chinese government initiated the Healthy China 2030 plan to align with the health-related agenda of the SDGs (Dai and Menhas, 2020). This programme is tailored to include the youth in the country in the plan of the Chinese government and the global SDGs agenda. At various international sports competitions such as the Olympic Games, the youth of China and the United States have been among the top-ranking sportspeople, winning numerous medals. Before the emergence of

China in the global sports space, the United States had always been at the top of these competitions. In the United States, youth are groomed from elementary schools to colleges and they are doing excellently in sporting events such as volleyball, basketball, swimming, American soccer (rugby), cricket and several others. They lift up the glory of their nation right from the high schools to colleges and to the national and international levels. The quantum leap in sports experienced in the United States cannot be separated from the involvement of the government in empowering the youth in that society.

Education has always been a viable tool for youth development all over the world. Quality education is the fourth SDG. Globally, policymakers and the other stakeholder have set off reforms to education to prepare the youth for the future. Reforms were made to afford the youth learning opportunities. The focus of the reforms has been for knowledge, skills and dispositions (Longview Foundation, 2021). The United States is one of the next stops for young people from around the world to get quality education. People move in large numbers from China and other parts of the world for quality education in the United States. There is a considerable decline in the rate of illiteracy in China, mostly among the youths. The Chinese government, in 2017, made public a 10-year youth development plan. Furthermore, medium- and long-term plans for youth development from 2016 to 2025 were initiated. The youth development plan's focus is to expand the employment frontier for the youth in various channels. The plan champions good and quality education, employment and health care for youth. As reported by Liangrong Zu, the unemployment rate of youth in China four years ago was 10.8%. In light of that, the unemployment issue then becomes one of the major issues for the Chinese government (Zu, 2020). These plans, in turn, will alleviate poverty and mediocrity among the youths in China.

Conclusion

This chapter established that youths are important and strategic engines of development in any nation. The inclusiveness of young people in the fabric of society will go a long way in helping society to reach its goals. China has the largest population in the world and is a country with a large youth population. Presently, the population of young people in China is more than the total population of one of the other populous nations in the world. Population growth use to be one of the banes of the development of China in the past, but now that weakness has been turned to strength. At the formation of the People's Republic of China, youth empowerment and inclusiveness through education and other forms were on the burner. On the other hand, youth empowerment has contributed immensely to the development of the United States. There are policies geared towards youth development and inclusiveness by the governments of both China and the United States. And China and the United States formulated policies to align youth development with the agenda of the UN's SDGs, championing the basic principles of global development goals not to leave anyone behind. This chapter discusses in brief the efforts of these countries' youth's involvement in education, health, economy and the like.

References

Asianinfo.org. 2021. Education and literacy in China, online material. Available at: http://www.asianinfo.org/asianinfo/china/pro-education.htm [Accessed 18 December 2021].

Dai, J. and Menhas, R. 2020. Sustainable development goals, sports and physical activity: the localization of health-related sustainable development goals through sports in China: a narrative review, *Risk Management and Healthcare Policy*, *13*, 1419–1430. https://doi.org/10.2147/RMHP.S257844

Gupta, M. D., Engelman, R., Levy, J., Luchsinger, G., Merrick, T. and Rosen., J. E. 2014. The state of world population 2014 – the power of 1.8 billion: adolescents, youth and the transformation of the future, *Prographics, Inc*, the state of world population, 136, Available at: www.unfpa.org [Accessed 10 December 2021].

Idike, A. and Eme, O. 2015. Role of the youths in nation building, *Journal of Policy and Development Studies*, *9*, 50–71. https://doi.org/10.12816/0018243

Longview Foundation. 2021. *Preparing Youth for the Global Age*, Falls Church, VA, Longview Foundation. Available at: https://longviewfdn.org/about/mission/ [Accessed 18 December 2021].

National Bureau of Statistics of China. 2021. Census, released on May 11, 2021, (Main Data of the Seventh National Population Census, n.d.).

Northway, R. 1997. Integration and inclusion: Illusion or progress in services for disabled people? *Social Policy and Administration*, *31*(2), 157–172. doi: 10.1111/1467-9515.00046. Available at: https://onlinelibrary.wiley.com/doi/10.1111/1467-9515.00046 [Accessed on 9 December 2021].

Ogundairo, J. A. and Ijimakinwa, F. 2020. Pastoralism and politics of exclusion in Ibarapa, Oyo State, Nigeria, *African Studies*, *79*(4), 428–443. https://doi.org/10.1080/000201 84.2020.1865789

Osotimehin, B. 2014. State of world population 2014 – the power of 1.8 billion: adolescents, youth and the transformation of the future [EN/FR/ES] – World, ReliefWeb. Available at: https://reliefweb.int/report/world/state-world-population-2014-power-18-billion-adolescents-youth-and-transformation [Accessed 10 December 2021].

Parent, D. and Lewis, B. F. 2003. The concept of social exclusion and rural development policy, *Journal of Rural Social Sciences*, *19*(2), Chapter 8. Available at: https://egrove.olemiss.edu/jrss/vol19/iss2/8

Samia, K. and Ingrid, H. 2019. Empowering youth decent and sustainable jobs and civic and political participation, *World Future Council Foundation*. Available at: www.worldfuturecouncil.org

Serpentza, F. 2019. China's awkward and disconnected youth. YouTube video. Available at: https://www.youtube.com/watch?v=kSRysotuYac [Accessed 18 December 2021].

Silver, H. 2019. *Social Exclusion*, pp. 1–6, New York, NY, Wiley. https://doi.org/10.1002/9781118568446.eurs0486

South China Morning Post. 2021, May 12. 'I don't want children': China's young shy from high costs. Available at: https://www.scmp.com/economy/china-economy/chapter/3133078/chinas-population-outlook-worrying-young-people-balk-high

Statista. 2018. *China: Population Density*, Published by Statista Research Department. Available at: https://www.statista.com/statistics/270130/population-density-in-china/ [Accessed 19 December 2021].

Statista. 2019. *Topic: Population in China*, Published by Statista Research Department. Available at: https://www.statista.com/topics/1276/population-in-china/ [Accessed 19 December 2021].

Statista. 2021. *Number of U.S. Youth and Young Adult Population by Age 2019*, Statista. Available at: https://www.statista.com/statistics/221852/number-of-youth-and-young-adult-population-in-the-us/ [Accessed 19 December 2021].

The Nation Newspaper. 2017. Youth and national development, *The Nation Newspaper* (blog), 7 September. Available at: https://thenationonlineng.net/youth-national-development/

The Organisation for Economic Co-operation and Development (OECD). 2017. People's Republic of China – OECD: Active with the People's Republic of China. Angel Gurría, OECD Secretary-General. Available at: https://www.oecd.org/china/ [Accessed 21 December 2021]

UNESCO. 2015. *Sustainable Development*. Online material. Available at: https://en.unesco.org/themes/education-sustainable-development/what-is-esd/sd [Accessed 20 December 2021].

UNFPA Report. 2014. The power of 1.8 million adolescents, youth and the transformation of the future. UNFPA State of World Population 2014. Available at: https://www.unfpa.org/sites/default/files/pub-pdf/EN-SWOP14-Report_FINAL-web.pdf

United Nations (UN). 2003. *Sport for Development and Peace Towards Achieving the Millennium Development Goals*. Available at: https://www.sportanddev.org/en/chapter/publication/sport-development-and-peace-towards-achieving-millennium-development-goals [Accessed 18 December 2021].

United Nations (UN). 2019. The United Nations sustainable development goals as a global content framework? *Journal of International Social Studies*, 9, 3–28. Available at: https://iajiss.org/index.php/iajiss/article/view/402 [Accessed on 21 December 2021].

United States Population. 2021. Worldometer. Available at: https://www.worldometers.info/world-population/us-population/ [Accessed 20 December 2021].

World Bank. 2017. *World Development Indicator (WDI) 2017. International Bank for Reconstruction and Development*, Washington, DC, The World Bank. Available at: www.worldbank.org

Xi, J. and Xia, Y. 2006. Introduction to Chinese youth (with a commentary). Faculty publications from Nebraska center for research on children, youth, families, and schools. Available at: https://digitalcommons.unl.edu/cyfsfacpub/2

Yeoh, E. K. and Chu, K. 2012. Literacy, education and economic development in contemporary China, *China-ASEAN Perspective Forum*, 2(1 and 2), 11–83. Available at: https://www.researchgate.net/publication/276355288_Emile_Kok-Kheng_Yeoh_and_Kah-Mun_Chu_2012_Literacy_Education_and_Economic_Development_in_Contemporary_China_China-ASEAN_Perspective_Forum_Volume_2_Numbers_1_and_2_pp_11-83

Zhou, Q. and Yang, J. 2016. Literacy education in China within an inclusive education context, *Per Linguam*, 32. doi: 10.5785/32-1-679. Available at: https://www.researchgate.net/publication/305311863_Literacy_education_in_China_within_an_Inclusive_Education_context [Accessed 14 January 2022].

Zu, L. 2020. Fostering social innovation and youth entrepreneurship for the achievement of the UN 2030 agenda: the Chinese way. In *The Future of the UN Sustainable Development Goals*, Eds Samuel O. Idowu, René Schmidpeter and Liangrong Zu, CSR, Sustainability, Ethics & Governance, pp. 341–365, Cham, Springer International Publishing. https://doi.org/10.1007/978-3-030-21154-7_17

Conclusion

Ọláyínká Àkànle

No generation confronts existential problems today as the youths even when the youths are the social and economic gauges, propellers, energies, passions and future of the world. There is no gainsaying the fact that the youths are very important generational cohorts, and they need careful handling if the world will know growth, peace and development particularly within the framework of development that is sustainable and not merely decorative and cosmetic development as it is currently the case. It can be categorically maintained that there can never be peace, growth, progress and development now and in the future if the youths are not well accommodated, accounted for and included in the development master plan and existences of nations across the world.

Unfortunately, in the context of exclusion and empowerment, the youths are the most endangered categories in the world today. The youths are systematically excluded and disempowered globally. Even in countries that pretend to be developed and inclusionary of the youths, many complicated elements of exclusion are present. The time is now for all countries to pay more objective and necessary attention to the plights of the youths as they battle widespread downplayed exclusion and dis/empowerment if there will ever be peace, justice and development in the world. What is certain is that there can never be peace and progress in the context of injustice, and social exclusion is injustice just as youth exclusion is arrogant and blatant injustice. All governments, institutions, people and groups are therefore called to soul searching through this book. All nations, groups and institutions need to answer the following question objectively, faithfully and honestly to gauge their youth inclusion status, performance and fill their youth exclusion/inclusion score cards: how well are the youths fairing in your space? How many youths are in governments? How many youths are gainfully employed? How many youths are in *real* position of leadership? How many youths live well above poverty line? How many youths are pleased with the current systems and social, political, economic, educational, religious, health, family, relational and digital schemes of things in your society/arrangement/establishment? Is the comparative access of the youths to justice in your society fair? How effectively empowered are the youths? Do the youths truly feel included or excluded in the systems at hand? How much opportunities do the youths have to contribute to the schemes

Youth Exclusion and Empowerment in the Contemporary Global Order:
Existentialities in Migrations, Identity and the Digital Space, 159–160
Copyright © 2022 by Ọláyínká Àkànle
Published under exclusive licence by Emerald Publishing Limited
doi:10.1108/978-1-80382-777-320221012

of events in your system? How well are the voices of the youths heard? Please ask the youths! Do not answer for them as usual!

This book is a clarion call to all stakeholders to re-strategize and be intentional in addressing the issue of youth exclusion and objective empowerment. Enough of playing lip service to the issue of youth exclusion and empowerment. The time for the right policies, practices, approaches and actions is now. For the world to move forward and for the future of everyone to be excellent in real time and term, the youths must be included and empowered and should no longer be treated as less important people anywhere in the world. That is it!

Index